Anonymous

The Dean of Coleraine

A moral history founded on the memoirs of an illustrious family in Ireland. Vol. 3

Anonymous

The Dean of Coleraine
A moral history founded on the memoirs of an illustrious family in Ireland. Vol. 3

ISBN/EAN: 9783337324179

Printed in Europe, USA, Canada, Australia, Japan

Cover: Foto ©ninafisch / pixelio.de

More available books at **www.hansebooks.com**

of Co[...]

A
MORAL HIS[TORY]

FOUNDED O[N]

MEMO[IRS]

OF AN

ILLUSTRIOUS FAMIL[Y]

A NEW EDI[TION]
Carefully Corrected and I[mproved]

IN THREE VO[LUMES]

VOL. III

LONDON:
Printed for F. JULLION, N°. 28, Holborn-Hill.
M.DCC.LXXX.

THE
DEAN of COLERAINE.

BOOK IX.

MY fears were soon dissipated, by meeting my Lord Tenermill, who was hurrying about the house with great forwardness, and, far from shewing any coldness at my approach, advanced towards me with an air that proclaimed friendship and satisfaction. As I expected as little to find in him an appearance of joy under such melancholy circumstances, as to see him so soon return to Paris, my surprise fixed me in the place in which I first perceived him. He did not from thence appear to be less eager in coming up to me; and embracing me with tenderness, his first expressions were made up of thanks for my cares, and testimonies of the great satisfaction he felt at his situation. The squadron he was in had been put back upon our coasts, by a storm so violent, that many ships, having lost their masts, were

forced

forced to return to the port of Dunkirk, to refit, in order to proceed on their voyage. He had taken advantage of this interval to make a journey to Paris, and, without stopping at the Count de S———'s, alighted at Fincer's house, which he easily found out, by the hints I had given him in my last letter.

This recital made me yet only comprehend the occasion of his journey; and his joy informed me at most of the renewal of his hopes. But far from suffering my curiosity to languish upon the point that was capable of enlivening it most, he continued to tell me, without giving me time to interrupt him, that having heard of the death of Fincer at his door, he was advertised at the same time of the escape of Patrick, and of the caution he was obliged to observe in relation to Sarah. He had been moved at the disaster of Fincer; but it being suitable to what he looked upon as a stroke too favourable for his hopes, to be too much afflicted at it, he had gathered from all occurring circumstances, that this accident had been no less a deliverance to him from the ever formidable competition of Patrick, than from all other obstacles that he apprehended from a furious father. Then informing me, that my sister being present with Sarah, he had managed a conversation with her to concert means for making his visit agreeable; and, under the flattering prepossessions in which Fincer's daughter yet was, he found little difficulty in giving a turn to his compliment in a manner proper to make her relish it. He had found the way of calming her imagination upon the sudden retreat of Patrick; and looking upon himself already as interested in the good order of a house, of which he doubted no longer but he should soon see himself master, he had began to assume an air of authority, to which the servants did not shew any reluctance.

There was nothing in this detail capable of augmenting my disquiet; and if I had not been sensible of some shame, in moulding together successively so many opposite desires, I should, on the contrary, have wished

wished that these new hopes of Tenermill should meet with all the success that might have filled his longing. I explained my thoughts to him in these terms, and not judging my presence to be very necessary to the repose of Sarah, I excused myself from going up to her apartment.

The return of Patrick's valet de chambre was speedy enough to save me from any impatience with which I should have waited for him. The uncertainty of my thoughts, that had made me turn my first steps towards Fincer's house, had diminished something from the natural ardour which I always felt for the interest of Patrick; but now not finding again any thing in my heart so pressing as this care, I ran immediately to his valet, as soon as I saw him at a distance. It seemed to me to be a matter of such importance to know what was become of Mademoiselle De L——, that asking him no other account, I made him twice repeat what he had discovered about that article. He had been informed at the convent, that she had gone from thence two hours before, and that in taking leave of the superior, she had shewn such marks of uneasiness and precipitation, that had caused astonishment through all the family. She had not taken this resolution, till after having some moments conversation with the man she had employed; but they could not discover whether it were from grief or joy she had so hastily determined to be gone.

I rested on this single point, which raised in me a thousand terrible ideas, from a foresight of all the consequences that might be drawn from it. Gone with so much haste, and so few reflections! and where could she have gone to, if she were not to Patrick, who without doubt had discovered that she was yet at Paris, and had given her assurances that she should find him again loving and faithful? What appearance was there, that in the resolution they were of going to Germany, they had deferred one moment to execute it after their reconciliation? I already

ready fancied them at a great diſtance, and I regreted bitterly the time I had loſt in my uſeleſs converſation with Tenermill.

In the mean-time, pierced through and through with this fear, I made haſte to their houſe, to learn at leaſt the circumſtances of their departure. The valet, to whom I had imparted my thoughts, and whom they had alarmed as much as me for his own intereſt, anticipated ſtill my diligence, and was at the gate ready to receive me, with ſome diſcoveries he had already drawn from another ſervant. They were more unlucky than any thing I had yet dreaded; although they had not made that impreſſion on him: ſatisfied enough to find that his maſter was not yet gone, and counting the reſt for nothing, he declared to me with a cheerful countenance, that far from being on the road to Germany, he was in the midſt of the delights of Paris; in one word, that he was in bed with Mademoiſelle De L——, and that having declared their marriage, all the houſe had prepared themſelves to celebrate it with rejoicings at their upriſing.

This news ſtruck me with ſuch an extraordinary medley of ſurpriſe and grief, that not having power to open my mouth, I continued for ſome time leaning againſt the gate, without being able to give an account to myſelf of the divers motions that diſturbed me. How! ſo near the unfortunate Sarah, and almoſt within ſight of the dead carcaſe of Fincer, whom he had juſt robbed of life, as much as if he had killed him with his own hands! Ah! why did not they go immediately to Germany? Why did they not remove themſelves out of the way of witneſſes, whoſe preſence ought to cover them with confuſion, and overburthen them with remorſe? Horrible tranſport of an imprudent paſſion, which ſhews neither decency to the living, nor reſpect to the dead! It was inwardly that I abandoned myſelf to theſe complaints; for I was ſurrounded by many ſervants, who ſeemed to wait my orders, and before whom

whom my own shame would not suffer me to make a noise with my thoughts. It came into my mind, nevertheless, to ask them, If they had, for any considerable time, been absent from their master and mistress? They answered, That they had only just come out of the apartment; and that the women of Mademoiselle De L—— were yet there. I had then a return of hopes; I flattered myself, that if I made haste to appear, I should come soon enough to stop a rash couple, who might be yet only on the edge of the precipice.

The valet de chambre consented to admit me, without penetrating my views. He went in first, and having told them that I was there, I heard my brother answer in an easy tone, and without appearing to have weighed the matter: Shew him in; without doubt, he shall be the first witness of my happiness. This easiness persuaded me fully, that I was not come too late. The door was opened to me; but with what anguish did I immediately find, that I had flattered myself with false hopes? I saw the two lovers peaceably lying in a very indifferent bed, that they had ordered to be prepared for them in haste. The vexation I as yet continued under at this scene, could not make me be silent on the glare that seemed to surround them in their situation. It would little become me to attempt a description of this nature; but I never saw a more perfect image of joy and happiness.

Nevertheless, what might have given me satisfaction in other circumstances, helped only to redouble the sorrowful thoughts with which I was now pierced. I approached the seat of their pleasures, and giving little attention to the toying of Patrick, who was willing to persuade himself, that I was come to wish him joy on the success of his desires, and who thanked me for it with affectation, I obliged him to change his tone and language, by addressing him in a discourse more serious than his: I leave it to Heaven, said I, to judge of the innocence of your conduct,

conduct, and at a time when my reproaches would
be as unprofitable as my counsels, I will not fatigue
you by a moral, which is no longer seasonable : But
what time and what place have you chosen to abandon yourselves to pleasures? Ah! why are you not
in the remotest part of Germany, added I, giving
greater force to my voice and looks? why have
you not made choice of another place than this to
insult an unfortunate woman, whose despair you
know, and the memory of Fincer, whose funeral
they are this moment preparing? You know not how
to disguise it, that the death of the father is your
handy-work ; and in the condition you have left the
sorrowful daughter, do you imagine she can be long
in following him? Go, be gone ; what pretence
remains for you to be in a place that you have filled
with horror? Since the evil is at the full, added I,
shedding a torrent of tears, which such a grievous
idea drew from me, we shall one day consider, if
your new engagements can be reduced to the rules
of religion and honour : But go, and do not draw
upon you the vengeance of Heaven, and of men,
by all those evils that your presence may yet cause
here.

This menace was a sort of prediction. Patrick
paused at it a little, and I was myself far from foreseeing that it would be verified by events, which
would follow it so close on the heels. But appearing nevertheless struck at the death of Fincer, and
the fresh troubles of Sarah, the image of which I
had laid in such lively colours before his eyes, he
demanded of me an explanation of an accident, of
which he was ignorant. I informed him of all the
circumstances of it. He agreed that decency should
have made him choose another time to give himself
up to joys; and having protested, that he had but
little thoughts of satisfying his passion, only by seal-
ing it in a manner irrevocable, he seemed disposed
to leave the bed off-hand, to deliberate with me
upon every thing he had just heard. Mademoiselle
De

De L———, in whom my words had caused some consternation, pressed him not to lose a moment. I went into the antichamber to give them liberty to put on their cloaths. They had no occasion, said they, but for an instant. Nevertheless they had scarce lost sight of me, when falling back into all their weaknesses, they seemed to forget that I was waiting for them. I had patience to attend for above an hour. At length lamenting for them their infatuation, and for myself an excess of complaisance, which made me lose time necessary for other cares, I called for a pen, which I made use of to explain my last thoughts. After I had reproached them with the hurry of an imprudent passion, which gave me room to expect nothing more considerate, or more moderate for the time to come, I repeated the advice I had given them at coming out of their chamber, and upon the whole recommended them to oppose the intention of their servants, who thought of celebrating their joy, by noisy and glaring mirth. Remove yourselves, said I, for your own proper safety, which is not so exempt from danger at Paris as you would represent to yourselves; and if in the transports you are in, there remain in you any sentiments of humanity, remove yourselves out of compassion for Sarah, who cannot learn what passes so near her without a mortal augmentation of her grief. And who knows, added I, of what love may make her capable, when she has nothing left but despair to consult? I prayed them to leave me the names of the places where I might address my letters to them; and making an effort to awaken in their favour some sentiments of my former affection, I promised them to employ all my cares to confirm their union, for as long time at least as they should not oblige me by other wanderings to abandon them to their own imprudence.

I did not go out of their house without advertising their servants, that they could do nothing more disagreeable to their master, nor more contrary to his intentions, than by publishing his marriage, and their joy. The valet de chambre coming to receive my orders, I renewed to him my desires, that he would inform me of the resolutions of my brother, and follow him with his ordinary affection. Without doubt the reason may be expected why I had not informed Patrick of the King's declared intentions of taking care of his fortune; but if it be considered what difference I put between the interest of his salvation, and that of his establishment, nobody can then be surprised, that in the eagerness I had to see the difficulties of his marriage finished, I had sacrificed all the ideas of grandeur and opulence to the urgent necessity of his departure. I saw no other than this way to cure Sarah of her unfortunate remains of hope, which had eternally nourished her obstinacy; and my thought always being, that without her consent we had nothing honest or lawful to pretend to, either for the solidity of Patrick's marriage, or for the success of Tenermill, I had nothing else in my thoughts but what might speedily conduct us to one or the other end.

The next moment gave me new subjects to confirm me in this way of reasoning, when being returned to Fincer's, his servants put into my hands some letters that had been sent to him by the post. I opened them in concert with Tenermill. One was from Dilnick, who upon the complaints Fincer had made him of our family, was determined to make a journey to France, to support there the interests of his. He had writ from Calais, on his coming out of the vessel that had brought him; and intending to ride post after a few hours rest, he might arrive at Paris almost as soon as his letter. What unforeseen alarms for me, who knew the boiling temper of Dilnick? He had made no scruple of turning his sword against Patrick upon an occasion, wherein the delicacy of his honour had been much less wounded; and what curb would be capable of bridling him,

him, when he had the death of Fincer, and the honour of Sarah, to revenge?

As, nevertheless, I had no hopes, that a motive of this nature could make any impression on Patrick from a principle of fear, I did not think at all of improving it; and the only resolution I formed upon the reading of this letter was, to return immediately to him, and press him by the same reasons I had done before, not to put off his departure to the next day. But this fatal day was marked out as a trial of all my virtues. Upon leaving Tenermill, after a short conversation, I met Dilnick at the gate, who was inquiring for Fincer's house. He knew me too easily to think he could be mistaken in it; and his prepossessions not hindering him from judging that I might have sided with his niece against the injustices of my brother, he shewed little surprise at seeing me come out from her with an air of freedom, which did not suppose either quarrel or anger.

Having embraced me nevertheless, the warmth of his resentment did not permit him to delay longer his complaints, and his expressions too plainly proclaimed with what dispositions he had left Ireland. Patrick was a man without honour and without truth, into whom he was resolved, in spite of him, to inspire other maxims; and I might declare to him beforehand, that he should find in the house of Fincer other defenders than women and old men. This was threatening us openly with all the violences I dreaded. But what had I not to fear from his fury, as soon as he should be informed of the bloody adventure of Sarah, and the tragical death of her father? By what charm could I hope to soften this savage heart, and what art had I not occasion of to enter into the explanation of a thousand things that were impossible for me to justify? Nevertheless, it was not at all to the story of a servant, that I ought to turn him over, and I ought yet less to suffer him to go into the apartment of his niece, without having prepared her by some cautious managements, which were more

necessary

necessary for her than ever. This was a situation full of grievous difficulties, and from whence I apprehended that no human assistance could bring me happily out.

I took him affectionately by the hand, and began to move him by my caresses; and while I was conducting him to a remote closet, without having the power to answer yet a single word to his menaces, I addressed to Heaven, from the bottom of my heart, an ardent prayer, to obtain from thence those succours, which I did not expect from my eloquence or understanding. In fine, being more at a loss, when I was at the point of opening my mouth, I did not think of humbling myself too much, by casting myself at his feet, to conjure him to make himself master of his first motions at every part of the discourse I should pray him to hear.

It is easy to imagine, that it was neither from the death of Fincer, nor the wound of Sarah, nor even from the confession of the new marriage of Patrick, that I began this moving apology. My integrity obliged me not to deviate in the least from the truth; but it was lawful for me to rank events in such an order as to make them appear under the most mild and favourable colours. In confessing to him the avowed infidelity of Patrick, I from thence hastened to the desires and intentions of Tenermill. Instead of a brother weak and inconstant, whose caprices I did not seek to excuse, I offered him one of a character more settled and steady, who burned with impatience to make a reparation for the injury the other had done to Sarah. I traced back all the steps that Tenermill had taken to insinuate himself into the esteem of Fincer and his daughter. It was she herself that put a perpetual obstacle in the way of her own happiness, and Fincer had so fully done us this justice, that he made his resentment fall only on her. Tenermill, myself, even Patrick, did any thing ever escape us that was capable of injuring him, and, knowing that the evil always proceeded from that source, have we

not

not always laboured to repair it by our submissions and tenders? Moreover, our family was beginning to be established in France in a manner splendid enough to make the eldest of it considered in a distinguished light; and though it were true, that the disgust of Patrick was an outrage on Sarah, the satisfaction she might receive in Tenermill was effectually capable of repairing it with great advantage. In fine, forgetting nothing that might at least put the sincerity of our intentions in a fair light, I thought to have led Dilnick to the point of being convinced, that the misfortunes I had yet to relate to him ought to be imputed to nothing but fortune.

He appeared indeed to listen to me with more tranquillity than I expected from him, and the proposal of Tenermill's marriage had made on him so sensible an impression, that his looks began to soften and grow mild; it was this hope also that made me heighten and set off the advantages of it with so much care. But it was necessary for me to pass to events less favourable, and my embarrassment redoubled at every word. I found my face all over in a sweat from my efforts to dispose my ideas and expressions in proper order. I began nevertheless this terrible relation without any other precautions than by representing resolutely the innocence of his heart in contradistinction to imprudence and weakness, and to improve the grief and repentance of a too guilty brother in proportion as I made a confession of his excesses. Thus the marriage of Patrick, the wound of Sarah, and the death of Fincer, found room successively in my recital. I saw more than once the front of Dilnick covered with gloominess, and his eyes inflamed by the motions which without doubt were raised in his heart. But it was then I redoubled the marks of my own grief, and laboured to make my discourse more moving by new humiliations. In fine, for the last impression on the heart of the formidable Dilnick, I alledged the cares and eager attendances of all my family since the misfortune of Sarah,

Sarah, those of Patrick himself, who had for three days even forgot his new spouse, and lost all relish for sleep and nourishment. You go to see my Lord Tenermill, said I, fixed to the bed of your niece with all the ardours of respect and love. You will there see my sister, who does not leave her one moment; your tenderness can add nothing to all the cares they have for her health and repose: And as to me, added I, who may without fear call up to your mind a thousand proofs of my sincerity and honour, which you cannot have forgotten, I call Heaven to witness, that your family has not among them a friend more zealous and tender than mine.

It was time for me to stop. Though I had something to add to the reasons I laboured to join together in my discourse, the efforts it cost me so exhausted my strength, that I could not continue it. I waited, trembling, to see on what point the first motions of Dilnick would bear; and if I laboured farther to bend him, it was by the consternation of my countenance and silence. He was not in haste to answer me. Without looking on him, I could discover from his agitations what furious combats passed in his heart. He seemed to reflect on every thing he had just heard and inquired after, and, notwithstanding his transports, appeared to regulate the tone of his voice he was going to speak to me in. So much slowness in a man so rough, began to raise in me some amazement. He at length took up the discourse, but in a voice more moderate than I durst have hoped for.

Thus, said he, the father, the daughter, the fortune, and perhaps the honour of my family, all appear an easy sacrifice to your brother, to gratify the irregularity of his passions. Hear me, said he; I charge no body with accidents of chance, and I can well distinguish between things that ought to be ascribed only to our misfortune, and those that deserve the name of insult and outrage. I even make a just distinction between the conduct of Patrick, and that of the rest of your family. But nothing shall stop my resentment against a base perfidious wretch, who has raised to us so many evils. If my Lord Tenermill maintains any pretensions to my niece, and you any design on my friendship, it is by abandoning Patrick to my revenge, that you can both of you give me proofs of the sincerity of your intentions.

Upon finishing this terrible discourse, he arose with a furious air. I should have thought him ready to go in quest of Patrick to decide the quarrel on the spot, if I could have imagined he knew where he lived. But the certainty I had, that he was but just come to Paris, relieved me from that fear, and the day beginning to approach towards an end, I flattered myself that before morning I should find means of hastening the departure of Patrick. This reflection was so much the more comfortable, as it made me look on it as an extreme happiness to see him turn all his fury on the sole object, which I hoped immediately to put under shelter from him, at least by removing it out of the way. I saw nothing to fear about myself, since he had excepted Tenermill from his hatred, and had in a manner approved the inclination he supposed in him for his niece. Whatever projects of revenge he might meditate against Patrick, I had room to hope, that during our continual commerce with him, by applying all our study to appease and please him, we should sooner or later succeed in making him assume other sentiments. I found myself so fortified by this way of reasoning, that avoiding every thing that might indulge him in his present notions, I proposed to him to go up to his niece's chamber, and to afford her by his presence a consolation she stood in need of. But notwithstanding the air of tenderness I affected in giving him this invitation, not being able to dispense with myself from prepossessing him with the necessity of concealing from Sarah the death of her father as long as her health required this caution, this advice

made

made me still endure some furious strokes of resentment against Patrick.

My Lord Tenermill and the Countess of S——, who were already informed of his arrival, and who had not doubted with what view I was retired aside with him, easily judged in seeing us appear together, that I had disposed him to receive their compliments civilly. They saluted him with marks of satisfaction and friendship, which confirmed what I had told him of their sentiments. Sarah was charmed to see him. She knew her father had persuaded to meet him at Paris, and his diligence did not seem to give her any surprise. But the joy she felt proceeded from a cause I did not at first perceive. In the sweet error she yet was under of flattering herself with hopes of Patrick's return, she thought obligingly that Dilnick, to whom her father had given no other reason for inviting him out of Ireland, than the desire of revenging himself on our family, was agreeably deceived to see us united together about her; and giving herself up to a thought so pleasing and satisfactory, she lamented that Patrick, whose absence they had hitherto luckily enough coloured over, was not with her. Alas! where is he? said she to me in a languishing voice. Dilnick fretted to see her in this error; and I perceived, that if he constrained himself to keep silence, it was only out of fear of injuring the recovery of a niece so dear. I answered in haste, that the three nights he had passed in watching with her, had made my brother stand in need of necessary rest; and then repenting myself for having said what might be looked upon as a falshood, since it only served to confirm her in her prepossessions without foundation, I changed what I had said with less violence to my sincerity, by speaking of a journey I had made to St. Germain, and of the intentions the King had shewed of advancing Patrick's fortune. What I added of the haste that prince was in to see him, and even of the orders he had given me to advertise him of it, was a preparation, of which the

effect

effect was very useful to us. It not only cast new
seeds of hope, and consequently of consolation, into
the heart of Sarah, but, in making her think that
he was obliged to go to St. Germain, in obedience
to the King's orders, it prevented the renewal of sorrow and trouble, which she would speedily have felt
for the continuance of his absence.

The moderation of Dilnick appeared to me to be
so good an omen, that, going into another apartment with him and Tenermill, I heaped on him my
compliments and caresses. He had the resolution
to let nothing escape him that might awaken my
fears on Patrick's score; and, on the contrary, the
thoughts of Tenermill's marriage possessing him entirely, he was the first to ask, Whether it were a resolution seriously formed? His tranquillity appeared
to increase yet more, by the ardour he saw in Tenermill to give him an answer. An alliance so sincerely coveted by persons on whom it might depend,
appeared to me so certain, as to have it concluded
on the spot, if circumstances had permitted; for necessity had become a law so indispensible for Sarah,
that it was no longer from her I expected any obstacles. What other resource could she have, when
she heard the confirmation of Patrick's marriage;
and could she fail of sacrificing all her repugnances
to her honour?

From the satisfaction this thought gave me, I
changed my design of pressing Patrick, by letter, to
be gone, into that of seeing him myself. It appeared
to me a matter of importance, that he should carry
with him some certainty of the marriage of his brother, and be disposed, by my exhortations, speedily to
repair the irregularity of his own. I was willing to
draw such a promise from him, that I might have
nothing to reproach myself with from a consent that
I gave to his departure, and which seemed to comprehend in it an open approbation of his conduct.
This was the first subject I accosted him upon; I did
not speak a word to him of Dilnick; and when I
though

thought myself ascertained by his answer, that he was not estranged from my proposal, I thought of nothing but retiring, to leave him at liberty to be gone.

He seemed to be taken up with nothing but his journey; and I could never imagine, how he came to change his mind all at once in so short a space. I had not got down to the foot of the stairs, before he sent one of his servants to call me back; and meeting me, I know not, said he, what it is obliges me to leave France, when you give me such formal assurances of my brother's marriage: Even supposing my presence should be an obstacle to it, what hinders me from retiring a few weeks to the country, and to spread abroad the report of my departure? You have not imparted to me, said he, the success of your journey to St. Germain, and the King's goodness to you. I have learned it all from my valet de chambre; and should not scruple to sacrifice the hopes that Prince has given you for me, if such a sacrifice were necessary for our common tranquillity. But one moment's reflection has made me believe, that all our interests may be easily reconciled. Tenermill shall become the husband of Sarah; I shall appear again after his marriage, and draw all the advantages I can hope from the King's favour. A proposal so little expected, surprised me enough to make me consider a long time upon my answer. He took me by the hand; Come with me, said he, and tell me what passed between the King and you more faithfully than I could hear it from my valet. I followed him, without losing sight of the first impression made on me by what he said, and which I had considered with all the attention I was capable. I found, that, in reality, the offer he made of retiring to the country being an answer beforehand to all my fears, he had but few hazards to run by delaying his departure. The country-house of the Count De S—— was a retreat, in which I was sure the secret would be kept: And when he could be in security from the menaces of Dilnick, what reason had I, at the

bottom,

bottom, to wish for his removal farther off? Even as
to the main design I had in view, of amending the
form of his marriage, had I not a more sure prospect of making him relish my advice when he was
within a few leagues of Paris, than at the distance
he was going to be from us in some town of Germany? And, on the other hand, of what importance
was it to Sarah, whether he were near or at a distance from her, when his presence or absence could
make no further alteration in her hopes? These
reflections, receiving strength, perhaps, from too
worldly a desire of not losing the opportunity of the
King's favour, for the advancement of my family,
made a revolution in my sentiments almost as quick
as what had just happened in those of Patrick. I sat
down near him with a tranquillity proceeding from
my joy; and having related to him, as he requested,
all the circumstances of my journey to St. Germain,
I confessed to him, upon winding up my story, that
I had few objections to make against what he proposed.'

Nevertheless, for ever alarmed with the menaces of
Dilnick, I added divers reasons, which, according to
his own scheme of retiring privately to the country,
ought to make him hasten his departure, as much as
if he was to go to Germany. I was happy enough to
make him relish these reasons; and the satisfaction
he shewed, in his turn, for my facility in approving
his desires, made him use all the diligence I could
expect for his entering into my views. Orders were
given, upon the spot, for the return of his goods,
which had already left Paris; and the other alterations were so easy, that they were made during the
night, with as much diligence as secrecy.

In the reflections I continued to make upon this
change, I found new reasons for approving it; but
still not forgetting the desire the King shewed to see
Patrick on the morrow, I was resolved to go myself to his levee, to make our excuses acceptable.
Arriving at St. Germain before the King was up, I
found

found many persons of rank in the antichamber; among whom I saw Anglesey, who came up to me as soon as he observed me. My perpetual troubles had given me few opportunities of visiting him since he came to Paris; and the strict friendship he had maintained with Mademoiselle De L―――― and Patrick, was the sole reason that made me a little strange to him. Nevertheless, not being able to refuse him those compliments, which the custom of the world has made a duty, he gave me the opportunity of seeing him sometimes at Saisons, and I never had given him room to think that I found his visits troublesome. I know not whether it were upon this foundation only that he thought himself authorised to make me a confidant of his designs, or whether he hoped to draw any advantage from my answers to give them success: But, after the first compliments, he took me aside, to entertain me with the following discourse.

You know, said he, the friendship I have sworn to your brother, and that which he hath honoured me with. Yesterday, when he was preparing to be gone, the night following, to Germany, he thought himself obliged, by our strict union, to give me notice of his departure; and the haste I made in going to his house, might demonstrate to him how sensible I was of this tender mark of his attention for me. He gave heaped measure to his favours, by discovering to me his situation. He informed me of the conclusion of his marriage with Mademoiselle De L――, and his resolution of retiring with her into Germany, to shelter himself from the resentment of Sarah Fincer; the place of his retreat; in fine, all the views he had formed for his new establishment. But, what I regarded as the most generous testimony of the goodness of his heart, among the reasons that obliged him to quit France, to separate himself from Sarah, he gave me to understand, that he took so much interest in her happiness as to employ himself still about it. He made me an encomium on all the perfections

tions he knew in her character, since the time he had bore the name of her husband; and seeing her worthy of a thousand passions, which he could not feel for her, he laboured to inspire me with them. As to the objection I drew from the concurrence of my Lord Tenermill, whose views and attempts he had informed me of a long time before; he answered, that unhappily for his brother, Sarah had shewn little taste for his person, and few compliances to his diligence and cares; that Tenermill was so well convinced of this himself, that he had in a manner renounced all hopes; that he had gone away suddenly to free himself from an unsuccessful passion; and that being embarked with his regiment for Ireland, there was great appearance, that his military occupations and absence would finish the healing of his heart, which was formed for ambition much more than for love. In fine, opening to me a course that he warranted to be free, he pressed me to enter courageously into it, and to trust the success of my boldness to my good fortune.

I cannot disavow, continued Anglesey, that independent of the charms of Sarah, which would be sufficient to make me aspire to the happiness of pleasing her, I look on her riches and birth, as two motives capable of animating me. I have but little estate, why then should I neglect the opportunity of making myself happy by fortune and love? In leaving your brother, I received from him, as his last favour, an advice, which I am going to execute. He has given me to understand, that in the trouble and weakness he had left Sarah, I had but one way to obtain access to her, and that was to support myself by the countenance of the King's recommendation. A stranger, and without alliances at Paris, the embarrassment in which she continues since the death of her father, would make her look upon the King's protection as a favour from Heaven; and I have no doubt, but that what I shall begin under such powerful auspices, I shall be able to bring to a happy
conclusion,

conclusion, by my address and pains. I only wait for the hour of the King's levee, to make a trial of my credit. Having got a sight of you, added he, I flatter myself, that you will not only receive in good part this overture, but that, seconding the intentions of your brother, you will employ for me all the weight that your merit has given you at court.

Whatever astonishment and vexation such strange proposals might give me, they were accompanied with so much respect, and so many polite compliments, that I could not assume a voice less civil to answer them. But I had taken my resolution from the first word, which had given me a foresight of their drift. It might have been easy for me to comprehend, that Patrick had given him notice to come to him in the interval of the two visits I had paid him, and that not being then informed either of the arrival of my Lord Tenermill, or the renewal of his love, he might have fancied that the project he had formed, in favour of his friend, might be of some advantage to Sarah. This reflection assured me also, that Anglesey was ignorant of the changes that had been brought about since; and to be able to reason upon these two foundations, would at least make him depart from his fixed point. I did not look farther for the means of delivering myself from such an unseasonable and unlucky accident. Having commended Patrick for his sentiments, which made him think of the happiness of Sarah, I laid before Anglesey all the reasons she herself had, not to be sensible of over much gratitude for a service of this nature; and confessing to him, without going about the bush, that he might indeed have chosen a confidant more disposed than I was to serve him, I informed him, that both he and Patrick were under an error that might be easily set right, if they thought that Tenermill was discouraged by some obstacles, which no longer subsisted. He is at Paris, said I; it is the force of his passion has brought him back to it; and

to

to conceal nothing from you, he is with Sarah, who receives his assiduities, and, in all appearance, finds an inclination to reward them. Spare yourself, added I, a step, of the unprofitableness of which I give you notice; and do not build upon hopes, which will be immediately destroyed by the recital I come now myself to make the King.

This, then, was indeed enough to banish all hopes from a man less animated than he, by a double motive, of which he had made me the confession. But, not being able so easily to consent to the loss of two advantages, which had all night flattered his imagination, he seemed less afflicted at my refusal to serve him, than at his own imprudence in opening himself to me so unwarily. He looked upon me with an irresolute eye; and, recovering himself, after some moments silence, It is of no importance, said he, with a peremptory air; I know no obstacle that can be capable of cooling me; and if you will give me leave to speak freely, added he, I have more reliance upon the notions of Patrick than upon yours. I was going to reply, and let him know, that what he called the notions of Patrick, supposed the absence and desisting of Tenermill; but, observing that the King's chamber was opened, he left me, and advanced nimbly towards the door: One word in the usher's ear obtained him the liberty of a private audience. I perceived all at once what advantage he was going to have by anticipating me, and I was vexed not to have made this reflection earlier.

In reality, he was sensible enough, that, not finding me disposed to second him, he could not be too speedy in bringing the King into his interest, and to assure himself of his protection by some formal promises, which would become a sacred engagement to this Prince. I further observed how deficient I was in the customs of the world upon this occasion. If I had known how to have profited by my prerogatives, my character, and the quality of almoner to his Majesty, I had opened to myself an entrance into his
chamber

chamber before him, who prevailed over me by his diligence. A false modesty stayed me, or, if I may confess it without shame, a motive yet more ridiculous, which was only a fear of injuring the gravity of my profession, by advancing as nimbly as Anglesey towards the door.

Whilst I was reproaching myself with this weakness, he took advantage of the honour he had of addressing himself to the King, by opening his designs, and interesting the goodness of that Prince to favour them to his power: The promise of attaching himself to the court was a motive so powerful, that it obtained him much more than he durst have hoped for. They looked at the court of St. Germain on these sort of conquests as so many advantages over the usurper. The King immediately ordered one of his principal gentlemen to be called, and charging him with his pleasure in terms most flattering for Anglesey and Sarah Fincer, he let him know, the success of his commission should be a merit for him that should not remain unrewarded. Anglesey went out with this lucky fruit of his haste, and being much above fearing my efforts, affected to pass near me with an haughty air, without imparting to me what he triumphed in having obtained.

Nevertheless, as I had acquired a little more boldness by my reflections, I took advantage from his example to demand a private audience after him. The facility they shewed in granting it, increased the vexation I felt for not having been earlier presented. The King did not give me time to declare what brought me back so soon to his court. If you had come one instant sooner, said he off-hand, you would have been a witness of the interest I take in all that belongs to you; for the daughter of Fincer ought yet to concern you: And giving himself the trouble to relate what he had done in my favour for the happiness of Anglesey, I wish, added he, that she may take a greater relish for him, than one of your brothers has had for her, or than she herself

has

has shewed for the other. I answered, that if I did not apprehend a failure in duty by my complaints, I would give a quite different name to what his Majesty willed me to look upon as a favour. My brother, added I, had hopes, which your Majesty has just now ruined by giving success to those of another. If the favour may contribute to the happiness of any one, it is not to that of my family, and the benefit is only for Anglesey, who must gather the fruit of it. This discourse, and the air of grief with which I accompanied it, gave the King so much surprise, that rising half up, he pressed me, continuing sitting on his bed, to explain to him a mystery, of which he assured me he did not comprehend one word. Is it not true, continued he, that my Lord Tenermill has broke with Fincer's daughter, and is he not gone to command his regiment? I then begged permission to enter into a detail of our domestick affairs, and taking up every thing that had happened since the arrival of Fincer, I prayed his Majesty to judge himself of the situation and hopes of Tenermill. Anglesey, added I, was not ignorant of his return; he knew it from myself a moment ago; and our misfortune is, that with more address, than I had, he found means of being presented to your Majesty before me. My sincerity appeared even in the tone that grief made me use. The King was so moved at it, that having ordered Anglesey to be recalled, he shewed himself much irritated against him, when being inquired after to no purpose, he was informed that he had already left St. Germain. He immediately ordered the gentleman, who had the charge of Anglesey's interests, to be recalled; but the hasty Anglesey had engaged him to be gone upon the spot; and the King, surprised at their haste, was reduced to the necessity of dispatching a courier, with orders for them to return to him immediately.

The goodness of this Prince would have been sufficient to console me, if I had considered in the marriage of my brother only the advantages he would find in it for his establishment. But in the disposition I knew Dilnick to be, I foresaw, that the only means I had to inspire him with more moderation coming to fail by these new views they were going to give him for his niece, it would be impossible, it may be, to make him drop his designs of revenge against Patrick. I confessed this to the King, and from thence took occasion to make apologies for this dear brother, who ought to have been at St. Germain to receive his orders. The advantageous touches, that friendship made me choose in praising at the same time his character, added to the impressions yet remaining on that good Prince from the moving recital I had made him of one part of his adventures, inspired him, with so much goodness for my brother, that he determined on the spot to give him an extraordinary mark of it. I approve, said he, the precautions you have taken to make him avoid meeting Dilnick; but I know more sure means to shelter him from his violence: That is, in the first place, to take upon myself the care of reconciling them: I will give notice to them both to appear here, and will oblige them to embrace one another and forget their quarrels. Then, to remove all opportunities of rekindling their hatred, I will send your brother to Spain, where I have some secret affairs to manage; so that what will conduce to his safety, will at the same time be useful for my interests and his own fortune. I embraced the knees of so excellent a King, to shew him the ardour of my gratitude; but appearing so sensible to his goodness for Patrick, I entreated him further to extend his favour to Tenermill.

The King's intention was sincere, and perhaps would have produced immediately some effect, if his commands had been fulfilled with more diligence; but Anglesey got the start of them by his. He went directly to Dilnick. The gentleman, who accompanied him, interested perhaps in his service by other hopes, had given such an artful turn to his commission, that Dilnick, whom necessity alone had
made

made hearken to our proposals, was in raptures to find so fair an opportunity of shaking off the yoke, and of preserving the honour of his niece, without being obliged to observe the least caution in respect of us. He gave his promise to Anglesey; and immediately assuming a right from this new engagement to deliver himself from Tenermill, he declared to him, that from his views, which he affected to wrap up in obscure terms, he was obliged to forbid him the house, and all access to his niece. Love, though mortally afflicting Tenermill, yet inspired him with moderation enough to keep in his complaints: I found him at the Count De S——'s on my arrival from St. Germain. He informed me what had thrown him into the agitations he was in, and my account augmented them; but I had so much hopes from the King's goodness, that my consolations had the power of calming his mind.

During this time, the same courier, who was charged to call back Anglesey and the gentleman employed in his favour, carried also an order to Dilnick to appear at St. Germain. This was in consequence of the King's promises, who seriously employed himself about the concerns of my brother, and was desirous of putting an end at once to the two affairs I had communicated to him. Dilnick, flattered with the attention they appeared to shew him, and looking on it as the consequences of the message he had just before received, left Paris in so much haste, that arriving above an hour before the other two, he heard from the King's own mouth the change that Prince had made in his first orders. Perhaps having made the best of the respect with which he had received them, the same reason would have had the power of keeping in his murmurs upon hearing they were changed; but the King passing immediately to the affair of Patrick, and exhorting him to put an end to it, by forgetting a quarrel, which it would be useless to revive, this mention of the most piercing of his vexations served as a

pretext

pretext to oppose openly what at first he had not durst to have rejected. He traced back with great warmth all the outrages he had received from my brother in the person of his niece, and not limiting himself to the pretence that his schemes of revenge were just, he had the boldness to demand of the King, if it were worthy of his goodness to propose to him the brother of his most mortal enemy for a husband to his niece. A King even more easy and condescending would have been offended at this question; but James the Second, whose sweetness of temper heightened and set off all his other virtues, did not answer this reproach otherwise than by persuasions founded upon maxims of religion, and upon the necessity of peace, even for the interest of both families. His instances were so pressing, that they put Dilnick to silence; and this was the greatest victory he could obtain over this inflexible heart; for his inward sentiments were not in the least softened by them. But the King, induced to believe that he submitted to his orders, thought no more than to confirm him in this disposition by all the caresses that were familiar to this great Prince.

In going out of the apartments, his misfortune and ours was, that he met Anglesey, who arrived with the gentleman dispatched with him. He took him aside to impart to him the King's intentions, but took care to assure him of his own; and having renewed to him all his promises, he easily made him understand, that if he wished for the execution of them, he ought not to go into the King's presence, who would infallibly oblige him to renounce his pretensions. Anglesey followed his advice without hesitation; they chose to return together to Paris, notwithstanding the King's express orders to Dilnick to wait for the arrival of Patrick, between whom he was willing to bring about a reconciliation. Upon my having acquainted this Prince with Patrick's retreat, he dispatched a courier to him, who went off immediately. Thus my brother was upon the road to St. Germain, while Dilnick and Anglefey retook that to Paris.

They met at a little diftance from the town. If Patrick could not fee Dilnick without feeling much emotion, anger was the fole paffion that took poffeffion of the other when he faw my brother. Neverthelefs, the prefence of Anglefey ftopped his firft tranfports. He fancied with juftice, that it was not in the fight of a common friend, that he ought to proceed to violence; and this thought obliging him to affume a calm air, he contented himfelf to come up to Patrick, and tell him in few words the defign he had to revenge himfelf. He made this declaration with fo much caution, that Anglefey taking no umbrage at it, my brother eafily found means of difguifing his anfwer. He promifed to go to Paris upon his leaving St. Germain, and to give Dilnick immediate notice of his arrival. What they added to this converfation related to nothing but the change made in the intended journey to Germany, which Anglefey complained of not having known earlier, and parting with the ufual appearances of friendfhip, they continued their refpective journies.

The King feemed extremely irritated againft Dilnick, when having feen my brother appear, he in vain had an enquiry made for his enemy. The gentleman, who had ferved for a guide to Anglefey, gave an account not only of the precipitation of his departure, but of the advice he had given Anglefey to follow him. This temerity could not but turn to the advantage of Patrick; fo that the goodnefs of the King appeared from thence more ardent in his favour. Having done him the honour of talking to him a long time, he laid open to him the occafion he had of his fervices in Spain; and although birth, faid the King obligingly, diftinguifhes itfelf more than all dignities, yet he invefted him with the title of Lord Chamberlain, to let him know what fhare he would henceforth give him in his confidence. In relation to Dilnick, he recommended to him to avoid meeting this furious man, and promised to take other measures to inspire him with more moderation. Patrick, bound by the common maxims of honour, made no answer to this exhortation, from the fear of drawing on himself a peremptory prohibition; but, lodging in the bottom of his heart the impression of Dilnick's menaces, he was not less urged with the desire of getting to Paris, to know without delay what his threats could have in them so terrible; and his impatience appeared so visible to the King's eyes, that this Prince having at length mistrusted what was the cause, he ordered him a guard, whom he commanded to follow him without intermission till his departure for Spain.

This obstacle did not hinder him from taking immediately the road to Paris; and thus overthrowing all my precautions, he went directly to Dilnick, with whom he had a very brisk conversation; they deceived the vigilance of the guard, by talking in the Irish language. The result of this heat was, that Dilnick should go secretly to the frontiers of Spain, and there wait for my brother. Besides the necessity the guard had laid him under, of constraining himself, Patrick did not forget what he had to fear in France from his first duel, and into what embarrassment he must of necessity cast himself in the courts of law by a new quarrel. But if it was prudence that made him think of turning over Dilnick to Spain for satisfaction, the same reason might have made Dilnick desire to battle it in France. The condition his niece was yet in, did not suffer him to remove far from her. He proposed to leave Paris in a litter under the guidance of Anglesey, and the same day to finish his difference with my brother. If the chance of arms declared for him, he reckoned upon it that he should be immediately able to get to the sea-side. Although he returned from St. Germain with this project, he was prevented from engaging by the presence of the guard, and was obliged to
change

change his thoughts at the desire of Patrick himself.

In the mean-time, when being alone at home he had made new reflections on the danger to which he should abandon his niece, and the delays he should be exposed to, his first design returned so strongly upon his mind, that he determined to pass over the considerations that had stopped him. Such a furious project could not come into the mind of any body but him; for the guard not losing sight of my brother a moment, another would have feared to have had an enemy more than one to combat, or at least to find himself taken and arrested upon any attempt to attack Patrick. Nothing was capable of dismaying him; discovering himself only to the faithless Anglesey, he did not refuse the request made him to embark in the quarrel; that is to say, Anglesey sacrificing all the rights of gratitude and friendship to love, should undertake to attack the guard, and lay him under the necessity of thinking of his own defence. Thus, by the most rash resolution in the world, they determined to go in quest of, and join their enemies on the spot, if it were possible, as they took their way out of Paris in the road to the castle of the Count De S———, to which they had no doubt but Patrick would make haste to return.

It was easy for them indeed to learn that Patrick was at the Count De S———'s house, and to have his departure watched. They followed him with so much precaution, that having chosen on the road the most proper place for executing their design, they had all the ease they could desire to overtake the chaise. The guard being on horse-back, Anglesey took him aside, while Dilnick pressed my brother to alight. The surprise he was in to see himself attacked against the faith of so late an agreement, did not hinder him from thinking to put himself upon his defence with a good grace. The combat was long and bold; at length the rash Dilnick found in it his punishment. He was pierced through with a mortal wound,

wound, having first received one more slight, which helped only to provoke his fury. Anglesey seeing him fall lifeless, left the guard, with whom he was less hurt than amused; he made some excuses to my brother, which he gave little ear to, but advised him immediately to remove himself by flight into a place of security.

Patrick and his guard had no other choice than to return directly to St. Germain, to give an account to the King of a mischance they could by no means avoid. Patrick put the corpse of Dilnick into his chaise, and mounted the horse of one of his servants, to whom he gave orders to return to Paris behind the chaise, and to go to the house of the Count De S——, where he had left me. The commission he had charged him with, was to inform me of this melancholy adventure, and to commit to me the care of burying the body he had sent me. I was with the Count and my Lord Temermill when this mournful present came to me. The care they took of drawing the curtains of the chaise took away all suspicion from the Count's servants, and Patrick's lacquey had discretion enough not to discover his master's orders to any body but me. I adored the dispositions of Providence, which did not leave me one moment to breathe after so many disturbances; and thinking I had no other choice to make in this matter than to bury Dilnick privately, I had him carried to Saisons, where I proposed to go immediately, and take that care on myself.

But going back to the Count and Temermill, I immediately informed them of what I had just learned. If the heart of a good man could feel any joy at the misfortune of another, when it might turn to his own advantage, I should have suspected Temermill not to have heard me without some return of complacency in relation to his own proper interests. But then he anticipated this suspicion by his answer; I lament the unfortunate Dilnick, said he, and I banish from me the memory of every thing that might
make

make me think of his death with other sentiments. Nevertheless, added he, you will not be surprised, that not having any thing farther to fear from the competition of Anglesey, I resume all my hopes, and am returning this moment to Sarah. I stopped him. You give little attention, said I, to a thousand difficulties, that ought to make you less hasty. What I fear from the very misfortune of her uncle, which may prove a new obstacle to your views, is not perhaps the most strong. But what are you going to say to Sarah, and how do you hope to conceal from her this new accident, which she cannot hear without being informed of more of the same kind of mischiefs? We are ignorant, continued I, whether she hath been told of the death of her father, of the last resolutions of Patrick; or, if it be probable that Dilnick might not have concealed for any time her misfortunes, we are yet more uncertain of the effect they have produced on her. Will you go and carry her news at a hazard capable of making her sink under the burden of it, and speak to her of marriage or of love, when she is not perhaps taken up with any thing but the horror of her fate? Having prevented him by these reflections, I proposed to him to abandon to me the conduct of an enterprise, that required a mind less disturbed than his; and I persuaded him to consent to remain with the Count, whilst I should go and inform myself of the condition, and feel the dispositions of the unfortunate Sarah.

Neither confidence nor courage were necessary for me in this enterprise; but I was sensible of the need I had of much precaution and address. Jacin, who followed me, did not seem proper for the discoveries I was willing to begin with. I must have a spy, who was not known to the servants, and who might assist me without giving them any suspicion of my design. I took advice of the Count, who offered me the services of a discreet and faithful friend, whose talents he had employed in carrying on the intrigue with my sister fister. Having given him notice to come immediately to us at his house, we instructed him in all the circumstances necessary for him to know, and told him every thing we desired to learn by his diligence. He put on the same disguise, under which he had formerly come to me from the Count to carry me to the Carthusian monastery, and not having known him at first sight, I recollected his air and figure with amazement, as soon as he had changed his dress.

I followed him till he had got to a certain distance from Sarah's house, and the time I passed in waiting for him was taken up by my sorrowful reflections. They did not hinder me, nevertheless, from keeping my eyes fixed on Sarah's door. I saw a chair carried into it, which soon after came out again. As I had observed, that it was empty when it went in, I saw as plainly, that it was not so coming out. But my curiosity would have proceeded no farther, if I had not perceived the Count's friend, who came out also to follow it. His eyes found me out in the retreat I had chosen, and I imagined, from a hasty beck he gave me with his hand, that notwithstanding the impatience he had to speak to me, he was obliged by a motive still more pressing not to quit the chair. I made no scruple to join him. Ah! said he, proceeding forward with me, could you ever imagine who it is I am taking care of, and where I am going? It is Sarah is in this chair; it is she herself, who upon the discourse I have had with her, has wished to be carried to the Count's, and has refused to return to Ireland with Anglesey, in order to desire a sanctuary in the bosom of your family.

If nothing could have happened to me more agreeable, nothing also was more capable of giving me greater surprise. I prayed this lucky negociator to inform me, as we walked along, by what art he had found the way of doing that in an instant, which I durst not have promised myself success in from all my endeavours and cares. He told me, that having posted himself at Sarah's door, under pretence of offering her
his

his services for Ireland, he had been received there with so much the more ease, as they were preparing every thing to undertake the same journey. This hint, which he had got from the servants, had at first embarrassed him; but becoming from thence more eager for the success of his commission, he pretended at all hazards, that he had come there on Anglesey's account, who being obliged to go before Sarah, the services he could do her related to her embarkment, upon which, Anglesey had given it him in charge to consult her. He had exposed himself to the imputation of an impostor, if Anglesey should have happened unluckily to be with her; but with the reasons he had to believe him far off, and not daring to use the name of Dilnick, because he was yet uncertain whether she were informed of his misfortune, nothing appeared to him more specious to improve upon, than the authority of a man, whose influences he had reason to suppose had a great share in the hurry he saw in the house. However it were, he found it very lucky that Anglesey had not in reality the hardiness to come back. Upon his coming into Paris he chose to write to Sarah, and to frame a story of an imaginary adventure, which had obliged Dilnick immediately to take post, and himself to make the sea-side with all expedition. But as they had both declared before they went to the combat, that they must return to Ireland, and that the preparations for their departure were not easy for strangers, who had resided so short a time at Paris, Anglesey had enlarged more than ever in his letter on the necessity there was for Sarah and her servants not to continue long at Paris. He had given her room to fear some part of the danger he supposed her uncle threatened with; and having sent to her a man of trust, whom he had charged to dispose her to the journey according to the first measures of Dilnick, he had reckoned that she would determine herself upon his word to follow an advice so urgent. One might moreover easily penetrate the principal motive that set him at work.

Yielding

Yielding with reason to the piercing alarms remaining from his wicked outrage, he was obliged, for the safety of his life, not to lose a moment in getting out of the way; and full of hopes, which he could not with any patience renounce, he would fain drag away Sarah after him, in order to draw all the advantage possible from what Dilnick had done in his favour, before she could get an account of his death.

The Count's friend having obtained liberty of seeing her, found her under the agitations into which this news had just then cast her. She had been prepared for these troubles by the measures Dilnick had taken for her departure, and by the orders he had given her to receive Anglesey as a man who must be her husband. But these two proposals throwing her at first into a mortal melancholy, every thing that tended to hasten the effects, was only fit to augment her trouble. In the mean-time, with the submission of an unfortunate victim, who could find no means to withdraw herself from her dependence, she had communicated Anglesey's letter to her servants; and not having power to declare her inclinations, she saw them make preparations for her departure with tears in her eyes, and despair in her heart. The death of her father, the absolute separation of Patrick, every thing that we had endeavoured to conceal from her with so much care, were not all the wounds she had yet to receive: The boisterous Dilnick had with all his skill endeavoured to make her relish more easily his new proposals, and reckoning as nothing the piercing of her by the most grievous strokes, he had interpreted the amazement that had checked the course of her tears, as the mark of a change he desired to find in her. In this situation, seeing the Count's friend come in, who had given her notice that he was a messenger from Anglesey and Dilnick, she expected nothing from his first words, but that he came to inform her that she must go, and that he was sent to serve her as a guide. I know not whether

ther she would have embraced the side of submission;
but she had scarce heard that he was come to her from
me, and from the Count and Countess of S——,
than opening her heart to hopes, she lifted herself
up on her bed with as much lightness and activity
as if she had no feeling from her wound; and taking
notice, by the windings he used in delivering himself, that he thought he risked something in speaking openly, she interrupted him with ardour, to conjure him to let her know, in two words, if she had
any ground of dependence remaining on my friendship, and on that of the Count and Countess. The
assurance she immediately received of it seemed to give
her as much strength as joy. She did not give him
leave to finish what he had to say. I am within a
moment, said she, of seeing myself forced to quit
Paris, and perhaps to accept a man for a husband
whom I detest. The only way open to preserve me
from the tyranny of my uncle, is to seek a sanctuary
in the generosity and friendship of the Countess of
S——. Go immediately and request this favour for
me. He, who judged from our own longings, that
we had nothing to hope for more happy, boldly took
on him to warrant our dispositions on that head, and,
perhaps flattered with the opinion he was going to
give us of his dexterity in returning so soon with
such good proofs of the success of his commission,
ordered chairmen to be called, and pressed Sarah to
make use of them that moment. The orders she
left with her servants were, not to slacken in the preparations for her departure; but, as they consisted in
nothing but packing up her luggage, and filling her
trunks, this care would equally serve the design of
removing them to the Count's.

Thus, without having executed his principal commission, our friend had in truth rendered to Tenermill and Sarah a service much more important than
I durst hope for. But the difficulty still remained
intire, to know from herself what she thought of the
irreparable step of Patrick, and how she was disposed

for

for Tenermill. I hugged myself with knowing, that she was already informed of what I should have had the most difficult task to communicate to her; for, with the subjects of complaint she had against Dilnick, I did not look on the news of his death as a discovery dangerous to her, or at least I did not fear from thence a renewal of grief, which could add any thing to what she had felt from the death of her father, and the last resolution of Patrick. We got to the Count of S———'s in the midst of these reflections. Her surprise was great to perceive me so near her chair; but that of Tenermill was much greater to see her, as it were, brought even to him into his apartment. Though he had a house of his own at Paris, finding himself in it without servants and without furniture, having left all his people at Dunkirk, he had taken no other lodging than that of the Count's.

Sarah was yet too weak to keep long out of bed; she accepted of one that was immediately offered her by the Countess. We had the discretion in this first moment not to let any thing drop from us that might recal her grief; and she herself, perceiving our views, thought of nothing but shewing her acknowledgments of gratitude for the services we were so ready to do her. But as soon as she had retired into the apartment that my sister had appointed for her, she prayed me to go in with her alone. The tears I saw burst out, and which, for some moments took from her the power of speaking, discovered the violence she had done herself in keeping them in. Alas! said she, after relieving herself by some sighs, do you know any one whose fate resembles mine? I am a stranger in a family, wherein I ought to hold the same rank with her, who has the generosity to afford me a sanctuary. I owe only to friendship, and perhaps to compassion, what I should hold by my own proper rights, if they had not been cruelly usurped. I have no longer any other pretension remaining to life or repose, but that which they would leave me by favour; and when the spite of my fate, and the cruelty

of

of men should cease to crush me with new wounds, that grief and bitterness, which yet always remains in the bottom of my heart, is sufficient to render me the most unfortunate of all my sex.

She stopped, being drowned in tears, and smothered even more by the multitude of her sorrowful reflections, than by the abundance of her sobs. A sight so moving had softened me even into tears, and I more than once took out my handkerchief to wipe them away. At length, resuming her words with a feeble and trembling voice, I have lost my father, continued she, I have lost my husband; the sense of finding in me so little obedience, is about losing me the esteem and affection of my uncle; I have lost every thing; I have nothing more remaining, my dear Dean, than to beg your aid to help me to die. Alas! hear me, added she, seeing me open my mouth to sweeten those black ideas by some words of consolation, suffer me to finish, and refer your exhortations and advice until I have acquainted you with all my sentiments. You ought not to doubt me, but that in retiring among you to avoid the persecutions of my uncle in favour of Anglesey, I did not reflect that this was to expose myself to those of my Lord Tenermill; and how are they perhaps going to be augmented, when they shall appear to him justified by the absolute loss of all my hopes? But I declare to you here, what will be more agreeable to him to hear from you than from me, I proclaim my eternal hatred to whoever shall dare to pronounce to me the name of Love; and this disposition shall infallibly continue all my life. Nevertheless, as I have nothing but the sentiments of my grief to object to him, and that after having lost the sole good that could make me happy, I would not refuse my happiness from him, if I were capable of accepting it from any one, I have no thought either to fly him, or to reject his cares: I even think of giving him a token of my gratitude, which he little expects. I know he is not rich. My estate is useless to me, as long as
the

the Count and his spouse will conserve the sentiments they have for me; which may he enjoy until death has delivered me from my pains, or till a change, that I do not foresee, shall have given me a relish for other pleasures than sorrow and tears. The sole condition I impose on him is, never to speak to me of marriage or love.

A declaration so formal, took from me the very desire of opposing her sentiments. But, in the name of Tenermill rejecting the offer she made of the use of her estate, I prayed her to believe us as capable as herself of a generous sentiment, and not to suspect any view of interest in our services. My brother, said I, aspires to the happiness of pleasing you. He will know how to retrench even from his cares every thing that might remove him from this aim, and I find him happy enough that you consent to endure them. It seemed to me at the bottom, that this preference she gave to him over Anglesey was flattering to him; and far from judging of it in another light, he confessed to me, when I went to inform him of what passed, that he drew from thence a very sweet omen for the success of his love. Nevertheless, upon some advice he had received from Dunkirk, he was obliged to be gone the day following to rejoin his squadron. The grief he had in leaving Sarah, and the instances with which he recommended to me to cultivate those seeds of goodness she had expressed for him, were perhaps the most tender sentiments that had ever disturbed his heart.

Anglesey, impatient of the delay which he ascribed to the daughter of Fincer, writ to her more than once to press her to make haste to Calais. He continued to use the name, and to lay a stress upon the commands of her uncle, whom he supposed to have crossed the seas, and to wait for her at Dover. At length, being informed by the letters of his agent whom he had left at Paris, of the resolution she had taken to retire into my family, and concluding, all at once, that she was no longer in the dark as to
the

the death of Dilnick, and that she had surrendered herself to Tenermill's passion, he sent for his sisters, and embarked himself with them for Ireland. I had opened all his letters by the orders of Sarah herself, who was willing to spare herself that trouble: I had found in the last, that he had spoke openly of the misfortune of Dilnick, from a supposition that the knowledge of this accident, which she might have received from somebody else, was the cause that hindered her from leaving Paris, and following the will of her uncle: This opportunity appeared to me so natural, to inform her in reality of her loss, that I thought it my duty to lay hold of it, without any other precaution than to add to my account the ordinary consolations of religion. I had to do with a heart so exercised in troubles, that a new misfortune could add but little bitterness to it. But the advantage I drew from doing this, was to fasten closer the bonds that had linked her to my family, by giving her room to think there scarce remained any thing in the world so near to her. She stretched out to me her hand, upon communicating this reflection, and conjured me to hold the place of the father and uncle she had lost.

I had the first day performed the funeral offices to Dilnick, and from an impatience to learn news of Patrick, had dispatched my valet to the castle of the Count de S——, to wait for his return. He had given me, the day following, a detail that had pleased me, for many reasons. The King had approved of my brother's vigorous defence, and had taken upon himself to put a stop to all the consequences of it. Nevertheless, conceiving that a rencounter of this nature might draw on him a prosecution at law, and revive the memory of his former actions, which might always expose him to some danger, he had given him orders to be gone two days after to Spain, and his instructions had been drawn up without any delay. Thus, there being nothing to call him back again to St. Germain, he had taken his licence

cence of abfence from the King. Whatever might now ſtop him was only decency to take his leave of us at Paris; but he had thought himſelf, that other confiderations ſhould hinder him from appearing there, and had taken the opportunity of Jacin to make his apologies. His commiſſion was to be of ſo ſhort a continuance, that he reckoned to be back in France in four months, and his intentions were not to carry his wife with him.

He would have been ſo unlucky as to have come to the Count's without knowing what he might have found there. I could not be too much pleaſed at the account that delivered me from this diſtreſs. Moreover, it ſeemed to me, that among the ſcruples yet remaining concerning his marriage, if the circumſtances of his departure did not give me room to propoſe the reparations I thought neceſſary to cover the reproach, yet his abſence would at leaſt leſſen what appeared criminal to my eyes, in a commerce that I could not bring myſelf to treat as lawful. I yet flattered myſelf, that this interval would give me time to obtain as formal a conſent as I could deſire from Sarah Fincer. Although ſuch a conſent might coſt her little, after the manner ſhe had explained herſelf to me, upon the loſs of all her hopes, neverthelefs I thought her affliction was yet too lively to permit her to conſent openly to the happineſs of her rival; and I hoped from time what the fear of irritating her grief had obliged me to retard.

Having communicated the report of Jacin to the Count de S———, and to Tenermill, who had prepared himſelf to go to Dunkirk, I had the ſatisfaction to ſee them enter into my views. We contented ourſelves in ſending back my valet to Patrick, to expreſs to him our concern, that we could not have the pleaſure of ſeeing him before his departure, and the reaſons that detained us at Paris. Our intention was to give him notice at the ſame time, that his wife ought not to think, during his abſence, of coming to the Count's. He went away indeed the day following, and the

the laſt letter of Angleſey arriving a few days after, I thought myſelf from every quarter at liberty enough to hope for a little tranquillity, after ſo many ſtorms and agitations.

I fancied at leaſt, that all my duties were going to be confined to the care of conſoling Sarah Fincer, and ſome journies to St. Germain, from which I could not diſpenſe with myſelf at times, to attend the duties of my new employment. I could not forget alſo another care, which was to write into Ireland, to make a reſignation of my benefice. My vicar had ſo well merited this favour by the conſtancy and zeal of his ſervices, that I did not look farther for a ſucceſſor. I was excited neverthelefs by the advice of ſeveral perſons, not to make too much haſte in taking this ſtep; and their reaſons would have made ſome impreſſion on me, had they been more conformable to my principles. They repreſented, that in the uncertain ſituation of the King's affairs, prudence ought not to make me look on the title and penſion he had granted me as a very ſolid eſtabliſhment; and if it ſhould happen to fail, I ſhould perhaps bitterly regret to be deprived of the only retreat, in which I might reckon my real ſettlement. I was ſenſible of the prudence of this reflection; but ſince I had accepted the King's favours, I did not think myſelf any longer at liberty to divide my cares. Religion and charity are rules ſo ſtrict, that I trembled to have been removed by ſo long an abſence from Coléraine. The debt I owed my flock could no longer ſquare with the engagements I had taken on me at court. In fine, whatever turn the King's affairs might take, had I not aſſurances enough in the friendſhip of the Count and Counteſs de S―― to look on their houſe as an agreeable retreat, from which I had no reaſon to fear being ſhut out? If I was obſtructed by any deſire, it was that of making a journey to Ireland, to turn over, in my own perſon, the precious burden on my vicar, of which I had thoughts of diſcharging myſelf. I foreſaw that the

King would, sooner or later, employ me in passing the seas, and bringing over into France Linch's treasure: His hints had made me judge, that he would with pleasure receive a proposal of this nature; and two motives of such importance had, without doubt, power enough to shake me. But since my affection for my family was the principal reason that stayed me in France, I looked upon that love as another duty that called for all my cares. Sarah could not be without my presence, and the marriage of Patrick had left in me so many scruples, that it did not give me liberty to absent myself voluntarily, before I was delivered from them. So I chose to resign my benefice by letter, and to wait the King's orders for Linch's treasure.

My life would have had nothing in it disagreeable during the absence of Patrick, if it had continued a long time such as I led for about eight days. All the time I did not pass at St. Germain was taken up with an extreme pleasure in consoling Sarah Fincer, or in the enjoyment of a society full of charms, in the conversation of the Count and Countess, or in the studies of my closet; occupations I should never be tired of. But when I had the spouse of Patrick (who had taken on her the title of my lady) least in my thoughts, I was informed by Jacin, that he had met her in Paris, in a very brilliant equipage; and that, having had the curiosity to follow her, he had learned from her servants, that she had there hired a very sumptuous house. I admired she was so soon weary of her solitude. Nevertheless, not daring to believe she had quitted it without the approbation of my brother, I charged my valet to dive more fully into her situation and conduct.

Jacin assured me two days after, that if she was sensible to any thing, it had little the appearance of being for the absence of her husband; or if such thoughts, added he maliciously, made the torment of her heart, she spared for nothing to sweeten them by all the consolations she could procure at Paris.

She

She had given herself up to all the pleasures that opportunity presented: The play-house, entertainments, brilliant assemblies, with her divided all the day: Those of the night were taken up either in giving suppers at her house, which lasted till daylight, or in being an ornament at the tables of others, and receiving the flatteries addressed to her sprightliness and beauty. I easily discovered from this detail, that Jacin was ill disposed to her, and that he took a pleasure in representing to me, under odious colours, circumstances that might be most unsuspected and innocent. His inclinations had always a bias for Sarah; he had seen her moaning, and as it were sinking under the weight of her misfortunes, while her rival was in a state of triumph and adoration. This, then, was enough to render the turn of his story suspected by me. Nevertheless, I could not imagine that he could have the impudence to alter the truth for the sake of gratifying his prepossessions, and I resolved at least to dive into the facts, but with which (I could not conceal it) I was deeply wounded.

I had never yet studied with care enough the character of Mademoiselle de L———, to flatter myself with having penetrated it. The opportunity I had of seeing her familiarly in Ireland, had led me only to judge of the vivacity of her mind, and the affections of her heart, from the sensibility I had seen in her for every thing that was capable of afflicting her. But this disposition is so common to women, that I was not from thence more ascertained of her principles. I knew she had been educated with too much constraint. Her praises, which I had heard my brother so often sound, had given me no surprise from the mouth of a lover. It might be true, that with the two qualities I have just now ascribed to her, she hath drawn both prudence and modesty from her education. She might even have received from nature as much integrity and goodness as charms; but Patrick himself had never seen
her

her in any of the circumstances, wherein to judge of the bottom of her sentiments from her deportment.

Could it be possible, said I, in my first reflections, that she could have looked upon two months solitude as a severe situation, to make the amusements of Paris necessary, if she had a heart so much filled with love, as she had persuaded my brother of? Or, if it be true, that her affection had been sincere, could she have a mind so full of levity, and an imagination so weak, as not to find a resource in herself, nor in the remembrance of what she loved, to support herself against tediousness? I could not suspect her of any thing that might wound her duty, and knowing Patrick, I could afflict myself only in his not having found in the companion of his life what I knew was most proper to please him.

I imparted to the Count and Countess De S—— the sorrow I felt from this conduct. They banished my suspicions by divers reasons, and I even found in those of the Count more of study and thought than my complaints appeared to call for. He laid before my eyes all the reasons that should seem to make me easy in the affection and fidelity of Mademoiselle De L—— for my brother; and not thinking her capable, said he, of losing so soon the memory of a man she adored, he exhorted me to be fully satisfied in the bottom of her sentiments. There remained yet with me a strong impression from this manner of defence; I stayed till I was alone with him. You have not spoke, said I, with all the openness that I expected from your friendship. This reproach made him agree, that he had concealed from me one part of his reflections, and excusing himself from the fear he had of being transported into any rash judgment, he confessed, that the doubts I had of the character of Mademoiselle De L—— were not a sentiment new to him. It was not curiosity, continued he, that made me observe her inclinations. I have seen her passionately in love with our dear Patrick, and I was charmed with the mutual

tual testimonies of their affections: But the opportunity I had of seeing her freely during her long residence at Saisons made me take notice of a thing which I took no pains to discover. She is indiscreet and sensual. These two defects are happily enough disguised by an air of modesty, which she is indebted for to her education; nevertheless the power of her natural constitution has seemed to me to hurry her away in a thousand circumstances; and I would not tell it you so freely, if I made my judgment only from the first of these defects. I have observed her relish for sensuality, which has surprised me to see in a young lady, in whom I could not suppose any knowledge of the pleasures of love. The Countess, who has seemed to you so reserved in speaking of her, has made the same observations; and we have sometimes admired together the prepossessions of Patrick, who always shut his eyes upon a thousand things, that could not please even a lover.

In truth, added the Count, whether it happened that the innocence of the thoughts of Mademoiselle De L⸺, or the continual presence of me and the Countess, had had the power of serving as a curb to her, she always contained herself within the bounds of prudence; and when, after her marriage, she chose to retire among the English nuns, I praised a resolution, that seemed to prove the injustice and temerity of my remarks. But what I have learned from you to-day, seems so contrary to all sorts of laws, that they have made me recollect things that were almost effaced in my memory; and my reflections have cast me, as it were in spite of myself, into all the mistrusts that you have taken notice of.

This confession was not sufficient to satisfy me. I represented to the Count, that having more understanding than I in the evil he seemed to fear, he ought to furnish me with his advice, and perhaps make some remonstrances to Mademoiselle De L⸺, from whence we may yet hope that she would take

no

no offence. He answered me, that the second of my demands embarrassed him; that a commission of such a delicate nature was as little agreeable to his humour as his age; but that my quality of an ecclesiastick, and as the first born of my family, authorising me to use a freedom of speech with the wife of my brother, he was persuaded, that advice of this nature could have no greater influence than from my mouth.

Nevertheless, as much as he thought such instances requisite, so much did he recommend to me to separate from them all harshness and sharpness. It is not always the force of reason, said he, that will prevail on a woman to condemn herself, and to change her thoughts or conduct. Pride and self-love, which watch incessantly at the entrance of her mind, will drive back all hints that injure them. But with a little address to gain these two guards, one may come to make her listen to reason, and not much fail intirely to gain those watches over by the tender methods of sweetness and pleasure. This advice, of which I was sensible of all the wisdom, became to me a rule, which held the place of experience.

The day following I determined to pay a visit to my sister-in-law; for I ought at length to pass over the repugnance I had to this time observed, and to give her that name, of which she had robbed Sarah. She seemed surprised to see me. The sanctuary we had given her rival was an offence, she was by no means disposed to forgive us easily; and her resolution upon her coming to Paris had been to keep up no commerce with us. I found her in the condition my valet described, adorned with every thing that might help to set off her charms, and less brilliant even by her dress, than by the air of joy that animated her eyes. As she had been prepared to go abroad with a gentleman who gave her his hand, the remembrance of the Count's maxim made me fear lest she took my visit as an
unseasonable

unseasonable accident, that might give her a prepossession against my remonstrances. But she pressed me herself to take a chair, and without appearing constrained at the presence of the gentleman, asked me with so free an air, to what it was she owed the honour of a visit she so little expected, that full of the ideas which possessed me intirely, I found myself under some perplexity to answer her. She perceived it herself, and imagining that I had something in private to communicate to her, she took me by the hand with the same air of freedom to lead me into her closet.

I confess this air of gaiety, so different from the sweet modest countenance I had always observed in her, and in the circumstances wherein I expected that my looks only might be thought a reproach to her, disconcerted me even to the taking away that presence of mind necessary to unfold myself to her. Moreover, what means had I of entering without preparation into a matter so odious, as that which brought me there? This was to lose sight of the advice the Count had given me a taste of; and I must of necessity have observed, that the moment she was going abroad, to give perhaps a loose to pleasures, was not that I ought to choose to load her with reproaches and lessons of morality. Thus I remained under the most painful uncertainty, and I did not deliver myself from it but by confessing, that I had an affair of importance to discourse with her upon, for which I requested a more favourable opportunity. She answered, that she would grant it to me freely, but did it with a wandering air, and an appearance of indifference, which persuaded me, that my request was the least thing in her thoughts.

The moment I prepared to leave her, she had notice given her that two persons, whom she expected, were in their coach at the door. She leaped joyfully at this news, and stretching out her hand to the gentleman, without giving further the least attention to me, she went down stairs to the coach that waited, and immediately drove off from her house.

In the amazement of so sudden a departure, having asked some of her servants, who continued about me, what was become of their mistress, they answered, that they could not tell. They knew however the two persons who came to take her up. One was her common companion, a woman of quality, of a general acquaintance, and who had obtained an extraordinary reputation for magnificence and gallantry. Her name was Madame De S———. For about eight days past there has been so strict a friendship struck up between her and my Lady, that they cannot live two hours asunder, and one or other of them always takes their friend in the coach. They could give me no further information. The two lacqueys who attended my Lady might be better informed; but they had orders to keep silence. And he who gave me the account added maliciously, that without doubt they were well paid for holding their tongues.

He could not tell me the names of the two gentlemen that accompanied the ladies. I returned to the Count's with this sole discovery, of which I was in great haste to give him an account. But he had scarce heard the name of Madame De S———, but lifting up his eyes to heaven; Good God! said he, what do you tell me? Are you sure you have been well informed? My memory not having deceived me, I asked in my turn the cause of such a sharp exclamation. You are going to hear it, said he, and without other preparation he continued to make me this recital.

Madame De S——— was one of those ladies of France, who, with a great estate and much wit and beauty, might have expected the highest fortune, and the most happy life, by some marriage suitable to such great favours of Heaven. She was educated with these hopes, and did not enter into the world without being proposed in a manner as a pattern to all the rich and illustrious
young

young ladies of Paris. But an excess of liberty, which her parents indulged her in too much, exposed her greatly to the desires of a thousand young gentlemen, who had not the same advantages; and her taste particularly declared itself for a musketeer, who had nothing else to recommend himself but his birth and person. Happy both one and the other, if, in surrendering themselves up to the pleasures of love with so little prudence, as to be soon compelled by necessity to a marriage, they had found their good fortune in the constancy of their passion; but the custom of seeing one another having in the end brought them to a disgust, Madame De S———, naturally haughty and proud, perceived the injury she had done herself by her imprudence, and pushed her resentment against her seducer even to disdain and hatred.

The first mark she shewed him of these was a comical reparation for all his rivals, to whom she reproached herself for having preferred him. She called to mind their names, and the greatest part of them being of known birth, there was no difficulty of finding them out at Paris. She found the means of getting them to her again one after the other, and lavishing her favours on them, she took care to let them know to what passion they were indebted for them. A confession of this nature, which she made them after glutting her revenge, took from almost all of them the appetite of keeping up the intrigue; and the numbers of those, to whom she had granted her favours, soon spread this adventure over Paris. I was among the number of those lovers one day, added the Count, and being more discreet than the rest, I never yet intrusted the matter to any body but you. Nevertheless, she found some among them, who got over the disgust of a declaration so capable of cooling them, and who seriously renewed their attachment for her. Among the rest she distinguished

distinguished one by a new caprice. This fresh passion became so strong, that not being more happy than at first in the choice of one more rich, she took up the humour of gratifying at least to the full her heart, by wasting riotously the best part of her estate with a man, whom she thought she loved exclusively of all others. This, besides, was a piece of revenge over and above what she desired to draw on her husband. She found such happy dispositions in her associate of this enterprise, that in the compass of a few years she sunk herself by expences and debts. Her husband, from whom it was impossible that the noise of her first adventure should be altogether concealed, dashed out of countenance with shame and grief, chose to go into the Emperor's service in the wars of Hungary.

This was about the time, continued the Count, that I married my first wife, with all the advantages that have led me to the happy situation I now enjoy. Madame De S———, being oftentimes reduced to her last shifts by an absolute disorder in her affairs, heard speak of my fortune, and did not at all despair to draw some part of it to herself. She fancied, that as I was condemned to live with an old and infirm woman, I should think myself too happy to receive new advances from a former mistress, whose charms I had known, and who, in promising me to carry on the intrigue with great secrecy, should induce me to accept of that consolation she tendered me under my circumstances. It was not nevertheless by open proposals that she tempted my fancy. She had in the neighbourhood of my castle a house, of which she had the enjoyment, though the rent of it was for a long time conveyed over to her creditors. She chose to retire here alone, and all the artifices she could invent for six weeks that I lived at my castle, she employed in persuading me, that it was her former inclination for me that confined her

to

to this solitude. I did not open my ears to her
flatteries; and I ought to hug myself for this
victory. The supreme art of Madame De S——,
and that by the exercise of which she has found
a resource in her misery, is to invade and possess
the mind and heart by her sweet and insinuat-
ing carriage. I should not have cast these things
as a reproach on her, if she had not made a
practice of them for her own sake only, or, to
explain myself more clearly, if she had never
abused them by inspiring people of rank with
tastes, for which she has made them pay most dear-
ly, not in their reputations only, but in their purses,
and has often by her extravagant expences brought
such to ruin, who have suffered her to take too
great an ascendant over them. Nobody could ever
more readily than she penetrate into the bottom of
a humour, in order to provoke all the passions,
and discover all the foibles of it. Thus she leads
on her cullies and her victims by roads so full
of charms, that though she thereby ruins their
fortunes and honour, yet they think themselves
still indebted to her zeal. I could bring you an
hundred examples of this, if I had need of other
proofs than my own testimony.

But what makes me tremble here, added the Count,
is, that not having discovered any other foible in
my Lady than a taste for sensuality, which I have
observed at Saisons, I already apprehend, that it is
by this way Madame De S——— will obtain her
confidence. Though my conjecture should be false,
an acquaintance so dangerous would be an evil always to be dreaded, and you cannot take too many
measures to break it; but if my reflections be just,
make all the haste you can, as to a danger the most
urgent, and fear lest your diligence should be too
late.

Under the alarms, into which this recital cast me
for Patrick, I did not stop a moment in demanding
any other explanations from the Count than such as
might

might shorten my labour in the execution of the advice he gave me. He proposed to me to make a second visit to my Lady, and to inform her without dissimulation to what she was exposed by linking herself to Madame De S———. The character of this woman being too flagrant to require any cautions, he was in hopes that the bare knowledge of the danger would make a young person open her eyes, who had not yet had time to harden herself against her duty. Try this way, said he; it is the most mild; and we will turn over to the last extremity those remedies, to which we may be compelled by the common interest of our honour.

This choice would without doubt have been the wisest, if I could have got an opportunity of unfolding myself openly to my Lady. But she had found my visit troublesome from the first moment; and when she had so readily offered to lead me into her closet to hear me, she thought only of more speedily getting rid of my company. She was accustomed for a long time to look on me as an impertinent censor, whose air and maxims without doubt agreed little with her inclinations. According to the new notions with which she was filled, I had become yet more terrible to her, and perhaps she had already objected to herself some weakness, of which my looks alone might seem to bear the condemnation: Moreover, having seen me a long time declare myself openly for Sarah Fincer, it was impossible but she should have some remains of resentment against me, which my late services had not intirely extinguished; and the resentment even of her husband, which he declared sufficiently in going away without seeing us, was a pretence she could always improve to cover her own. Be that as it will, the same day I saw her, and that she appeared disposed to receive me with pleasure, she did not go abroad till she had given orders to her porter to free her from my visits, and to have always some fair excuse in reserve to refuse me her door.

I endured

I endured a thousand times this refusal, without imagining the cause of it. But the impatience of my zeal increasing the more from this reason, I made my complaints of it to the Count, who saw more clearly than I did into a conduct so affected. The resolution I took by his advice was to take assistance from my pen. I writ to my Lady in terms the most circumspect I could possibly use, and sparing Madame De S——— with as much caution, I spoke to her of the strict friendship she had made with her, as of an imprudence, the blame of which I cast less upon the conduct of her friend, than upon the malignity of the public, who sometimes without reason set themselves up in opposition to innocence; and without examining into the bottom of my advice, I exhorted her to take some informations upon the character of this lady, before she pushed her friendship or confidence further with her. My motives, said I, in assuming a liberty, which I prayed her to take in good part, were not only my zeal and tenderness, which were not capable of being lulled asleep when she was concerned, but even the lively interest I ought to take in the satisfaction of my brother, whose love without doubt was subject to all the inconveniences of absence, that is to say, to a thousand passionate inquietudes for a spouse, whom he only cherished. This reflection, being the only one with which I apprehended she could be injured, I added, to sweeten it, every thing that friendship and politeness could find out most flattering, and I prayed her in the conclusion to grant me the opportunity of a conversation, in which I promised to be explicit.

I received no answer to this letter, and I many times requested it in vain. In fine, foreseeing nothing happy from so much obstinacy, and giving way to my fears, which augmented perpetually, I resolved, with the participation of the Count, to see Madame De S———, less for the sake of discovering myself to her, than for drawing some light from what she

she should say, and to let her know, that my family had their eyes open to the conduct of my sister-in-law, and that if she should engage her in any false step, we knew on what side our resentment ought to fall.

I chose an hour for my visit, which I proposed to make very short; and it was in the morning, with the view of being more sure to find Madame De S———. She was at home, and the readiness, with which I was admitted, made me judge, that my name, which I told at the door, was not unknown to her. But I owe little thanks to my Lady, who had informed her of it, and had joined to her account the portrait of my person and character. She had painted me with features, that must have made a lively impression on Madame De S——, since her first motion, after having seen who I was, had been to rise briskly off her chair, and run directly into her closet, doubting whether she could have courage enough to endure my deformity. I judged of her thoughts by her posture. She held the door of her closet half open, and only thrusting out her head with an air of curiosity and fear, she seemed to be puzzled at the first glance, whether she should resolve to return into the room, or hide herself altogether. The moment she looked at me, I could see her eyes, which she opened with a new effort. In fine, having considered me a moment, she found me without doubt less frightful than ridiculous; for breaking out into laughter without respect or caution, she ran forward to meet me with the most extravagant tokens of admiration, and for a quarter of an hour did not cease clapping her hands, and asking those who were about her, if ever they saw a sight so fantastical.

I cannot at all disown but my figure might make such an impression upon a sprightly and polite woman at her first seeing me. This was the thought I had myself of it. Thus, far from being disconcerted at the reception she gave me, I only smiled

at

at this excefs of pleafantry; and praying Madame De S⸺ to give me a moment's converfation, I made a fign with my hand to her fervants, that I defired to be alone with her. My courage turned the fcene to my advantage. It was not the impreffion before her that induced Madame De S⸺ to receive me with fo little refpect to my character. The plan of it had been formed between her and my Lady; though they had not forefeen the opportunity they would have to execute it. My letter had almoft equally offended them. They had judged by agreement, that not being able to anfwer me with good manners, without betraying their refentment, nor in a harfh and angry ftile, without taking from me perhaps the courage of feeing them again, they refolved to difpenfe with themfelves abfolutely from making me any anfwer, with the hopes that I fhould myfelf come to demand one; and the order of refufing me entrance into my Lady's houfe had been fuperfeded at the gate. Among many projects of revenge, they refolved upon that of turning me into ridicule by an extravagant raillery on my figure. Madame De S⸺ had paffed three days at her friend's houfe in expectation of me, and being prepared for the outrage intended me, the unexpected vifit I paid at her houfe raifed in her a defire of acting one part of the comedy fhe had ftudied.

In the mean-time, when I had invited her with a grave and preffing voice to be feated, in order to hear me, I faw her countenance change, and obferved embarraffment enough in her eyes, to flatter myfelf that I fhould foon gain fome afcendant over her. A woman without wit would have appeared to me more difficult to reclaim, becaufe I fhould have defpaired to make her fenfible of the force of my reafons. But the Count having prepoffeffed me with the character of Madame De S⸺, I did not doubt but in fpight of the irregularity of her manners I might engage her in a folid converfation, from whence I hoped

hoped to draw as much advantage for herself as for my sister-in-law. In one word, I had proposed to employ all my talents and zeal to make her ashamed of the disorder of her conduct; and not being discouraged at the reception she gave me, I hoped even more to bring her to a submission, when I saw I had so easily prevailed in gaining from her some respect.

This hope was natural enough from the consideration only of the common rules by which the heart and mind are conducted; but I was quite out in my judgment to suppose, that a coquette, long exercised in the art of masking her notions and opinions by perpetual impostures, could have honesty enough to submit to truth, even at the time she should gain light and understanding sufficient to see and be sensible of it. Madame De S—— listened to me. Perhaps she was at first hurried away by the air of authority that I affected to maintain, and I thought I observed this for some moments during the continuation of her embarrassment, from which she had not yet had time to recover. But soon recovering her assurance, she had at the same time resumed an air of licentiousness and gaiety familiar to her. I took notice of this change. My discourse heating her already, I should have expected from it an effect quite contrary. Nevertheless, I pursued the motions of my zeal, and in all the complaints I made of my sister-in-law, I not only without scruple named the cause that alarmed me for her conduct, but taking occasion from my reproaches to add to them what I thought most powerful in the principles of religion and morality, I flattered myself after a long harangue, which she listened to with the same affectation of sweetness and complaisance, that she had at least taken some relish for hearing me, and I had the credulity to interpret it as the first mark of success I had to desire.

She appeared indeed glad to hear me, and perhaps had found justice and method enough in my expressions to form to herself an agreeable appearance of the warmth and zeal with which I explained myself.

self. But the approbation she seemed to give to my discourse proceeded from a source quite foreign to my notions. I should have had a difficulty to be persuaded to this, if the experience I had of it had not been a proof that admitted of no reply. In hearing me, Madame De S—— had thought me very comical to undertake her conversion, and struck with this notion, had lent her attention to my reasons and proofs, much less than to a very whimsical project that came into her mind. The accounts she received from my sister-in-law, and even the ardour of my zeal, of which she had received a convincing testimony, making her easily judge, that the love of honour and religion was my predominant passion, she thought herself capable of assuming some empire over me by these two foibles; and, pushing her views much further, she imagined, that with a man of my figure nothing could be more glorious for her, nor help better to confirm the opinion she had of her own artifices, than to employ the notion she had taken of my character by inspiring me with sentiments of love for her. This thought had so much force over her mind in its birth, that immediately referring to it all her pains, she had power enough over herself not only to hear me with the appearance of a passionate satisfaction, but in the end to give her approbation to every part of my discourse. The snare was not at all palpable or gross: Her first expressions were as moderate, as her looks and the tone of her voice appeared to be stripped of all artifice. For some moments she fixed her eyes on me, as if, in the novelty of the impulses which she felt, she had been searching into the cause of an impression that had filled her with amazement. In fine, appearing to surrender herself to the power of those truths she had just heard, she stooped her head towards me: My dear, said she, with an affectionate tone, as it is impossible for truth to employ expressions more powerful to make itself heard, I confess also that it never before made so great an impression on me. Oh! that

that this were the moment, that heaven had marked out for my converſion, added ſhe, appearing to admire what paſſed in her heart! You will have at leaſt the glory of having ſtrongly ſtaggered me, and I begin by promiſing you, that I will give a faithful account of this converſation to my Lady. She thought alſo of improving the opportunity of ſeeing me again by my approbation; and I avow, that in the joy I felt of finding her enter ſo freely into my views, I had not the leaſt diffidence in her ſincerity.

Nevertheleſs, relying little on the work I had begun, if I did not draw an abſolute promiſe from her to be conducted by my advice, I furniſhed her againſt myſelf with arms which were yet more infallible, by propoſing to her two things, which ſhe deſired as ardently as I; the one was, to receive my viſits, in order to enſure the fruit that I aſcribed to my firſt exhortations; and the other, to diſpoſe my Lady to afford me an opportunity of converſation, from whence I had already hoped to obtain the ſame advantages over her, and to make her return as eaſily within the bounds from whence ſhe had wandered. Madame De S———, though ſure enough of making her conſent to every thing ſhe ſhould propoſe, yet laid a ſtreſs on the efforts, ſhe pretended ſhe ſhould have occaſion to uſe, to engage her to receive me at her houſe; and the reaſon ſhe gave me for this repugnance being only the reſentment ſhe ſuppoſed ſhe had againſt my family, ſhe compleated my perſuaſion, that ſhe had towards it as much honour in her ſentiments, as I found probability in her diſcourſe.

The ſame day I communicated to the Count the hopes I had taken up upon ſuch ſlight grounds. They appeared ſuſpicious to him, and friendſhip not ſuffering him to diſguiſe from me his jealouſies, he inſpired me with a diffidence that I yet had the fooliſhneſs to upbraid myſelf with. The ground of it nevertheleſs remained in me, notwithſtanding the efforts with which I thought myſelf obliged to oppoſe it; and charity, that made me fear to make a raſh judgment,

ment, not being able to efface the traces of it, which continued at least in my memory, this aid, that Providence had laid up in store for me, served to save me harmless from the most dreadful snare to which the bias of nature had ever yet exposed my virtue. I should have drawn a veil over this profane scene, if there had not been a necessary connection between it and the history of my brothers; and further, if I did not flatter myself that the reflections it raised would be of some utility to my readers.

The day following I received a message from Madame de S——.——, that my Lady would receive my visit at her request; and the hour being appointed for that afternoon, I did not fail to follow the Instructions given me in her letter. I found her at my sister-in-law's. They had two gentlemen with them, one of whom I knew to be him I had seen there the first time. Although they were both dressed out with great neatness, and that their appearance discovered some air of distinction, they affected nevertheless to behave to me with such submission and respect, that I could not long believe them to be of a rank equal to my own. My Lady also soon put an end to my doubts, by declaring that one of them was her master of musick, and the other her master of languages, from whom she was learning English: and acting over with the same air the part she had without doubt studied with Madame de S——, I think, Monsieur, said she, to make you easy all at once. I have been informed by Madame, that some reproaches you have made me in a letter were not at all a banter, and that very black suspicions of my conduct have taken hold of your mind. I would fain ease you of them, by informing you that it is a desire of acquiring new knowledge, or perfecting myself in what I had, that made me choose to quit the country; and I thought that the absence of my husband could not be better employed. In regard to your religious maxims, of which Madame de S—— hath given me such a faithful account, I do not imagine, that, at my age, you will think to make me follow

low them in all their rigour; and if Madame, added she, is so moved at them as to put them in practice, and be already determined to put herself under your direction, I shall entreat both one and the other of you not to disturb my mind with ideas of perfection, which at present surpass my strength.

This discourse, pronounced with the most easy air, had all the effect that was expected from it. I found in it as much innocence in the conduct of my sister-in-law, as sincerity in the conversion of Madame de S———. I made them both apologies for having given too much credit to the impulses of an indiscreet zeal; and even fearing to explain myself too openly before the master of languages and the musician, I contented myself with offers of service and friendship, which were accepted without affectation. I would very willingly forget, said my sister-in-law, the just complaints, which cannot pass so soon out of my memory. You shall be free to come here as often as you shall find any satisfaction in it; and if your zeal, or the new-born piety of Madame de S———, do not confine themselves to exhortations which you are engaged to make her at her house, you may continue them here, when she happens to be here with you. But never expect, added she, that I will be a witness of those mysterious obscurities, that will make my mind gloomy, and chill my blood.

The liberty they both wished for the success of their private views could not be better established. Nothing presented itself to my mind that could awaken the diffidence with which the Count had inspired me. Thus, during the time that my sister-in-law hugged herself for having disposed me to serve as a cloak before the eyes of the publick, and even before those of her husband, I looked on this liberty she had granted me (to be with her at all hours of the day) on my side as an advantage for her, and for the honour of our family; and I did not doubt but it was sufficient to silence all sorts of suspicions. The Count surrendered himself to this way of reasoning. The
opinion

opinion he always had of Madame de S―――― had made him wish, that this commerce might be absolutely broken off; but I talked to him with so much force of a conversion, whereof I congratulated myself for being the minister, that, yielding at length to my hopes, he agreed, that a woman of that merit might become as dear to people of honour, when she should change her principles and manners, as she would appear odious and contemptible in their eyes with the conduct she had hitherto observed.

I should enter badly into the circumstances of this unlucky adventure, if I should too far put off to give some eclaircissements necessary in this place for the understanding it. Madame de S――――, who had a little house in the Count's neighbourhood, having been not at all discouraged at the efforts she had in vain made to infinuate herself into his esteem, had hopes of succeeding better with Patrick, when he was retired there with his spouse. It had been no difficult matter for her to strike up an acquaintance with a man, who sought to amuse himself in his solitude; but his departure for Spain interrupted her projects, and making her put off her hopes to another season, she had fancied, that for her principal end, which was to repair the disorder of her fortune, by sharing a little in that of another, she had not less advantages for that end to promise herself from his absence. A young and amiable woman, such as his spouse was, appeared to her an easy conquest, and the rather when a few days of familiarity and acquaintance had given her the opportunity of unravelling the bottom of a character, which she had not the art to disguise. She thought herself sure of success, as soon as she had discovered in her a brisk relish for pleasure. All her discourses related only to that end; she often had stirred up in the heart of my Lady a passion to share in some part of the diversions of Paris, so much the more ardent, as, in the absence of her husband, she could find nothing in the country to serve as a remedy against tediousness.

Never-

Nevertheless, she proposed at first only to pass a few days in town; and Madame de S———, who had formed much more extensive schemes, was well upon her guard to combat this resolution. Not having any longer the house she lived in after she had left her own for making the journey to Germany, she took furnished lodgings, which agreed very well with her intentions of continuing in town but a short time; but the forecast of her companion had so well provided for every thing to encourage her stay, that two days after her arrival she found in the neighbourhood a house to be let ready furnished, and the rent appeared so moderate to my Lady, that, added to the advantage of being absolutely at liberty within herself, it determined her to accommodate herself with it for some months. The truth was, this house and furniture were prepared by the artifices of Madame de S———. But this was not the most impoisoned part of her services. She had thought, that to secure a long time her prey, and to engage her in that sort of disorder, from which a woman scarce ever recovers, something was wanting more lively and poignant, than balls, shews, and all the common diversions of the town. It was necessary she should have love. She had, by long experience, known all the irregularities of that fatal passion; and without the assistances of her reason, she had no need of any other lessons than her own example. It was upon her own lovers she had cast her eyes to try this enterprize. With the knowledge she had of mankind, her passion always predominant for the same pleasures that had began her ruin, she could not fail having under her banners a well chosen militia. She detached then two of them, in whom she found by experience (added to all the qualities that could please the sex) all the wit and address that could conduct her to her views. She associated them in this enterprize by the common hopes, and finding lucky opportunities to introduce them succeffively to my sister-in-law, she did not in the least doubt, but if one them did

not

not carry away her heart, she should not escape the other.

It was true my Lady loved Patrick tenderly. A passion of so long continuance, and strengthened by so many adventures and obstacles, must in a manner have penetrated into the bottom of her heart. But she was such a woman as the Count had observed, too much given to sensuality and pleasures. The very power of her sensations was a perpetual danger to which her virtue was exposed, from the necessity it laid her under of employing them; and over a heart of this frame the present object has always those powers and advantages, against which it is very difficult to make a defence. The first of these lovers, that Madame de S⸺ raised up for her, seemed to be led only by the power of love. A pretended chance brought him to a party at a ball, where my sister-in-law was flattered by receiving those praises that her beauty deserved. She saw him come in at a time when perhaps her self-love was best satisfied, adorned with every thing that could set off his person, and without doubt, if she wished to see him among the number of her admirers; he affected so well his surprise and admiration at the first looks he cast on her, that she thought him more agreeable than any body else, from the tribute he paid to her charms. The union of esteem was formed at that instant. She became much more free, as soon as she understood that he was one of the best friends of Madame de S⸺, and the day following he obtained leave of paying regular visits to my Lady.

I say nothing but what she told me herself, in too lively circumstances ever to slip out of my memory. It was, nevertheless, not all at once that she suffered him to assume an empire over her heart; and the subtile Madame de S⸺, who was such an understanding judge of the power and progress of love, despaired so much for some days of the success of this first attack, that she made haste to form a second. She had taken care to make choice of two

men

men of different miens and conftitutions, to give, under one or the other form, a fure aim to the fhafts of love. The one was fair, the other brown. Strength and vivacity appeared to be the character of the one, and all the delicacies and graces feemed to fall to the lot of the other. It was neverthelefs with extraordinary preparations that the fecond was brought upon the ftage. The marvellous ftrikes apparently on the imaginations of women. A duel was counterfeited near my Lady's door, at the moment fhe had withdrawn at night. Madame de S——— knew the wounded combatant, who lay ftretched at length two paces from the door, and who had taken care to make a flight fcratch on himfelf, after having blooded on purpofe his fhirt and cloaths. They feemed to be in doubt whether he were not actually dead. Generofity and compaffion did not fuffer her to refufe a fanctuary to a man of quality, who ran an equal hazard for his life either from the law or his wound. He was taken into the houfe of my fifter-in-law. The ftory of his quarrel foon became the moft moving part of his adventure. His character was tendernefs and fweetnefs itfelf. He had drawn this misfortune on him by having too eagerly efpoufed the intereft of an unfortunate woman. He had to do with the moft hot-brained brute, and moft formidable fwordfman of all Paris. In fine, the furgeon, who had been gained over, not thinking he could be removed without imminent danger, my Lady was obliged, by her natural goodnefs, to give him an apartment in her houfe, and in the condition he was in, Madame de S——— had given her opinion, that this favour might be granted without fcandal.

Such were the enemies fhe let loofe againft the virtue of my fifter-in-law. The names they had affumed, of mafters of languages and mufick, impofed in reality on my credulity, and the fubmiffive behaviour they always fhewed me, confirmed me a long time in that error. Neverthelefs, I could not but be much furprifed, from the firft moment, to fee them

them use an extraordinary familiarity with the two ladies; and if I from thence suspected nothing that was capable of alarming me, I did not less condemn it as one of those excesses of prepossession and taste for talents, which sometimes allow too great a consideration and favour for the possessors of them.

I was always ignorant what progress they had made in the heart of my Lady, and the very conclusion of this sorrowful adventure did not inspire me with curiosity enough of seeking after further lights into it. But I remarked, that they always regulated her business; and, under pretence of music meetings, and other assemblies, which, as they said, had some relation to their studies, they manifestly engaged her in all the parties of pleasure suitable to their views or particular tastes. Even the very dexterous colours that Madame De S—— gave to such continual disorders, took away all suspicions that might have raised in me a desire to watch them; and being gained over, (for I owe this confession to truth) by the hopes of her conversion, with which she wonderfully fortified me, I sometimes reproached myself for having had such a bad opinion of her conduct, taken up from stories and testimonies, that I could not accuse of any thing but rashness. To make me open my eyes, I stood in need of an adventure as dreadful as what I have to relate.

I was often at the house of Madame De S——, or at that of my sister-in-law; and the more effectually to banish all mistrusts, they agreed to give me notice of the times they could receive me with freedom. Thus, under the pretext of providing for the quiet and calmness necessary for such serious conversations as ours ought to be, they found means of getting me out of the way at all times wherein my presence might be troublesome; yet nevertheless they every day gave me notice so unaffectedly of the hour they expected to see me the day following, and they appeared so satisfied with my visits,

that

that it never once came into my mind, that this exact order of them might be a concerted game. I passed whole hours with Madame De S———; and if my zeal made me think them short, the desire she had of bringing her adventure to a happy conclusion, or perhaps the satisfaction that fed her vanity, by reasoning with me upon the most important points of religion and morality, and receiving the praises that I often could not refuse to her wit, hindered her from thinking them tedious. It was easy for me to observe in her behaviour, and even in her looks, an air of complaisance and affection, that I found sometimes carried too far: but, in a woman who had been given up all her life to the vain amusements of the world, I looked on it as the remains of her ancient customs. If I was deceived so dangerously by her exterior appearance, which, on the contrary, was not made up of so much affectation as to endeavour to gain any empire over my senses, yet she fell into a much more ridiculous error in relation to my behaviour, in which she could not have discovered any thing but an ardour for the interest of her soul. The fire, that the warmth of a long conversation made sparkle in my eyes, and a Christian love and benevolence, from whence possibly some expressions less circumspect than my thoughts might have escaped, appeared to her as so many marks of the progress she made in my heart. She did not in the least doubt but I had penetrated the design she had to please me, and that stopping at that point which was most flattering in it for me, according to this way of thinking, that I had the weakness to be sensible of it; in so much, that, having begun on both sides to take our mutual motions from the meaning suitable to our desires, we should soon come to the point of thinking ourselves equally sure of victory. Perhaps Madame De S——— did not at first propose to push her enterprise so far. Her notions were corrupted, without doubt, by degrees; and in the mind of an artful coquette, the sole desire

of

of amusing herself with so ridiculous an adventure, was a motive capable of making her forget all decency and decorum. However that be, having one day tendered me her hand, upon which I imprudently let fall my head, without any intention of touching it with my lips, but, on the contrary, to dispense with myself from receiving it in mine, she took this over-hasty bowing of my head for the motions of a heart that trembled to explain itself more openly and apparently, and, with a design of letting me know she understood me, she stretched her hand forward to my face, and laying her fingers to my mouth, pressed them against my lips for a moment. If this familiarity gave me some surprise, I neverthelefs considered it as a light transport, which proceeded from the satisfaction of a heart, wherein a relish for virtue was beginning to arise from the influence of my advice. This reflection, which was not mixed with any doubt, was confirmed immediately by a proposal that Madame De S—— made with some air of embarrassment. As I had pressed her often to a review of all the irregularities of her life, and that she had always made some pretence for retarding that mortifying action, the meaning of her discourse did not appear to me at all ambiguous. Come to me, said she, sinking her voice, at ten o'clock this night, I will open to you my heart; and you shall not have the least reason to complain of my sincerity. I immediately was convinced, that she at length had vanquished all the difficulties she had to combat, and, that if she took the night-time to discharge her conscience of the load of her sins, it was owing to the remains of confusion, of which her springing piety had not yet the power to shake off the yoke.

It would be drawing an ill picture of her character, to imagine that her disposition was that of love, and her design that of leading me from weakness to weakness, to the point of inspiring me with inclinations, from whence she expected to gather the fruit.

In

In flattering herself with having softened my heart, she proposed no other pleasure from it than to triumph over the chastity of a mortified and austere man, who had himself attempted to triumph over her. She would humble him, who thought himself capable of instructing her, and who, after having endeavoured to frighten her by his menaces, had hopes of gaining the power of moving and convincing her by his reasons. In fancying she had seduced my mind and heart, she did not in the least think of taking any advantage of her victory; but a cruel malignity had put it into her mind, to make my weakness serve to divert as well as to revenge her. She had communicated this scheme to my sister-in-law; and the empire she already had over her, made her easily succeed in assuring herself of her consent, and even assistance. They had agreed, that as soon as my virtue should have abandoned me, Madame De S—— should propose the assignation, which she had already effectually appointed me at her house, and that, instead of coming to it herself, she should send in her place a woman extremely deformed, that care should be taken, (to deceive me more readily) that the place of rendezvous should be dark; and when they should think me given up to all the licentiousness of my appetites, as they imagined, the two ladies should appear with lights, and load me with justly merited reproaches. It was conceived, that this scene would afford some pleasure to the ladies, without obliging them to a conduct, from whence I had been desirous of laying down lessons of prudence; and following this plan, I should even have thanks to give them for keeping measures with me, in order to save at least my reputation. In the mean-time, Madame De S—— no sooner thought herself sure of my defeat, than she changed her thoughts; and nothing was more worthy of the corruption of her heart, than the new project she formed. She resolved, without discovering herself to my sister-in-law, to push the adventure herself

self to a conclusion, as much to make a trial of my conduct in an experiment, wherein she had reason to think me a great novice, as to enjoy her triumph in greater perfection; and, in the end, to make the advantages she should acquire over me serviceable to her other views.

The integrity of my heart having then banished all shadow of suspicion, I did not fail to attend punctually at the assignation. All my zeal in a manner reviving at the approach of the hour, I prepared for the ministry, which I thought myself ready to exercise, by redoubling my prayers. I appeared at Madame De S⎯⎯⎯'s door, and found there a woman who seemed to expect me, and who introduced me, with many circumspections, up a pair of privy stairs that led to her apartment. She recommended nothing to me but silence; and I was not a little surprised, that a ceremony, not usual in such a house, was accompanied with some air of mystery. The door of the apartment being open, I was desired to walk into the closet with the same cautions. At length I perceived Madame De S⎯⎯⎯, who was seated in a negligent posture, but adorned and set off with all the care, and less decency, than I ought to have expected. The only thought this affectation raised in me, was a reflection upon the ascendant of vanity, that does not abandon a woman, even in the most holy exercises of religion. In fine, the door of the closet being shut on me by the chamber-maid who introduced me, I was all alone with Madame De S⎯⎯⎯.

I rejected an impulse of my mind, that inclined me to reproach her for the ornaments of her dress; and, thinking some indulgence due to those remains of weakness, I approached her, and desired to know, if the dispositions of her heart corresponded with those she had taken up for employing the solitude and tranquillity we now enjoyed. This discourse was perhaps equivocal, although the circumstances had inspired me naturally with it. It might without doubt

doubt have been taken in a sense directly contrary to my thoughts, since helping to confirm Madame De S———— in hers, it gave room for some moments to the most extravagant conversation. Her answer was such, as one may imagine it to be, from the prepossession she was in. She talked to me of the dispositions of her heart, as of a love the most lively and impatient. What had it not cost her to delay the happy moment we were arrived at? and if my ardour was equal to hers, what could be wanting to the perfection of her happiness? Upon discovering herself with so much warmth, she took me by the hand, and pressing me to sit down near her, she possibly would have opened my eyes all at once by the vivacity of her action, if in the thoughts she was in, that I burned for her with an ardent passion, she had not desired to have an agreeable sight in the unravelling of my own projects. Thus with the appearance of moderating herself all at once, she complained only of not seeing my eagerness correspond better to hers; she even drew back her hand, with which she had yet held mine, and looking on me with a tender air on the elbow-chair whereon I sat, she immediately asked me, for what reason, with the views that brought me there, I had come in a long gown, which was so little suitable to such circumstances? I justified my garb from the reasons of decency, that even obliged me to wear it on this occasion, if I had not been accustomed to do it at all times. Our discourse upon this matter became a series of obscurities, into which I could not fancy she saw more clearly than I did. However, she had this advantage over me, of persuading herself, that she comprehended something in my reasons, that thinking me withheld by a remainder of modesty and fear, she could understand the most obscure of my expressions as a veil, in which I wrapped up my true sentiments; in lieu of which, not suspecting her at all of any other views than of speedily disburdening her memory of a load of faults, it happened almost at every word she pronounced,

that

that I was stopped by some difficulties of which I did not understand one word.

I attributed her motions at first to an impatience, and even a trouble, of which the soul is sometimes capable in the first approaches of zeal; but I began to fear at last, that in an imagination overheated by the grand objects with which I thought it filled, there was some resolution made that reason was little sensible of.

During this time she held the end of my girdle, which she rolled about her fingers, sometimes pretending only to amuse herself with it, sometimes squeezing it close, and drawing to her, with looks in which her ardour seemed to redouble. Tired at length with an excess of reservedness, of which she nevertheless accused my bashfulness, she got up, saying, that these men were strange creatures, to employ all their artifices to seduce the heart of a poor woman, and then to take advantage of their gravity and strength of mind to abuse their victory. This was a mischievous irony, which she thought to uphold by a thousand passionate caresses, with which she bore me down all at once.

The first efforts I made to defend myself from her, being taken (it may be) for an effect of the same embarrassment to which she had attributed my coldness, and the silence that my surprise hindered me from breaking, helping yet to maintain her in the same thoughts, she did enough, in a few moments to have made my reason rebel in her favour; and this was without doubt a more powerful succour, than that of my feeble virtue, which delivered me from such a frightful peril. I summoned up all my strength to tear myself from her arms; and all out of breath as I was, recovering with difficulty the power of speaking, I seated her in an elbow chair, where her own confusion detained her as much perhaps as the words I spoke. Madam, said I, with a disturbed voice, if it be a straying of your mind, an illusion of the enemy of your salvation, or any other forgetfulness of yourself, that in spite of your teeth transports you from your first resolutions into such unworthy excesses, recal your judgment, arm yourself with those great principles which I have laboured to instil into you, and be persuaded, that the assistance of Heaven is always superior to temptation. I perceive, added I, the wrong I have done by swerving from the ordinary custom to hear your confession: I ought, as much for myself as for you, to fear the danger of solitude. But if the corruption of our nature sometimes makes our falls so sudden, we can raise ourselves as speedily by repentance; and from one single motion of the heart often proceeds both sin and innocence.

As I made her this discourse, I had my hand leaning on her arm, from a remainder of mistrust that made me fear, lest she should fall again into a new fit; and I observed even her eyes, from thence to discover, from what new species of transport I had to save myself harmless. I know not whether this patience, with which I continued near her, gave her room to believe, that I might yet be vanquished, or whether she took (it may be) the softness of my reproaches only for the disguise of an hypocrite, who feared to discover himself with too little caution; but taking advantage of the situation I was in to attack me with more success, she gave greater strength than ever to the temptation, both by her caresses and looks. Some tender and animated reproaches, that she added to them at intervals, her sighs, that seemed to arise from the bottom of her heart, an air of languor diffused over her countenance, and all her attitude; in fine, the whole equipage of softness and sensuality, which she seemed to reunite about her, might perhaps have made me sensible, that man is always too weak when he voluntarily exposes himself to danger; if the thought itself, which came into my mind from the expressions of the sacred pages, had not made me take a resolution of retiring hastily. A short apostrophe, addressed to my enemy on turning my back to her, gave her to underſtand how remote ſhe was from her triumph. However, there was leſs of anger and harſhneſs, than of compaſſion in what I ſaid. I pity you, ſaid I, from whatever ſource this exceſs of corruption comes; and if you are ignorant of the judgments of heaven, I muſt tell you, that they are terrible againſt a hardening of the heart, which proceeds even to a contempt of its warnings and graces.

I haſtened to get out of this infected place, thanking the Author of my ſtrength, which ſupported a faithful Chriſtian in the love of virtue; and being as little ſenſible of the ſhame of being deceived, as not fearing to give up to Heaven the judgment of my intentions, I prayed him, out of his infinite mercies, to place to my account the ardour and purity of my zeal. But having deplored the melancholy ſucceſs of ſo great hopes, I did not fail to let my reflections fall on my Lady, and I began again to ſee with another eye all thoſe things that my illuſion had as it were accuſtomed me to look upon without diffidence or alarms. My firſt ſuſpicions nevertheleſs did not at all turn upon her two lovers: On the contrary, I did not forbear to take them for what I was told they were; and I was pleaſed in the midſt of my fears, to find yet the ſame likelihood in the reaſons that brought my ſiſter-in-law to Paris. Suppoſing, ſaid I, to hearten myſelf, that her intimacy with Madame de S―― may have a little diſordered her principles and conduct, yet the evil is not ſo inveterate as to be afraid already of its progreſs. Her deſign in quitting the country was not at all a formed reſolution of giving herſelf up to diſorder. She had in it an intention, which ſhe is carrying into execution; and when her unworthy friend had raiſed in her a deſire of it, to take occaſion from thence to engage her inſenſibly in the ſame corruption, even the neceſſity under which ſhe thought herſelf to employ this pretence, ſhews ſufficiently that ſhe had need of time and labour to ſucceed in ſuch a horrible project. I encouraged myſelf also to hope something from her motives of coming to town, which were not absolutely without probability and force; but I should have made one reflection much more just, if I had thought, that vice is not so slow in its progress as virtue, and that the bias of nature, which so often is of itself sufficient to hurry us along, will become a torrent by its rapidity, where it has received the unhappy instigation of counsel and example.

Self-love never had dominion enough over my mind to make me look on the confession I had made the Count of the mortifying success of my adventure, as a great sacrifice. He always had his mistrust of it, which he in vain laboured to communicate to me. I confessed to him, that his eyes were more penetrating than mine, and that this adventure was a new lesson to me, of which I humbly acknowledged the usefulness. My frankness proceeded even to discover to him the reasons I had to dispel my fears as to the conduct of my sister-in-law, without which I still confessed to him, that I should have thought myself the most culpable and unhappy of all men, to have by my mistake deferred those remedies, which we might with ease have applied earlier to the disorders. He let nothing drop in his answer that could increase the grief I felt at finding myself deceived; but recollecting one part of the advice he had given me, when I had declared my first fears, he added, that if decency had permitted him at that time to enter deeper into the conduct of that affair, he would have begun with every thing that would have forced my Lady to break with Madame de S———. Though, said he, the union that attaches me to you be very strict, yet it would not be proper for me to take up the voice of a reformer in your family, especially in regard to a woman, who has entered into it, as I have done, only by alliance. But to whatever degree the evil be spread, you may be assured, added he, that if there remains any hope of reforming it, yet it is not to be done, but by re-

moving

moving the productive cause thereof. He paused a moment, as if it were to give himself up to his own reflections. If I might explain myself with freedom, said he, you are not from henceforth a more proper person than I am to undertake the enterprise in which you appear to be employed: As to me, I must have a right to interfere, which I have not: As to you, since the ill success of your unlucky experiment, as you must have lost all hopes that exhortations of zeal, and maxims of religion, can be sufficient to reclaim minds but little sensible of them; as to you, I say, you must have an air of boldness and courage, which, in a man of your gown and character, cannot be such as the occasion calls for. Consider, added he, still, that of the two means, which are only proper to heal the disorders of which you complain, there is not one of them can become you. In truth, the first can be proper for nobody, and I should think it almost as dangerous as the evil we fain would cure; that is, to employ the authority of the court, or that of the law, to oblige my Lady to enter into a convent, until the return of her husband: And this method cannot be undertaken without making a great noise, which may cause us more confusion and grief, than we hope to avoid. But the second way, and consequently the only one that remains to be taken, and which consists not only in expostulating with my Lady boldly, but in using some vigorous means to banish all persons from her house of either sex, that may not be thought convenient to be suffered in it: This way requires a man of the sword, who may join, to the right you have, expressions, and perhaps actions, that your profession excludes you from. Thus, added the Count, as long as we would avoid making a noise, in taking care of and conducting our honour, I see nobody but my Lord Tenermill who can be charged with an affair of such a delicate nature with any hopes of success.

I found prudence and truth in this counsel; but to what point did it reduce us? To remain in a state of inaction till the return of Tenermill, of which the time was very uncertain. It was even probable that Patrick would return before him; and one of my views had always been to spare this dear brother the concern and vexation he would infallibly feel, to find so great an alteration in the character and conduct of his wife. I was not at all discouraged at the objection the Count made against himself, although it seemed to carry in it a formal refusal of interfering in the interests of Patrick. I thought him more proper than he appeared to think himself for this enterprise. In agreeing with him, that it no longer required a man of my profession; Think, said I to him, that though you belong only by alliance to my family, you are nevertheless, in the absence of Tenermill, the nearest person to it. You consequently succeed in all the rights of my brother, and, in the case we now are, his duties become yours. I added to this way of reasoning such strong and pressing instances, that they determined him at length to acquiesce in them.

He demanded a delay of a few days to give him time to obtain more knowledge in the habitual actions and conduct of my Lady. Without having ever known what ways he employed, he informed me a few days after what I have related of the two lovers. Surprise and grief raised a cruel revolution in all my senses. But this was not all he had to tell me. From whatever quarter he had got this information, he had learned, that my Lady had already consumed, in less than two months, all the ready money she had at the departure of her husband; and those could not be small sums, since, over and above her current yearly rents, we remembered that she had 50,000 franks in her coffers, when the affairs of the Count had made his friends believe that he stood in need of a pecuniary assistance to put an end to his law-suit. This waste and consumption not making her think of diminishing her expences, she had already been obliged to the common expedients, such as as taking up money on high interest, and the pawning of many valuable jewels. As she had no passion for gaming, and that her table was not regular enough to throw her into so considerable expences, it seemed manifest to the Count, that all these sums had been lavished away on love; that is to say, either on Madame De S———, who was a great woman at laying out for pleasures, or on her fortunate gallants, whose assiduities and cares she apparently paid for: And to give more credit to this odious imputation, the Count had been assured, that among a great number of lovers, who perpetually swelled my Lady's court, there were many who had the reputation of being well with her, and who had from thence taken occasion to appear with a more magnificent retinue. I took great care, said the Count, perceiving the impression this frightful relation had made on me, how I blindly believed the slander. It magnified every object, especially when added to the vanity and indiscretion familiar in the mouths of young people. But reuniting all my present informations to my former conjectures, I had no room for doubts left me, but that there was a strange alteration made in the behaviour of my Lady, and that this corruption gained ground daily.

It remained for him to inform me, in what manner he proposed to break this matter to my Lady. I received yesterday, said he, a letter from Patrick, who, supposing her yet at my castle, prayed me to be watchful over her health, and to see her myself, notwithstanding our domestick coldness. He complained of not having often enough received letters from her. This forgetfulness would appear to him surprising, if he had the misfortune of knowing the cause of it. But this gives such a natural opportunity to me to go and see her, that I reject all the other schemes I have formed. Be assured, added he, that having once consented to do him the service you desire, I will leave nothing undone about her, until I acquit myself of my commission. He

confessed

confessed to me nevertheless, that with the view of inspiring some terror into the guilty, he had already given notice to Madame de S———, that she was already threatened with some disgrace, which would be the effect of her intimacy with a lady, whom the world accused her of having hurried into disorderly courses. He told me, he did not at all doubt, but that this advice had immediately been communicated to my sister-in-law, and that finding herself perhaps already greatly alarmed, he should from thence have the greater ease in staggering her upon his first visit. He had even flattered himself, that if he should have put her into this disposition, it would not be impossible for him, by magnifying a little the motives of terror, to engage her on the spot to quit Paris, and to wait the return of Patrick in the country.

He chose the day following for his visit. Fatal day! After so many circumstances he had related to me, he did not tell me, that he had discovered the favourite lover of my sister-in-law, and that he had already had a very warm expostulation with him. This was the first object he met in her apartment. Passion has no curb upon such violent occasions. Seeing him come out alone from my Lady's closet, he stopped him boldly, and without using the least caution in his expressions, he forbid him with the most violent menaces ever again to put his foot within a house he had dishonoured. This miserable wretch, who was little acquainted with the sentiments of honour, pretended to go out without making any answer. A scene so little foreseen had heated the Count. He went into the closet with the remainder of the same warmth, and observing fewer measures than he had at first proposed, he reproached my Lady openly with a conduct, of which it did not appear to him that she even feared the scandal. The name of her husband, that of her brothers-in-law, all was employed to augment her fear and confusion. In fine, having laid before her eyes every thing

thing that he had judged most certain from the informations he had procured of the disorder of her manners, he declared, that, from the right he had over her in the absence of Patrick and my Lord Tenermill, he gave her the choice of two things, either to return immediately to his castle, there to take up a resolution of living a more regular life, till the return of her husband, or to retire into a convent, which he would leave her the liberty of choosing.

The evil he pretended to cure was great enough to require a remedy of such violence; but the habit of the disorder not being yet strong enough in my Lady to have hardened her front against such severe reproaches, the first impression she felt was more piercing than perhaps the Count had reason to apprehend. Under so terrible an embarrassment she had neither the presence nor instigations of Madame De S———— to support her. The Count had not yet familiarity enough with her to inure himself to use a noble and lofty tone with her, which he knew how to assume in his reprimands and menaces better than any person in the world. She thought she saw all the evils together ready to tumble down upon her head; and whether she was in reality as guilty as we fancied, or whether remorse and fear had magnified her faults in her own eyes, she remained under a deep silence, that seemed to amount to a confession of every thing with which she heard herself reproached. In the mean-time the Count pressing her to come to some resolution, she opened her mouth with an air of confusion and fear, to entreat for time to recover herself. He was unwilling to push his rigour so far as to refuse her so slight a favour; but mistrusting that she had thoughts of consulting Madame De S————, he declared to her, that she must renounce all such hopes, and that, during two hours he gave her to deliberate upon those two proposals, he would go to that lady, and would not conceal from her, that it was to her he ascribed all those disorders. If he added a few

D 5   words,

words, it was only to lay before her the shame of giving herself up to a woman so odiously infamous, with the hopes of hastening her repentance by increasing her confusion.

He went out indeed in order to go to Madame de S———, to whom he was willing to renew openly the advice he had given her by better. The impatience I had to know, with what air she would receive his visit, had made me wait at some distance from my Lady's house. I got into his coach: he embraced me, and at the same time congratulated me for his having found less resistance than he had foreseen, and for being near the point of executing his commission without violence and noise. Such agreeable news raised in me all the joy that I ought to feel from it. I approved the design that led him to Madame de S———'s, and left him to wait for the success of it with the same hopes.

It being agreed that we should return to my Lady's together, and offer her in concert our services and cares for either of the choices she should make, he took me up in the same place he had left me. I was but little amazed at what he related to me of Madame de S————, after the experience I had of her character. She received his menaces and reproaches like a woman above such little adventures, and even confessing with a malicious jest, that my Lady had in a short time made an extraordinary progress in gallantry, she excused herself from having had the least share in any thing that had the appearance of disorder or excess. Facts of this nature being difficult to be verified by proofs, the Count had been obliged to hold to his first declarations; and the principal advantage he thought he had drawn from this visit was, to prevent so dangerous a woman from infecting the mind of my Lady by new advice.

Not above an hour had passed during the interval of these two expeditions. We proceeded to the house of my sister-in-law. The door of it was freely thrown open to us, and we went up into her apartment,

ment, without finding any further obstacles. The Count, finding the door of the closet shut, suffered no more than one lacquey to go forward and give notice that we were there. We must conceal, said he, with great prudence, as much as is possible of this grievous scene from the servants. This is a precaution, added he, that I should have recommended to my Lady herself, and shall be vexed if she has not observed it. We knocked softly at the door. No body made haste to open it. The Count having raised his voice to give notice who was there, we heard that of my sister-in-law, who after some obscure words, one part of which even escaped us, gave orders to her chamber-maid to let us in.

She was alone with this woman sitting at a table, and holding a pen in her hand, with which she was writing. With difficulty she got up to receive us, and we soon remarked, that she had scarce strength enough for any further motion. Her countenance had a paleness in it, that I could compare to nothing but that of death. The alteration in all her features, the disorder of her eyes, in fine, an air of astonishment and fright, that spread itself over her whole form, gave us sensibly to understand, that she was agitated by something more terrible than confusion and grief. The Count, to whom the office of unfolding our thoughts seemed to belong, began by observing some marks of disturbance we were in for her health, and asked her chamber-maid how she could suffer her mistress to be in this condition, without proposing to her to send for help. Alas! answered this woman, she would by no means suffer me; and she has obliged me to stay here this hour past, whether I would or not. To what the Count said to herself to draw from her a confession of her misfortune, she answered nothing, but by stretching out her arm before her, with a sign of aversion to all our cares, which seemed to make her fear the seeing us too near her. In fine, as it was of her own accord she had ordered the door to be opened to us, she prayed us to hearken to what she intended to say to us, without any other precaution than by ordering her chamber-maid to go out of the closet, and attend a little from the door.

If you have brought Mr. Dean here, said she to the Count, casting down her eyes, only to redouble my confusion by his presence, you lose your labour; I am in a condition which must make me insensible to those little considerations; and my shame or your reproaches cannot be an evil very insupportable to me, with the certainty I have of seeing them very soon at an end. On the contrary, I rejoice in having you both witnesses of my last thoughts. You will apprehend better from my mouth, than from the letter I was about writing to you, what passes this moment in my heart; and if you condemn the excess or despair coming to hurry me away, you are at free liberty to make what use you please of my secret.

As the astonishment the Count and I were in obliged us almost at every word to cast our eyes on each other, I know not, said she, what signify so many looks; but if they proceed from the obscurity of what I say, which possibly may cause you some embarrassment, I have occasion but for one moment to clear them up, and I will then leave you to determine whether I merit your horror or compassion. It is true, continued she, that the attractions of pleasure, and the miserable counsels of Madame De S———, have made me swerve from my duty. Give, if you will, to my disorders the name of infatuation or blindness, but do not be so unjust as to think, that the forgetfulness of myself, into which I have fallen by degrees, has been ever voluntary: Circumstances have every day contributed to this depravation, and I have been surprised myself to see myself in the midst of the abyss, without having once opened my eyes to see the way that led me into it: How, for example, the love and veneration with which I was filled for my husband, have not

better

better defended me against the first motions of a diffolute love; and if I was capable of any weakness, ought I to have been at the expence of a taste so dear, which time and my own choice had so perfectly confirmed? Without acknowledging myself so criminal as you have supposed by your reproaches, I confess, added she, that you have not been deceived in one part of the excess you have imputed to me. I owe this confession to truth, in the dreadful moment I am in; but it dispenses with me from giving you a detail, which, without doubt, would bring a torment to my husband.

We interrupted her, by shewing strong proofs of our compassion, in order to banish that diffidence she seemed to remark of our discretion. If you had known us to have been men of honour, said the Count, you would not be apprehensive, that your husband could ever hear from us what you yourself are going to make us forget by such strong marks of your repentance. Ah! replied she, interrupting us in her turn, you are ignorant of my situation, when you ascribe any thing to my fear. I have nothing further to expect, when I have no longer any claim to life; and praying us to hear what she would tell us in two words, she informed us, that far from thinking we had any knowledge of her intrigues, she had been so terrified at the Count's reproaches, that her spirits, which had supported her during his discourse, intirely failed her the moment he went out of the closet. Remaining some time in a swoon, the wretch, whom the Count had forbid ever to appear again in the house, and who nevertheless had only retired into a chamber hard by, returned into the closet as soon as he had seen the person go out of it, the sight of whom he durst not bear. He did not in the least doubt, seeing my Lady in such a deep swoon, but that some scene had passed between her and the Count, which was the consequence of that he had just before been exposed to from him, and of which the effect would infallibly be

the

the loss of those resources he had hitherto found in the credulity of my sister-in-law. The same fund of artifice and knavery, that had attached him to her, inspired him with the detestable thought of taking advantage of her condition to rob her all at once of what she had already much impaired by the help of Madame De S———, and which they had fully made sure of carrying off by degrees. From a long familiarity he had known the casket in which my Lady, together with her jewels, kept all the deeds and contracts that were the sureties of her estate. He seized them, and as he got into the street, meeting nobody but the chamber-maid, who was accidentally going in to her mistress, he pretended, smiling, that my sister-in-law had given it him in charge to secure that precious burden, out of fear, lest the Count de S———, who had some difference with her, might so far assume the ascendant he desired over her, even to the seizing of her papers.

The chamber-maid went in to my Lady, who had recovered out of her swoon the instant she entered the closet, and perceiving in her only the remains of a paleness, which is the consequence of such accidents, she had so much the less mistrust of the cause, as her mistress restrained herself enough from giving her any room of making a discovery of it. Nevertheless, as she was busied about her, she could not forbear mixing in her words what she had just seen and heard. My Lady, as it were thunder-struck, by immediately seeing a proof of the robbery before her eyes, nevertheless had power enough in the excess of her trouble to become mistress of her first transports; yet she had too quick a sense of her misfortune. All things, capable of casting despair and consternation into her soul, joined together to overwhelm her. Together with the terrible consequences, with which she thought herself threatened from her husband, she found herself reduced in a moment to indigence by the only man of the world on whom she had most extravagantly lavished

her

her substance and confidence. Being without experience or understanding in the practice of affairs, she could see no remedy for recovering the loss of the casket, and stopping the consequences of the robbery. In fine, seeing no appearance of hopes, and preferring death to a thousand fatal extremities that she thought inevitable, the only thought from whence she drew any consolation was to remember, that among many elixirs come to her from her father, and which she had choicely preserved, she had a poison, of which he had boasted of the virtue. She did not hesitate a moment in swallowing it, without giving the least notice of it to her chambermaid, who on the contrary imagined that what she had taken was some remedy for her health. She afterwards called for a pen to give us an account of the reasons she had to put an end to her life, and to interest us, even for the honour of our family, not to reveal such a tragical adventure.

What she could add to this account seeming to us of less importance than the necessity of giving her assistance, we cut her words short to call in her chamber-maid, whom we ordered in the most pressing terms, immediately to send for the first physician could be got; and, to neglect nothing in the interval, the Count, visiting the casket of elixirs, luckily found among them divers counter-poisons, with their names and distinguishing marks, and forced my Lady to take this assistance. Her opposition was long and obstinate: But she yielded at last, from two hopes he gave her; one, that if she were resolved to reassume a relish for her duty, her husband should never be informed of the misfortune she had of injuring it in his absence; the other, that the very robbery of her papers was not yet an irreparable mischief; because the duplicates of them were for the most part preserved in the public registries; and as to those that it was impossible to make good this way, they had at least the remedy of giving out public and particular advertisements, which would
infallibly

infallibly secure the best part of them. These two motives prevailing on her to take the assistances that might recal her to life, she cast herself at our knees, and her promises appeared to us to be as sincere as her thanks.

There was so little to fear, in the disposition I now saw her, that she would make any difficulty in following my advice or orders, which only tended to engage her to take medicines, and even quit Paris immediately, if her situation should permit her, I pressed the Count not to delay a moment in taking the necessary measures for preventing the consequences of the robbery. He went off with this design. The physicians, who came immediately, found the effects of the poison less advanced than I could fancy from the appearances. Whether the elixir had already lost its strength, or whether it required a longer time to work, they assured me, that it had not yet communicated itself to the vitals, and that they would easily master it. In reality, my Lady found herself so much relieved by their care, that in less than an hour she was in a condition to get into her coach with me, and drive to the Count's castle. This alteration was made with so many precautions, and such decency, that her servants not having any more suspicion of the cause of her departure, than of the reasons of her sickness, I still comforted her by improving the present blessing into the most favourable omens of what was to come; and I persuaded her at length that she had nothing to fear from the secrets lodged in the Count's and my hands.

Nothing could excuse me from passing some time with her, as much to keep from her Madame De S———, whose indiscretion I feared would yet attempt to seek the means of seeing her again, as to confirm her in those resolutions she had taken, in which I was not yet convinced that necessity had not a greater share than the inclinations of her heart. So my abode with her was a continual exercise of charity and zeal, by the care I took constantly to lay
before

before her eyes every thing that might call her back to herself, and make her forget what she had lost. She opened her mind to me in such a manner as left me not the least doubt of her repentance, and which would have convinced me what strong dependence I might have on her resolutions, if on the other side her very frankness had not helped to inspire me with a fresh diffidence of the future, by giving me room to penetrate more and more into the natural bottom of her character. With the first hints given me by the Count, and those of a fatal experience, which had but too well confirmed them, I could not lay hold of her change, nor she indeed give it me, as an alteration in the least of her inclinations. I was as well acquainted with her heart as with my own. I saw in it a sincere resolution of vanquishing those inclinations, with which she accused herself for having had too much indulgence; but this only helped me to discover, that she yet had them, and that she would perhaps be always obliged to a conflict with them. Her condition, on which she had the ingenuity to open herself, was only a violent condition, which consequently supposed that she was not in the least what she had an inclination to be, and which must make it doubtful, as long as the combat should last, to what side the balance would one day incline: And if this observation was indubitable, I had nothing to expect either from her proper efforts, or from the ardour of my zeal, to heal the evil in its source. That had been to attempt to change nature; an enterprize surpassing the power of man, and which Heaven is not even engaged to place always among the miracles of its grace.

Nevertheless, it was of so little importance for the honour or repose of a husband, whether his wife were reclaimed to virtue by a natural relish, or an effort of reason, and I had so little doubt of my Lady's knowing how to triumph over herself, when she should have for a curb not only the presence and looks, but even the love and complaisance of my
brother,

brother, that if I had any scruple upon the renewal of their union, it was not from a doubt of the love of the one, or the fidelity of the other they sprang. I only applied myself to consider what the lot of Patrick was going to be, who finding his wife the same in appearance as he had left her at his departure, was about lavishing on her all the caresses that a husband owes to a constancy of duty and love, whilst she had abused them so cruelly, that, according to the common precedents of honour, what was his duty to her was perhaps a cruel death, or a punishment which made his life more insupportable than death. This reflection did not at all proceed from an inclination I sometimes had of raising or magnifying difficulties; it is the common manner of thinking upon events of this nature. The most contemptible and mean of all men, being consulted upon the situation of Patrick at his return, would judge that no condition could be so cruel; and consequently to reduce him to it with as much freedom as knowledge, would not this be to betray him with the utmost cruelty? I did not examine this question by the laws of men, which would have given me too much perplexity; and moreover I had no occasion to consult them, when Patrick's misfortune being unknown, it was not the impression it might make on another, that I ought to take for the foundation of my reflections. I turned myself to Heaven, the laws of which are never equivocal, even when they do not accord with the opinions of men. It seemed to me, that the faults of a woman not diminishing either the rights, or property, or relish of a husband, they draw their enormity less from the wrong they do him, than from the corruption of the heart that made her commit them. Thus when ignorance on one side puts the imagination under shelter, and on the other side no change is observed to make it doubted whether a woman has been faithful to her duty, there is in this nothing of the situation of a man betrayed, to make it as cruel as
people

people fancy. The crime and her shame appear in the eyes of God only from what she has committed; and both the one and the other should vanish equally when they are effaced by repentance.

But I confined myself to useless discussions; and I should have been excused from them by the disposition Heaven had given to these events, if I had been able to have penetrated them. With whatever hopes I had laboured to soothe my sister-in-law's mind, a remorse for her weakness, and a fear of her husband, had acted upon it with more force than all my consolations. If the diligence of the Count De S— had preserved one part of her wealth, it nevertheless could not prevent many considerable bills from passing immediately into strange countries with him who had stole them away, and who had taken care to make sure of all the profit he could draw from his crime. The sums which there were no hopes of recovering, amounted to more than two hundred thousand franks. It was not possible but Patrick, perceiving such a considerable loss, should shew a great deal of curiosity, by inquiring into the circumstances of the robbery; and that he would sooner or later come at further intelligence. This thought, joined to a thousand inquietudes, which augmented in proportion as the return of my brother drew near, joined to a continual remorse for having failed in love and fidelity to a husband so worthy of those two sentiments, joined, perhaps, to the effects of the poison, of which it was hard to think but that some part of it had deceived the care and skill of the physicians, threw her into a languishing sickness, which made me believe, from the beginning of it, that her death was not far off. Nothing was neglected for the recovery of her health. I did not leave her one moment; and my services were as eager, as if I had the most precious life in the world to preserve. The Count and his spouse paid her as much attendance, and with as great ardour, as they could have done to Patrick himself. She seemed to have suffered much

disturbance

disturbance from the first visit of the Countess; and I easily observed, that the presence of a virtuous woman was to her a dreadful sight. Nevertheless, I disburdened her imagination from one part of this load, by assuring her, that my sister was entirely ignorant of her adventure. This persuasion, that seemed to her a security for the same discretion in respect to her husband, appeared to make her last breath undisturbed enough. She conjured me not to leave her bed-side. All the intervals of strength and freedom of mind, that her distemper left her, were employed in regretting her crimes. She prayed me to count over her misfortunes, by that means to soften the horror of them in her own eyes; and she told me, that, knowing she had not resolution enough to endure the looks of her husband, without expiring for shame and grief; she considered it as a favour from Heaven to spare her this punishment, by taking away her life during his absence.

The Count and I lamented her sincerely: A woman so amiable merited a different fate; and it is yet to me an impenetrable mystery, that the most perfect qualities of nature are sometimes matched with odious vices that disfigure them. The Count pushed this reflection further. In a material body, said he, wherein every thing depends on mechanism, which has not rules absolutely certain, and whose different movements form nevertheless what they call the passions, it does not appear to me so surprising as to you, that the inclination to vice or virtue should be subject to great variety and alteration; but what I admire, added he, is, that women have found the art of disguising their most contradictory inclinations, under appearances, nevertheless, resembling each other; insomuch, that nothing can aid us in piercing this deceitful veil, which gives to their most irregular inclinations the same outside as to their virtues. Would Patrick, added he, have been deceived by his wife, if length of time and observations could have given him room to penetrate with a sharp eye through those thick darknesses?

darknesses? Without opposing the Count's reflection, I desired him only to observe, that the difference he made between what he called an inclination to vice or to virtue, proceeded less from nature, than from a thousand circumstances, that are the sources of our habits. These two natural inclinations of love and hatred, to which all the others may be referred, never in themselves deserved the name of vicious inclinations; they only become so by the evil quality of objects, towards which we direct our intentions: This is so true, that of what nature soever these objects be, the affection of the heart is always the same. Why do you hold then, added I, that nature has given different appearances to one thing that is not at all capable of change? The change at least, if we must acknowledge one, not proceeding but from exterior causes, which justly or without reason excite the natural desires and affections, it is not more unreasonable to wish, that the change should manifest itself outwardly and by sensible differences, than it would be to hold, that fire takes the colour of the objects before it, and upon which its action is always alike, although the difference be sometimes very wide in the effects.

We immediately passed from these abstracted ideas to considerations more urgent. Although the sickness of my sister-in-law had been long enough to give time to advise Patrick of it, yet the embarrassment that her adventure gave us, and, if I durst say it, even the hopes we had to get out of it by her death, made us choose intirely to conceal it from him in our letters. But if every thing had changed its face by this event, we were under no less difficulties what address we had need to use in communicating to him such sorrowful news. His journey, which was intended to continue but four months, was prolonged by new negotiations, with which he was commissioned by the King to the court of Spain. His impatience to return to Paris was nevertheless the only thought uppermost in his
letters.

letters. What means had we to inform him by ours of an accident so much the more terrible to him, as prudence, which was yet more necessary, did not permit us to add to it other eclaircissements? That common griefs have their bounds, we knew well enough by domestic experiences: But, in the heart of so tender a brother, the Count (as uncertain as I) asked me, If I did not apprehend, that it was capable of vast excess? And both of us trembling for the consequences, that from thence stared us in the face, we were a long time in taking a resolution, which did not at first strike our minds.

In fine, not fearing that he would have so little moderation as to reproach me for it, when the question only was to give a demonstration of my affection and zeal to my brothers, I thought myself to make the journey to Madrid: Pretences could not be wanting to a man so curious as I to get experience: This was the sole motive I resolved to make use of to the King; for I was willing to avoid every thing that might diminish the opinion his Majesty had of my brother's steadiness and resolution. My sister-in-law was not enough known to excite the attention of the public by her sickness and death; this news had not yet reached St. Germain; and I did not doubt but we might also keep it concealed as long as we thought convenient for our interests. The day following I went to court, and, without any explanation, obtained of the King his licence to make a journey to Spain. He nevertheless assigned bounds to my absence, but still with an obliging motive for it. According to the hopes he had of seeing his arms succeed happily in Ireland, he asked me, if I would not make haste enough to swell his court, when the success of his affairs would enable him to take possession of his kingdoms. He fixed my return to the beginning of winter, that is to say, when at the end of the campaign he should be able to make a judgment of his fortune. Vain expectation, which failed by a train of events quite opposite! But, for the same reason, he

some

some weeks before dropped the design of sending me to Ireland, to bring over my Lord Lynch's treasure. Whatever facility he had found in doing so according to his first views, when he imagined that I might have been seconded by his troops, he then judged so favourably of this expedition, that, thinking himself every day at the eve of a signal victory, he reckoned upon going to receive this treasure with his own hands.

BOOK X.

I Was confidently determined to go to Madrid; and my preparations never requiring much time or pains, I did not put off my departure further than the day following. An accident, that never so much as came into my mind, delayed my journey, and very near obliged me to abandon it altogether. Could any one imagine what obstacles they were that had been capable of stopping me, if I did not declare beforehand, that this was the only one that could make me relinquish any thing even more urgent; or, with the same view, form enterprises a thousand times more toilsome and difficult?

Nothing appearing to lay us under the obligation of imparting the death of my sister-in-law, nor the design of my journey, to Sarah Fincer, I proposed to take my leave of her with the ordinary marks of esteem and affection, without speaking to her otherwise of my departure, than to recommend to her the care of her health during my absence. Nevertheless, upon my arrival from St. Germain, I understood that she had inquired for me several times with great eagerness; and, going to her, my astonishment was extremely great, to hear her speak not only of the death of my sister-in-law, but of the project of my journey, as if she had been informed of it by myself, or by the Count, even in the most minute circumstances. Some words, which escaped her in the warmth of divers motions, of which I did not of a sudden discover the nature, gave me also to understand, that she was not at all ignorant of the adventures of her rival, or that she knew at least every thing relating to them, which had not been confided only to the Count's and my discretion. I looked on her with surprise, expecting where this prelude would end: At length rising off her chair with so brisk an action, that I could not for a long time understand myself to be the cause of it: Ah! my dear Dean, said she, do you think I will let you go alone to Spain, and when Heaven restores me to life by such happy events, is there any person else in the world to whom I can trust the success of my hopes? I am acquainted with your friendship by the most generous proofs, and if I could choose to repose my interests on any other than myself, I should not go farther to look for a protector or agent. But what I ask of you at present is to be my guide. Lead me, added she, with a more open and declared ardour; I have no more obstacles to vanquish than in demanding the conduct of your prudence; I wish for nothing but to arrive at Madrid, and I dare from thenceforth hope every thing from the sole power of honour and love.

Having had time to recover myself during this discourse, I apprehended a thing, which I now confess, that the multitude of my notions and occupations did not hitherto permit me to consider of; that is to say, that the death of my sister-in-law gave just hopes to Sarah, and that in effect not having any thing more than grief to combat in my brother's heart, it was not impossible but he might take for her those sentiments, which, as I have remarked a thousand times, it had afflicted him not to be in a capacity of paying her. Why should he continue obstinate in refusing her his heart? Would he not find there all the virtues,

tues and charms that he could not possibly forbear admiring? I even thought that her patience, in the midst of so many misfortunes, had given to them a new lustre; and, whether it were that my love for her had magnified her accomplishments in my eyes, or whether she had really drawn these advantages from adversity, I had remarked a thousand times since she had been at the Count's, that her wit, her sweetness, her politeness, were improved and wrought up to perfection by continual advancements. The moment I was making these reflections on what was past, I could not avoid one remark on the present, that struck all my attention. As I perceived she was informed of the irregularities of my sister-in-law, I could not but admire, that she never dropped an ill-natured reflection, or shewed the least mark of that insulting joy, which ladies so commonly do over the misfortunes of a rival. Scarce did she pronounce her name; and this effort on herself redoubled the opinion I always had of her mildness and modesty.

In the mean time, her proposals, which I so little expected, threw me into a perplexity from whence I could not easily recover. I had need of some deliberation to examine whether they did not injure any right. Could a marriage dissolved with a good deal of noise be renewed? And if the divorce had been lawful, could it be cemented together again by a new tie? Moreover, what appearance was there of disposing Patrick to receive a new spouse, the moment he heard of the loss of her whom he had loved exclusive of all others? This last thought being sufficient of itself to furnish me with an answer, I turned over the discussion of the others to a season more free; and, without making any further objection to Sarah, than what so naturally occurred, I asked her, If the first moments of grief were a proper time to give a good issue to her hopes? She agreed in the force of this obstacle; but, not continuing from thence less steady in her resolution, she proposed to me a thousand expedients, that she thought capable of reconciling

conciling all difficulties. I will be exactly careful, said she, not to appear at first with you. You shall see him alone, and inform him of his loss. Your zeal and prudence shall be bestowed in moderating the first motions of his grief; and when you think him disposed to receive my visit, I will labour in my turn to make him relish my consolations. If it be the pleasure of being beloved that he regrets, alas! he shall soon see, that what he has remaining of that pleasure, surpasses every thing he has lost.

This excess of love and goodness drew tears from my eyes, and compliments and praises from my lips; but, still afraid of a project, in which I thought I saw a thousand insurmountable difficulties, if I was not stiff in condemning it, I at least insisted, that it should be communicated to the Count and Countess of S——, and I made my consent depend on their answer. How great was the grief of Sarah, when she found them in no less opposition to her desires! In her first motions, she protested to me, that nothing was capable of staying her; and that if I refused to serve her as a guide, she should know how to find the road to Spain without me, and to get to Madrid as quickly as I should. I considered then whether her interest itself and that of Patrick should not oblige me to abandon the design of my journey. My letters might lead my brother, by degrees, into the knowledge of his loss, and, in like manner, insensibly inspire into him those consolations that might restore peace to his mind. I imagined I had a foresight, that, after having, as it were, exhausted in his absence the first impetuosity of his grief, he would be satisfied enough to find here a more agreeable remedy in the love of a lady, whom he never had hated, and by whom he was sure of having been constantly beloved. I should perhaps have fixed in this resolution, if the Countess had not succeeded, by other motives, to make Sarah change hers. She represented to her, that, without looking on her as a woman that had any other relation to my brother than from the desires of love,

decency

decency imposed laws on her, which she seemed to forget. This advice, without perhaps having all the solidity in it that the Countess persuaded herself it had, made so great an impression on a nature so virtuous as Sarah's, that it stifled her most impetuous desires. But with what ardour did she not then conjure me to embrace her interests, since she had lost the hopes of soliciting them herself! She repeated to me twenty times even the terms and expressions with which she desired me to serve her. She would write them down, and charge me with her letter. It was after a thousand reasonings, and a thousand efforts, that I obliged her to own the power of my first objections, and confess, that precipitation was no way expedient for her hopes.

In fine, I had the liberty to gone alone; and my diligence corresponding with my zeal, I scarce took any necessary rest during so long a journey. Patrick received me with an openness of heart, which all at once gave me room to judge, that I should find in this amiable brother all the good qualities that had rendered his friendship so precious to me. There did not subsist in his memory the least traces of our differences. But the haste and eagerness with which he inquired after news from his spouse, declared to me almost as speedily all the difficulties of my enterprise. He renewed the complaints, which he had often made by letters, of the too long time she took in answering his; and all in a breath asking me a hundred questions of her health, her employments, and her love for him, he did not relieve my embarrassment otherwise than by the right he gave me of answering him with the same confusion. I had less difficulty in giving a probable colour to my journey. The desire of seeing him, and the opportunity that his residence at Madrid had given me to get some knowledge of Spain, were such natural reasons, that thereby persuading him of my views, they inspired him with all the warmth I wished to give me satisfaction. It was in the wanderings and absence of mind that this exercise might cause him, wherein I hoped to find a favourable moment for my design, and not being pressed by time, which afforded me as many days to choose out of as he had till his return to France, I had not the least doubt but that an enterprise conducted by so many steps and precautions would in the end have the success that I had ventured to promise myself from it.

This facility in flattering myself, increased yet more by a discovery I made during my first days, and which an appearance of truth made me take in a sense proper indeed to augment it. By the care I took of informing myself from my brother's servants, what acquaintance he had made at Madrid, I understood that he familiarly visited a young lady, whose merit had made an impression on him. She was a widow, and that condition giving her the freedom of receiving strangers, he spent at her house almost all the time he did not employ in his business. Perhaps I should have relaxed a little from my principles by desiring that he had taken an inclination for her; and even the interest of Sarah Fincer did not prevent me in the least from wishing her this obstacle. Besides, as I could not have a fancy strong enough to make me fear any considerable difficulty to overcome, this was the surmounting one so powerful as the making myself master of his grief, that all the rest appeared to me a mere jest. If I had not been assured by himself all at once of his inclinations for a woman, whose charms were so highly exalted, this was only to draw from thence more advantage, in making subservient to my designs those lights and hints that I would have endeavoured to have procured some other way, without his having the least mistrust of it.

Many persons being named to me from whom I might procure informations, I contented myself in making an acquaintance with a Spanish gentleman, who often visited the same lady, and who, speaking French, every one had an easy access to him who
could

could discourse him in that language. From the only quality of friend to this lady, I should have thought him linked to her by the same motives, that I desired Patrick should be, if in the first opportunity I had to talk to him of her, he had not drawn a potrait of the lady that did not appear to me to proceed from the pencil of a lover. He represented her to me as an experienced and disciplined coquette, who under a false semblance of modesty and gentleness concealed all the artifice, of which a woman seeking only to please, is capable, and who not limiting herself to hold a single lover in her chains, laboured continually to extend her conquests, with the care only of disguising herself with such address, that every one of her favourites might think himself confident of having no rival. He himself had been cured of an unhappy passion (that he had a long time nourished for her) by the experience he had found of her treachery, which nevertheless did not hinder but that the esteem he had of her wit, and a hundred uncommon qualities, which he yet acknowledged in her, had made him conserve for her a kind of attachment, which he rather chose to call a fancy or relish for her than a friendship. When he understood from me, in the sequel of our conversation, that Patrick was my brother, he plainly declared, that seeing him very assiduous about this fair widow, he little doubted but that love had the greatest share in his visits; and he counselled me moreover to give him such advice, as I should think proper to preserve him from the danger. At least I am convinced, added he, that he makes it his study to please her, and offered to make me judge of it by my own eyesight.

Far from being affrighted at this picture, it was exactly an inclination of this sort, that I should have thought capable of amusing Patrick enough to render him less sensible of the wound I was about giving him; without exposing him nevertheless to the softening of his heart enough, so as not easily to receive a

remedy,

remedy, which would be perhaps in the end much
stronger than the evil. I accepted the Spanish gentleman's offer with joy, and the same day informing my brother of the opportunity I had of con-
versing with a lady of his acquaintance, I put off
my visit no farther than to the next day. You will
see, said he coldly, a lady of distinguished merit,
and you will have no need of any other person than
me to introduce you to her. I found in what he said
an air of confidence, that confirmed all my notions.
I had even so little doubt thereof, that I could not
defend myself from some reflections upon the inconstancy of the heart, which one single passion was not
sufficient to possess intirely; and if this thought gave
me more hope than ever of adjusting matters easily
with Patrick, it perhaps served to inspire me with a
more strong compassion than I had ever felt for my
sister-in-law.

Patrick put me in mind himself of the engagements he was under with me. Having presented me
to Donna Figuerrez with a character, such as was decent from the mouth of a brother, he gave me room
soon to perceive the consideration she had for him.
I should have began my observations from the first
moment, if the Spanish gentleman, who was already
in the assembly, had not come up to me so near as
to engage me in a particular conversation, which I
could not avoid. The remains of the vexation,
which he yet preserved from his adventure, without
doubt induced him to give me a character of his
rivals. One of them, whose mien and figure were
very prepossessing, had been the first lover of Donna
Figuerrez, after the death, and perhaps, added he
maliciously, in the last season of her husband's
life. Possibly he is the only person whom she has
ever loved sincerely; but being without any estate,
it would become too great a clog to her, in the moderate fortune she possesses, if she should be touched
with a constancy, so as not to make her think of any
body but him. It would not be impossible in this

manner

manner to juſtify her coquetry in its ſource. However that may be, a misfortune, ſtill worſe than poverty, obliged this lover to remove from Madrid the moment ſhe had ſubjected to her charms a rich old man, whom you ſee there, whoſe wealth poſſibly might have afforded her more pleaſure than ſhe could have found in her firſt engagement. She conſequently loſt on the ſide of love as much as ſhe gained on the ſide of fortune: But, to repair this damage, ſhe immediately made a new ſlave of that officer, continued he, pointing to him oppoſite to me, whom ſhe has deſtined to fulfil the functions of the abſent. It was about this juncture, added he, that I took up for her that fatal paſſion, which has a long time blinded me. I am rich, and of an age that has nothing in it forbidding, no more than there is in my form. She appeared to be charmed with my application and diligence, and all the addreſs in the world was employed to confirm my defeat. Ignorant of what the ſequel made me luckily diſcover, I thought myſelf the ſole maſter of a heart, that I judged to be of an ineſtimable price, or at leaſt I had but a ſlight jealouſy on the ſcore of the old man, who had not ſteadineſs of mind enough to diſguiſe a good fortune, of which he thought himſelf the ſole poſſeſſor. I remarked to her ſome alarms, which ſhe turned into banter. In one word, the officer being more reſerved, and enjoying in private thoſe rights he had acquired, and the old man paſſing in my eyes for a rival little dangerous in her wiſhes, whom I ſaw reduced to ſome favourable looks, we aſſociated ourſelves all three in the ſame happineſs; and perhaps my illuſion would have yet continued, if the firſt lover had not come to draw me out of it againſt my will. Having obtained licence to return to Madrid, he immediately took the place he had abandoned; and if he perceived he had got competitors, the preſence of the old man and mine, which was always accompanied with many liberalities, of which he had a ſhare, did not at all wound his delicacy. But not thinking himself in the least obliged to the same constraint, which she had the art of exacting from others, he betrayed himself by so many indiscretions, that they opened my eyes; and without breaking too harshly with the lady, I retrenched myself insensibly in a commerce of friendship with her, in which I have yet the weakness to find some pleasure. The tranquillity of this affection makes me relish without bitterness all the good qualities, that I cannot help observing in her. I join to this satisfaction a pleasure, which you perhaps will think less innocent; that is, of watching her conduct, and observing with what address she swells every day the train of her lovers. A collection of my discoveries would compose an engaging history full of variety and pleasure. But what I have not yet penetrated, added he, are the views she has on my Lord, your brother, and the manner in which he answers them. I know the original of their acquaintance. She is niece and heiress of our ambassador in France; the opportunity of living in the same neighbourhood gave her the means of making an acquaintance with an amiable man, under pretence of enquiring after the health of her uncle. See with what care she seeks to please him; observe the attention she shews for every word that drops out of his mouth, and the air of flattery that accompanies all her answers. He will fall into the snare, if he has not the misfortune to be already caught, and you will do him a brotherly office by giving him notice of it.

I perceived indeed that Donna Figuerrez was wholly taken up by her attentions on Patrick. The moment I turned my eyes on her, having done hearkening to the gentleman, I observed the tone she used in shewing her satisfaction or admiration. Prepossessed by the account I had just heard, and even full of my adventure with Madame de S——, I thought I penetrated into this disguised cheat, and did not find her as deceitful as she was represented to me.

Nevertheless,

Nevertheless, the posture and discourse of Patrick continued to make me think that he was more dazzled than I; and I did not in the least doubt, in seeing him sustain the same air of prepossession, but that he was more deeply engaged than perhaps he imagined himself.

In the evening, having the liberty of a private conversation with him, he did not wait till by my questions I should lay him under the necessity of discovering himself. You have seen Donna Figuerrez, said he, with a serious air, and you have found her, without doubt, of a merit superior to her sex. I was willing to give you time to know her, before I informed you of the reasons I have for seeing her. He continued to tell me, that, having made an acquaintance with her on occasion of some letters he had received from the Spanish ambassador at Paris, he had taken such a relish for her wit, that in the conversations they had together, he had discovered to her a share of the events of his life. The history of his marriage had not been forgotten, and not having, in the sequel, the power of dissembling from her his chagrin of having received so little news of his spouse; this confidence had engaged Donna Figuerrez to offer him the assistance of the ambassador to procure an account of her. Although it was not very natural to employ a way so foreign, when he had all his family at Paris, the fear lest we should still retain some resentment against his spouse, which might make us too cold in his service, had made him accept her offer, which could be inconvenient or improper for nobody to do. The first letters of the ambassador had filled him with a thousand notions, which he could not yet clear up. They had represented my sister-in-law in a condition so brilliant, that he could not again know the situation he had left her in. The ambassador, in praising her charms, of which he affirmed he had the knowledge by his own eye-sight, had spoken of the agreeable life she led at Paris,

and

and had laid her down as a pattern of graces united to fortune and beauty. This letter, of which she had read only the articles of this nature to Patrick, had raised in him some inquietudes, which Donna Figuerrez had observed. She had made but little advantage from thence, towards penetrating deeper into the secrets of my brother; and putting those things which seemed to disturb him in a better light, she had employed all her address, to repair the evil she had imprudently done. The letters which came afterwards, had never brought any accounts that were not conformable to the desires and ideas of Patrick, and as we had in all our letters avoided with care to inform him of any thing that might to no purpose trouble his repose, he had come to that pass as to be convinced, that the ambassador was deceived in his first relation.

You conceive, said he, that with the tender alarms I continually have for my spouse, I ought to be fond of an acquaintance, which procures me every week such certain news of her health and situation. I have had the injustice to believe them less certain from your hand, and from that of my sister; and I have had the vexation to receive accounts but seldom from my spouse herself, who manifestly does not find the same pleasure in an epistolary correspondence as I do. Nevertheless, the ambassador has constantly taken the pains to inform me of every thing that relates to her; and this notice has served me as a remedy against the torments of absence, and consoles me for the new orders of the King, which detain me yet here in his service. I see Donna Figuerrez, added he, as a resource, which in favour of my love I have husbanded at Madrid. I speak less frequently to her of herself than of my spouse; and the agreeableness of her conversation serves me instead of a happiness, which I can find no where but in France.

It may easily be imagined, how much admiration this discourse, which supposed my sister-in-law living, and her conduct still as regular as her affections, must
raise

raise in me. The fidelity of my brother frightened me; and from the indignation I had of seeing him so cruelly deceived by strangers, in whom I could not suppose the same motives as I had for suspending the eclaircissement of his fate, I was ready to dissipate all such dangerous darkness from his eyes, that seemed necessarily to conceal some odious mystery. Nevertheless, a moment's reflection on the importance of the matter he had to penetrate, made me immediately moderate this warmth. I even affected to enter into Patrick's ideas, and without imparting to him what I had learned of the character of Donna Figuerrez, I avoided every thing that could lead us to that conversation, in order to obtain the liberty of diving, the day following, into artifices that I would not willingly remain ignorant of.

No other way offered to procure me those discoveries, than by means of the Spanish gentleman, to whom I was under the obligations I have related. Notwithstanding the attachment he preserved to his former mistress, I had perceived in him a fund of resentment, which disposed him always to give ear to every new proof he could discover of her perfidy, and to set it off in the strongest colours, apparently to confirm himself in the resolution he had taken, never so have any thing more to say to her in the way of love. I perceived the same also by other proofs, if I had been deceived in this conjecture; and thinking I might open myself to him without any hazard, I related to him all I had learned from my brother, without concealing from him that many certain facts, absolutely destroying all Patrick's suppositions, made me suspect Donna Figuerrez of some black imposture. A scene so new to him excited all his ardour to discover the secret wheels of this machine. As it was not from herself he could expect any insight, he concluded, after a number of reflections, that he could hope for no more certain discovery of it, than from her letters. He knew the place where she kept them; and the pleasure he had already formed within himself

from

from finding her guilty of some new treachery, was such a powerful motive, that he resolved to risk every thing to make himself master of her secrets, by stealing them. I admired, that the same day he found the means of succeeding in an attempt, of which he was sensible of the difficulty himself. He gave me notice to come to him, and triumphing in what he had already discovered, as soon as he perceived me at a distance, he shewed me a packet of letters which he had carried off, with the casket containing them.

He did not inform me of the way he had employed to serve me; and whatever satisfaction I felt in seeing such sure proofs in his hands, I durst not commend his rashness, which had something grating in it according to my principles. I even began by reproaching him for an action so little weighed, and insisted, that at least all the letters that had no relation to our view should have remained inviolably safe. He was obliged to read a great number of them, to get to the bottom of a horrible combination. The ambassador had conceived a violent passion for my sister-in-law, at the same time that Donna Figuerrez had taken up the same sentiments for Patrick. The first news he sent to Madrid was attended with the confession of his love, which she took care not to read to my brother. Observing, on the contrary, that the plain relation of my sister-in-law's diversions had made a deep impression on him, and that the disquiet he seemed to shew might become strong enough to make him speedily leave Spain, she had taken the advantage of the hints she had drawn from him to engage the ambassador to write nothing but what corresponded with the ideas my brother had of his spouse. Her hope was to soften his heart insensibly, whilst the ambassador should have the same liberty of forming his attacks against that of my sister-in-law; and when, after divers events, of which I have related only those that to that time had come to my knowledge, she had learned the unfortunate death of my

Lady,

Lady, she from thence conceived but too lively hopes of subduing Patrick, and of bringing him perhaps to offer her his hand with his heart.

The ambassador was then among the number of those who had conspired against the virtue of my sister-in-law; and his letters afforded a proof that he had not thought himself the most unhappy of them. He often lamented nevertheless, in the answers to his niece's questions, that the object of his passion had not taken up such serious sentiments for him, as he could have desired to compleat his happiness. He represented her as a fickle and capricious woman, who seemed to look for nothing but amusements in her pleasures, and who made the repose and satisfaction of a lover the least part of her cares. These complaints were capable of re-establishing her a little in my opinion: I thought I discovered, from an unsuspected testimony, that though she had shewed some irregularity in her conduct, yet she had not taken up a gross relish for debauchery, otherwise than from the levity of her humour, or as the Count De S——— had thought, from the luxury and softness of her passions. Whatever idea might be formed from my recital, I owe her this justice, that the ambassador, in confessing the degree of favour he thought he had in her, hugged himself on his relish for a lady so charming, as if it had been the most glorious fortune love could offer him in France. What way nevetheless was there to conceive, that she could have the power of concealing from him her commerce with another lover, without believing her to have subtilty enough to deceive him by a false outside? And under this supposition, must not he have looked on her as a coquette so much the more refined, as in such a tender age being indebted only to her address for her experience, he must have ascribed her practices to the corruption of her mind, and the natural perversity of her disposition? unless one would do honour to the great artifice and cunning of Madame De S———, who had no occasion perhaps of a very long space of time to form her pupils.

But

But what was Patrick's fate, to find himself fallen again in Spain into the hands of a woman of the same character? He had nothing but the integrity of his heart to defend himself from it: For being so methodically attacked by a lady of such expert address as Donna Figuerrez, I never conceived he had any other means to save himself from a danger, that gained fresh strength every day. Filled with the idea of his spouse, he could not so entirely lose the memory of her, as to leave room for another woman to think of pleasing him. Thus the coquetries and advances of the Spanish lady were all lost labour. He did not ascribe her behaviour and most flattering expressions to any thing but the natural allurements of her wit, and the gallant turn of her imagination, which prevail commonly enough in Spain. This reason, added to the pleasure he had of receiving news of his wife through her conveyance, gave him more satisfaction in her company, than in all the assemblies in Madrid, where his merit and birth had given him a distinguished reception. He had not taken the same care, as I had, in gaining informations, which would have made him look on his acquaintance with a woman so irregular with another eye. He was then her sincere friend, and all the shifts of coquetry had never raised in him a more tender passion.

Having read over all the ambassador's letters with great attention, I engaged the gentleman to dispose again in order all those that had no relation to our design into the casket, and prevailing on him to leave the others with me, I thanked him for a service, by which I was fully convinced he sought to satisfy his own curiosity rather than mine. It remained for me to turn so many important pieces to account. I represented to my imagination, what had been the confusion of Donna Figuerrez, when learning from my brother that I was come from Paris, and that not having been ignorant of the death of my sister-in-law, it had likely been the first news I had imparted to him on my arrival. She had thought indeed all her designs overturned; but
one

one glance of her eye having given her room to remark the tranquillity of Patrick, she had immediately judged, that for some reasons I had to conceal her death from him, it was impossible he was informed of it; and keeping close to this thought, she had made no change in her ordinary gaiety. Nevertheless, she did not think my silence to be without some mystery, and her impatience to discover it left her no rest. Thus at the very time I thought myself of visiting her privately, to engage her perhaps, whether she would or no, in being serviceable to my principal design, she had the same passion to talk to me; and at my return to Patrick's, I found a billet whereby she pressed me to go to her house.

I went there immediately. The advantage she might be to me reduced me to conduct with address the sorrowful overtures she had to make to Patrick. I made light of her designs, which did not seem much to be feared on that side; and knowing nevertheless the power she had over his mind, I did not doubt but she would have the same cunning to console as to please him. It was of little importance to whom I was to have been indebted for this obligation, and she who was capable of inspiring with gratitude, laid me under no necessity of granting her my esteem. She received me with an air of sweetness and insinuation, which obliged me to be watchful over her views. The example of Madame De S——— returned to my mind without intermission. It gave me nevertheless great advantages over her, that she confessed upon beginning our conversation, that she built great hopes upon my goodness; and continuing in the same tone, she told me, that she had sufficient esteem for my brother to wish, that he would take an inclination for her; that having been informed of the death of his spouse, she had not judged it seasonable to give him an account of it, and that I had apparently some reason to keep it a secret from him, since it did not appear that I had given him the least hint of it; that her reason for concealing it was the

fear

fear of giving too great an affliction to a man, for whom she had the most tender affection, though she had not been happy enough to touch his heart; that she knew from his continual confessions the lively passion he was prepossessed with, and that foreseeing the excess of grief to which he would abandon himself upon discovering her death, she had wished to inspire him a little with love, before she opened his misfortune to him, with the view of fortifying him against such unforeseen strokes; that if I would lend my assistance to her design, by deferring in concert with her those discoveries that might be easily suspended, she did not despair of triumphing in the end over his heart; and that by informing myself of her birth and rank in the world, I might find perhaps, that she was not altogether unworthy of bearing one day the name of my sister-in-law.

From these words, and a thousand persuasions she added to them during the doubt I left her in for some time by my silence, I paused only on the proposal for deferring the discovery I was to make my brother for as long a time as she wished for the success of her views. Setting all the rest aside, I answered her, after some moments consideration, that my brother thinking his spouse yet alive, his error obliged him to the same fidelity for his matrimonial engagements, and that consequently I could not enter into a combination, which exposed him to wander from his duty. But for what reason, said I, should we take so long and so uncertain a time? Is it not more natural, and more conformable to your desires, to take advantage from the discovery that we now stop at, of the present relish my brother has for your merit, and to postpone inspiring him with more tender sentiments till after the service you shall have done him by making your wit and the power of your charms help to his consolation? Gratitude will perhaps procure you that favour, which you lament not to have obtained from his love. The end of these words had not all my ordinary sincerity in them;

but

but it was sufficient at the same time that my sincerity was not injured by them with a woman from whom I had nothing to expect but artifice. She seemed to relish my advice, and without informing me what means she intended to employ, she took upon her the charge of acquainting my brother with his loss, and the reason of my journey.

For some days I avoided going to her house. But, whatever method she had chosen to begin with, I perceived Patrick did not enjoy his usual tranquillity; and not doubting the cause of his troubles, I was surprised he did not open himself to me by more professed declarations of his disquiet. In fine, four days had not passed over, when returning in the evening to his house, from whence I took care not to be absent, he came up into my apartment with a furious air, and his voice being in a manner stifled by the violence of his agitations, he threw himself into an elbow chair, where he continued some time without the power of speaking a word. He recovered his speech nevertheless, but it was to address Heaven with a thousand complaints of his fate, before he once turned his eyes on me. I prevented him. What transport! said I, and what have you heard terrible enough to disturb you to this excess? Ah! all your conjectures will never come near it, answered he, redoubling his fury, and if you knew with what horrors they come to empoison my mind, you would detest the malice of men, which seems to employ itself against nothing but innocence and virtue. Hear me, hear me, added he with an air that did not promise a very coherent discourse, and you who make honour and virtue your profession, learn from the example of another what recompence you are to expect for them. Are not all men of honour and women of virtue in the world interested herein? and mingling his words with a great number of exclamations, he told me, that Donna Figuerrez, having for many days past given him a foresight of an important secret, which she seemed under a perplexity to
impart

impart to him, had at length juſt then made him a horrible relation of his wife; that ſuch black impoſtures had not given him one moment's trouble, ſince they were not attended with the leaſt air of probability; that he would make me judge of it myſelf, me, who had ſo long and familiar an acquaintance with her, and who had always had ſo many lights to let me into the bottom of her character; that inſtead of that modeſty, which I knew ſhe had, and whereof one might ſay ſhe was a finiſhed model for her ſex, Donna Figuerrez had aſcribed to her a laſcivious and diſſolute conduct; that they had repreſented her at Paris as having a reliſh for all ſorts of debauchery, ſhe, whom he had left, as I well knew, at the Count's caſtle, and who had always preferred the ſolitude of the country to her living at Paris. But, what he could not repeat without indignation and fury, ſhe ſpoke of her as of a woman of intrigue, who was well known by more than one affair of gallantry, and who did not pique herſelf upon treating her lovers with too great rigour. It was Donna Figuerrez, who had vomited out to him all theſe horrors, and who had ſo little ſhame as to lay a ſtreſs upon them, as upon a piece of important ſervice; ſhe, whom he had taken hitherto for his friend, and whom he had judged to have as much goodneſs and candour, as wit and charms. He could not nevertheleſs accuſe her of being the author of ſuch a black exceſs of calumny, and knowing that ſhe had a correſpondence by letters from France, he choſe rather to perſuade himſelf, that ſhe had been deceived by ſome ſcandalous intelligence: But in the heat wherewith he was raiſed by ſo many infernal accuſations, ſhe proteſted that ſhe had advanced nothing of which ſhe had not the proof and particulars in a number of letters. She imagined, continued Patrick, that I ſhould have the credulity to believe her on her word. I demanded the proof ſhe offered by her letters, and I ſhould have been willing indeed to have acknowledged, that it was ſome perfidious wretch that

that durst so impudently trust the malignity of his heart to paper. But what is it come to? Donna Figuerrez, having excused herself a long time under the pretence of not setting people together by the ears, at length pretended to go search for the pretended letters, and returning the same instant with dissembled exclamations, complained of the loss of a casket wherein all her papers were locked up. Judge, added Patrick, what an impression such a course artifice must make on me. I quitted her immediately, thinking I did her a favour in not loading her with injuries; and I have sworn never to see her more.

Nevertheless, added he, looking on me with a mournful eye, is it not true that I am the most unhappy of all men living? What would this Figuerrez have with me? What reason has induced her to destroy the reputation of my wife, and to fill my imagination with such dreadful chimeras? Is it she who has invented them? Has she in reality received them from the Spanish ambassador, or from some other correspondent? Ah! if I durst think that Sarah Fincer had been capable of such an unworthy revenge———

I interrupted him, and this respectable name seemed to me to be so unseasonably mixed among such a number of invectives, that I made him ashamed of a suspicion unworthy of him. I had listened patiently till now, and reflecting upon every word I heard, I found no difficulty in comprehending the full meaning of what he had related. It was evident to me, that Donna Figuerrez had thought she had taken the most prudent course to prepare him for the news of his loss, by informing him that his wife deserved to be little regretted. The letters she would have produced were those I had in my hands. So Patrick, who did not see me give any sign of amazement, nor any other mark of disturbance and heat, but at the name of Sarah Fincer, appeared to look on me with some air of confusion. It

seemed,

seemed, notwithstanding all his prepossessions in favour of his wife, that my silence raised some doubt in his heart, and that he waited for my explanations to get rid of this uncertainty. And was my perplexity much less troublesome? What could I answer him, without engaging too far, or without being laid under the necessity of coming all at once to a point, which I would willingly avoid till he were properly prepared by some new and discreet management? Far from thinking, as Donna Figuerrez did, that it was necessary to begin with the infidelity of his wife, I had thought it my duty to leave him in eternal ignorance of this odious article; and without having any experimental knowledge of love, I judged, that of all losses, those that are experienced by perfidy, are the most mortifying and the most cruel. But was it possible to repair an indiscretion, which I had not in the least foreseen? Could I do it at least without falsifying truth, which deserved even yet to be better husbanded? And since sooner or later he must inevitably come to the knowledge of the whole, why should I neglect an opportunity that Patrick himself threw in my way, and by which I should have spared him in some sort all the troubles he had hitherto felt?

Nevertheless, the reasons that had till now hindered me from this course, still continued more forcible. I found in them even a new motive in the injurious doubt he had raised in regard to Sarah Fincer. Being easily prepossessed against those whom he thought ill disposed to his wife, who could be my security, that he would not have the same injustice for me, and that I should not become odious to him all at once from the only reason that I could not appear under as much affliction as he for his misfortune? It seemed moreover, that Donna Figuerrez, for the readiness she shewed in following my advice, did not deserve to remain under the embarrassment into which I had cast her by keeping her letters; and though her coquetry deserved to be punished by some mortification,

mortification, yet I had no reason to contribute to her correction. It depended on me, by causing her letters to be privately returned, to put her in a condition not only of justifying the truth of her story, but of finishing all at once the attempt she had undertaken; and if there was any fear that Patrick should take up too violent a hatred against the source from whence those frightful discoveries should come, there was yet some reason to desire, that his resentment should fall on a coquette, who sought less to serve him, than to gratify her own vanity and ambition by labouring to seduce his heart.

My answer then bore such an equivocal turn, that Patrick, being eager to lay hold of every thing that flattered his notions, saw nothing in it but the refutation of the injurious secret of Donna Figuerrez. A husband, less blinded by love, would have had some mistrust of the air and tone I affected; for not only my expressions, but all the exterior motions that accompanied my voice, were conducted with circumspection and care enough not to expose me to the reproach of having deceived him by false appearances; and I reckoned less upon what I laid before him in a favourable light, than upon his disposition in hearing me: So his reflections themselves had a tendency to the betraying me into danger. I could not hear him speak of his happiness in transports, and to pretend to be so much the more happy in proportion as he stirred up envy enough in people to provoke their calumny and spight, without lamenting his blindness, and exhorting him in a manner openly to moderate the opinion of his happiness, which the inconstancy of human affairs made subject to great revolutions and crosses. Nothing was capable of making him have any suspicion of his prepossessions. He called me a thousand times as a witness of the modesty and virtue of his wife; and not giving any attention whether I answered or not, he continued to hug himself in having a woman

fall

fall to his lot, whose prudence was at least equal to her charms.

I abandoned to Heaven the care of healing such powerful prejudices without violence; and the day following I employed all my address in procuring the ambassador's letters to be returned to Donna Figuerrez, without her suspecting to whom she was indebted for this restitution. I had foreseen very justly that she should no sooner see this treasure again in her hands, but she would give notice of it to my brother. He hesitated whether he would return to her house again; and informing me of the motives he had by intreaty to do so, he jested with me on her obstinacy, which began to give him a suspicion that there was some medley of love in it. His visit was short. I saw him return, pensive indeed, and his countenance enough dejected to persuade me, that his mind was not in a state of tranquillity; but so determined nevertheless to reject all kinds of discoveries, that affecting a smile, as soon as he saw me, he said in an ironical tone, that he had just come from seeing the master-piece of the malignity. I have read many letters, added he, which indeed contain part of what she has related to me; yet you will not have a moment's doubt, but that Donna Figuerrez has had them written since yesterday, to repair her imprudence in having been a little too forward.

I confess this great trust raised my embarrassment to the height; I made no reply but by a motion of my head, which did not hinder him from proceeding. But, added he, what you will have a difficulty to comprehend, it is so extraordinary, she has carried her assurance so far, that being piqued at my refusal to give my assent to what she affirmed, and apparently to strengthen her calumnies, she maintained to my face that my wife is dead. Moved with indignation in spite of me at this ridiculous piece of news, I could not forbear answering her most seriously, that you had arrived very lately from France,

and

and that without doubt she had forgot to have seen you at her house within these two days. She told me, that you knew, as well as she did, of the death of my wife, and that I might have from you the same assurances. This extravagant effrontery made me leave her apartment without making any reply.

Notwithstanding the undisturbed and smiling air he yet laboured to maintain, he looked on me so attentively during his discourse, that I stood in need of all my steadiness to keep me from changing countenance. I considered, as I listened to him, what tone I should use in making him an answer; and when he had done, I found nothing more ready to say to him, than to make a simple reflection upon the ardour of Donna Figuerrez, whose motives I ascribed to those sentiments of love, of which she was already suspected. My coldness, added to the address I used in avoiding to answer him directly, convinced him so well, that all he had come from hearing were so many chimeras, that if he added any words, it was only to pity Donna Figuerrez, whose head he imagined to be more disturbed by an excess of folly, than her heart was by love.

If any body should be surprised, after I had wished he might receive from her those discoveries I had so much repugnance to make myself, that I took no advantage of a beginning which she had carried so far, and especially when there was no question but one word from me would finish her work, I cannot justify myself but from the astonishment I was in to see him as far from opening his eyes, upon his return from her house, as he was when he went there. In truth, there was need but of one word to give him those fatal discoveries, against which he so stedfastly armed himself; but on this word hung all the effects that I was in fear of producing. Thus returning to my first notions, that had brought me into Spain, I resolved to wait till the ripeness of time, and the further removal from him of his loss, should make the enterprize more
easy

fy. It was not indeed a very small advantage to
give him room to think at least, that the misfortunes
declared to him were possible; and I did not doubt
but that his having had a sight of them under some
uncertainty, would be a reason of consoling him
more easily, when he should find without any doubt
that they were only too true.

He broke off all acquaintance with Donna Figuerrez, and during some weeks of intermission from
his public business, he proposed to me to visit with
him the parts adjacent to Madrid. I consented freely to attend him; but not being able to excuse myself from seeing again the Spanish lady, I stole some
moments before our departure to acquit myself of
that visit. She was under an extreme impatience to
hear the success of her discoveries; and I struck her
speechless with astonishment, by assuring her that
they had not made any impression on the mind of
my brother. But have you then added nothing, said
she, to confirm my testimony? She was offended at
my sincerity in answering her, that very powerful
reasons, of which I prayed her to spare me the
detail, had made me suspend my resolutions; and
protesting to me, that she knew how to take other
measures to let my brother know, that she had deceived him less than I had done, she threw me into a
new disturbance, which I could not get rid of during the whole course of our journey. I observed
during the last conversation, that Patrick had been
more in her affections, than I could have imagined
from a coquette so subtle and refined, as the Spanish
gentleman had described her to me. She spoke to
me of him with so tender an air of interest; she set
off his good qualities with so many praises; she
appeared so afflicted at the opinion he had entertained
of her, since he had thought her capable of imposing
on him by calumnies; and so piqued against me,
whom she with reason accused of having forsaken
her in the precipice into which I had engaged her,

that

that I could not doubt but the merit of my brother had made a real impreſſion on her heart.

The king's orders, the execution of which detained Patrick in Spain, had been fulfilled with zeal, and the ſole cauſe of his ſtay was the ---- of the Spaniſh miniſters, who had fixed him at a place remote enough to receive their maſter's anſwer. I was induced, from the fear I had of the menaces of Donna Figuerrez, to lengthen out our jaunt to the time in which I foreſaw our return into France might be retarded. My brother, to whom I made this propoſal, reliſhed it without penetrating into the motives thereof. We left one of our ſervants at Madrid, with orders to hold our equipages in readineſs againſt the day we had appointed for our return; and the anſwer of the court being an affair of moment, we reckoned to begin our journey to France the day after it. Nothing could further flatter the impatience Patrick had to ſee Paris again.

During the continuance of our little journey, a thouſand circumſtances offered me the opportunity to diſcover myſelf to him; but having deferred it ſo long, I did not think I had any reaſon to be in haſte: and length of time ſince his misfortune adding ſtill weight to the delay by its continuance, I perſuaded myſelf in the end, that it would not be too late to come to the laſt diſcoveries, when we were upon the road from Madrid to Paris. Our converſation, during the jaunt we made to ſatisfy our curioſity in the places adjacent to the capital of Spain, rolled upon ſubjects quite oppoſite to the principal object of which I was full. The natural qualities of the country, their policies, religion, learning, daily furniſhed over-abundant matter to two travellers, who endeavoured by their application to acquire ſome knowledge. We had not a moment's trial of the languiſhment of tireſomeneſs. Nevertheleſs, I could not be always near Patrick, and ſee him in ſuch tranquillity, without lamenting his ſituation. Sorrow, death, all the violent paſſions ſeemed to me without ceaſing

...ing to flutter about him, with a cruel eagerness to ... entrance into his heart. I had this melancholy ... perpetually before my eyes, and in the bit... ... from it, my love and zeal made me of... ... ardent prayers to heaven, which cost ... effort to conceal from my unfortunate brother.

... executed without any obstacles, we ... almost as soon as we arrived there; and our ... to hasten our journey was proportioned to Patrick's ardour to see once more what he held most dear. It was time to think that delays, dissimulation, lenitives themselves, could be no longer of any use to me. It was not nevertheless the first day of our journey that I undertook the sorrowful office, which for a long time had been the torment of my heart. I let eight days of it pass over, which I employed as much in overcoming my repugnances, as in preparing my expressions. It seemed to me, that it was gaining something to defer it. In fine, a little village, wherein bad weather obliged us to pass the night, gave me that opportunity which I had before a thousand times rejected, by the philosophical turn our conversation took there. I interrupted Patrick in the midst of an excellent reflection, and forseeing the point to which what he had already said might lead him, stop, dear brother, said I with a deep sigh, and make no difficulty of telling me your mind sincerely: Are you sensible of all the courage and steadiness that appear in your principles; and do you think, that the practice of so high a philosophy does not surpass your strength? He seemed to be surprised at this question. Nevertheless, without hesitating on his answer, Perhaps, said he, I cannot promise you, that I have the same strength and vigour of mind every moment of the day; and I remember a thousand fatal occasions, in which I have found myself more feeble than my maxims: But in an instant such as this, filled as I am with all the ideas we have just debated, and in the degree of heat with which they have animated my

reason,

reason, there are few trials which I should not think myself able enough to resist. Ah! D[...]ick, added I, make then a good use this mo[...] your courage. I have concealed it from yo[...]nt; (and heaven is my witness, that all my d[...] and delays had no other source than the ten[...]ship I have for you;) but you are drawing [...]n[...], in which you will have it cleared u[...] [...] I will or not. Your wife is dead, and h[...] so for some months past; and if it be any co[...] to you to know, that her conduct has not rendered her worthy of your affliction, I confirm at least one part of the accusations of Donna Figguerrez. I should have continued, if the motion I saw him make had not been capable of inspiring me with terror. A furious air of trouble and despair at first chased away that sweetness, which was the natural ornament of his countenance; which nevertheless, did not hinder him from lending all his attention even to my last word: But having in appearance joined together the facts and proofs of them, not seeing any pretence to mistrust me, and recollecting all the accounts of Donna Figuerrez, of which I had so precisely confirmed the greater part, he lost for a moment all government of himself, even so far as to clap his hand hastily on the hilt of his sword, as if he had thought of nothing but thrusting it into his own heart. I could ascribe his second motion, by which he supported himself against the first, to nothing but the assistance of heaven, or the real strength of his mind; for I was too far from him to put a stop to so bold a transport. If he put his hand with so much fury to his sword, he drew it back with the same air after a moment's reflection; and throwing himself on the first chair, lifting up his eyes and stretching out his hands to heaven, he continued a long time without speaking one word, or fetching one sigh. I came near him; he thrust me back with one hand, whilst he covered his eyes with the other. One would have taken him for a criminal, who was under the terrors of his own conscience;

and the crime of another raised in him as much horror as his own could have done, had he been guilty.

The motion of his hand did not at all escape my observation, and convinced by that which immediately succeeded it, that he had rejected the first transport of his heart, I made no haste in shewing any desire of dissipating the grief and confusion in which I saw him swallowed up. These were thoughts from whence I apprehended no longer the same violence. I affected even to observe for a long time a mournful silence, to give him room to perceive, that I sincerely took a share in his grief; and that if I had shewed a cruelty in causing them, I had began much sooner than he to feel them. I expected, that after having abandoned himself inwardly to the full impression of a stroke so terrible, he would begin to address me with just imprecations against her perfidy, or complaints more sorrowful and tender, which I should take care how I opposed or condemned; but rising after a quarter of an hour's silence, and continuing to cover his eyes with his hand, he made a sign to his valet de chambre, whom I had already called to attend him, to shew him into the room where he was to pass the night. As he went by me he made a respectful bow, which encouraged me to use some persuasions to detain him. The same sign of his hand, by which he had already removed me from him, gave me to understand, that it was in vain I should attempt to follow him. I gave orders to his servants to remove from him all his arms, and every thing else that sometimes serve too readily as a relief to grief.

Having retired to my chamber, to what an excess of bitterness did I not deliver myself up? What exclamations did I not use? What tender and doleful cries did I not address to heaven? Oh! brother, worthy of a better fate? What sweetness would you not have found in my compassion, if you had seen all the excess of it, or if it were any consolation to you under your extreme misfortune to see a tender heart, who shares it with you?

I added

I added to the orders I had given his servants that of watching at the door of his chamber, and to go in without affecting to do it on purpose, at the least motion they should hear. During the whole night, which I spent on my knees before heaven, my heart big with groans, that vented themselves only by the ardour of my prayers, it came a thousand times into my mind to go and surprize him, and make him, whether he would or not, receive the assistances of my zeal. But I knew his humour incapable of betraying himself outwardly, when his mind was taken up with any affection; jealous in solitude even of the most slight interests capable of moving his heart; how then would my importunity redouble his grief? I expected nevertheless, that he would the next day grant me the liberty of seeing him, and I had already prepared a discourse suitable to my sentiments and his situation. My hopes were vain. Coming to his door in the morning, I was informed by his valet de chambre, that his desire was to remain absolutely alone, and that I was not excepted out of this order. I did not insist further on seeing him, contented enough with the moderation he had passed the night in; his sighs being the only noise he made. All the day was to me a new exercise of compassion and grief. My troubles redoubled in the evening, upon hearing from his valet de chambre, that he was attacked by a dangerous fever, and that upon touching his hands, as if by chance, he had found them so burning, that he could scarce bear the heat. I made a new attempt to see him, and if he did not reject my proposal with too much harshness, yet he ordered an answer to be given me that was a law even more powerful for the affection of my heart. He ordered me to be told, that he could easily fancy how highly I was moved at his grief, and he had a just sense of my compassion; but in the violent transports he had to combat with, he was resolved not to go out of his chamber but dead, or in a state of tranquillity. All the compassion I was pierced with did not hinder me from smiling tenderly at this answer. I chose to trust him to the excellence of his natural temper; being as sure that he would render himself worthy of the protection of heaven, as I was that heaven would not abandon so much integrity and goodness.

We had already passed a day and two nights in a miserable place, where we scarce found the conveniences most necessary for life. In the morning of the second day, going out of the inn to take the air, I saw at a distance a chaise driving in post-haste; before and after which, were many servants on horseback, who gave an air of importance to the owner of the equipage. A motion of curiosity having made me wait to observe the retinue as it passed by me, I was surprised to hear myself called by name, and still much more to see Donna Figuerrez appear at the boot of the chaise, who added divers signs of joy and friendship to the cries by which she endeavoured all at once to make herself known to me, and to stop her postilion.

Although in my first thoughts I looked on her appearance as an unseasonable and cross accident, I could not nevertheless refuse her those compliments that I owed as much to our acquaintance as her sex. She was earnest in asking whether my brother was with me. I must have done too great a violence to truth to conceal it. I answered, that we arrived together at that village, and that a sudden disorder, which fixed him to his bed, obliged us to stay there. Then recollecting immediately the vexation she must have felt to have passed in his eyes, as the author or accomplice of a multitude of calumnies, I thought that chance having thus brought her on our heels, I ought to take advantage of the opportunity to repair the share I had in her trouble. It entered readily into my first reflections, that since she had shewn such a great esteem and relish for my brother, her zeal might be of some service to his consolation; and from all these notions I concluded, that without injuring decency, I might invite her to alight, and repose herself a moment in
the

the same place: O heaven! cried she out immediately, Do you doubt that my journey is not at an end, when I have met with what made me undertake it? This village is my limit, since I find you here. And giving me her hand to help her out, she embraced me with as much affection and ardour, as if she had taken me for the object of her journey and caresses.

She began by expostulating with me on the wrong I had done her, as much in having left my brother in an error, which she took to heart from the loss of his esteem, as in obliging him so speedily to leave Madrid, that he had neglected to take leave of a great number of his best friends. I interrupted her complaints by my apologies that I thought I owed her on the first particular, and confessed, without going about the bush, that if I was guilty of any thing at Madrid, I had repaired my fault within these two days by the discovery I had made my brother. You will judge, said I, by the condition you are going to see my brother in, of the reasons I had to delay my discovery. Her impatience increasing, she spoke of nothing but being shewed directly to his chamber; but I moderated this heat by informing her, that he could not be seen but with great precautions, and that I myself, who flattered myself with being beloved, had been two days solliciting leave to see him. She promised me to observe the same measures, and following me on foot to the inn, she had time to relate the motives that engaged her to come to France. I have three motives for this journey, said she with those graces that never forsook her, and I confess that I stood in need of the first to serve as a veil to cover the other two. The ambassador being my nearest relation, I anticipated a design I had a long time of taking the opportunity of his embassage to make a journey to Paris. But why should I dissemble? I have the image of your brother in my heart: I cannot be comforted under the opinion he has conceived of me. I would go to the end of the world to follow him, and prevail on him to do justice to my intentions. You, who have drawn on me his hatred, are not you obliged, added she, to use means to convince him of my innocence? I could not disown but that this was a duty incumbent on me, and had been at length fulfilled by my discovery to my brother. We arrived at the inn. I sent a message to Patrick to know if he would receive our visit. The name of Donna Figuerrez, and her unexpected arrival, awakened him from his deadly heaviness. He not only reproached himself for having treated her with scorn, but calling to mind all the measures she had observed in giving him the first news of his misfortune, he with that gratitude, that he thought due to her friendship, resumed all the sentiments of esteem that he ever had for her merit: Nevertheless, he contented himself to give her these assurances by his valet de chambre; and excusing himself on the score of his disorder, with which she could not doubt but he was afflicted, he prayed her to take in good part his excuses for not admitting her.

She did not seem offended at this refusal: On the contrary, lamenting her situation, of which she drew a sorrowful picture, she said to me in a tone that already supposed a familiarity well established: Ah! My dear dean, we will wait until he consents to see us, and we will have the pleasure of thinking that he knows we are very near him. I did not oppose her resolution to stay with us. The solitude of Patrick could not continue so long as he seemed to propose to himself. The king's affairs necessarily called him to St Germain; and if his fever should not become a distemper important enough to justify his delay, I knew, that having given notice to the king of our departure from Madrid, he must be persuaded his majesty would count the days of our journey. I charged his valet to put him in mind of this particular, and I even looked upon this advice as a matter

ter that would give me room to make a judgment of the depth and danger of his wounds. He made no answer to the meſſage of his valet de chambre, as if he had been equally infenfible to the cares of his duty and his life.

This obſtinacy appeared to me to be ſo dangerous an effect of his grief, that I began to conſider more ſeriouſly on the means of drawing him out of his lethargy ; but the day was not ended before Donna Figuerrez, more dextrous, or leſs reſerved than I, had found means to be admitted into his chamber, and relying on the familiarity in which ſhe had lived with him a long time, obtained by her infinuating carriage, as much as by the ſurpriſe her preſence had raiſed in him, to oblige him patiently to hear her. She informed me herſelf, when ſhe came from him, what paſſed in this converſation. He had made her very humble amends for the difficulty he had ſhewed in giving credit to her teſtimony ; and ſpeaking of his misfortune, like a man who did not hope to ſurvive it, he prayed her to charge me with a commiſſion, which, ſaid ſhe, he had not the power to acquit himſelf of in perſon. The ſight of the dean, did he ſay, is a torment more inſupportable to me than death. He triumphs without doubt, in the ſubject of my troubles. I always found him in a conſtant oppoſition to my marriage. He muſt for the ſame reaſon have wiſhed to ſee it turn out unluckily. And how will he ever perſuade me, that having my wife before his eyes, and being a witneſs of her conduct, he might not have given an oppoſition to every thing that you have related to me of her irregularities ? he, to whom the voice of a cenſor is ſo natural, and who has all his life made it his ſtudy to vex and perplex his family by the exceſs of his morals! Depend upon it, he has taken a malicious pleaſure in ſeeing my wife fall by degrees, and in reality hugs himſelf at an effect that ſeems to prove the ſuperiority of his views to mine. I do not, continued he, intruſt this with you as a

ſecret ;

secret; tell him from me, that I cannot have the courage to reproach a brother; but that I am sure I shall never pardon him. And, as I have the charge of the king's affairs, which consist only in putting into his hands the treaty I have just made in his name with the court of Spain, desire my brother to finish my commission, by carrying it to the court of St Germain. I shall owe him a double obligation, by delivering me from his presence, and procuring me the liberty of flying equally from the sight of all mankind, with whom I will not any further have the least commerce.

Donna Figuerrez, flattered by the confidence he had expressed for her in these words, and without doubt foreseeing, that to cure him of his melancholy, as much as to aid the design she had in gaining his heart, it would be more easy in my absence to employ all her wit and artifice, had made no answer otherwise than by approving his intentions, and exhorting him not to change them. In giving me this account, wherein she affected not to soften any thing that was mortifying in it by the least compliment, she endeavoured to persuade me also, that rest and solitude being what was most suitable to his situation, I ought to agree to the satisfaction he required, and repose on her the care of calming his mind. Then, thinking to give a greater probability to this promise by a formal confession of her affections, she declared to me, that not thinking herself unworthy of the love of a man of honour, her hope was to merit that of my brother by all the marks she could give him of a virtuous passion, to bring him, if it were possible, one day or other to grant her the name of his spouse. You shall, said she, see me engaged from this view not only to spare nothing for the recovery of his health and repose, but to bring him to change his disposition towards you, and to make a merit in conserving peace and amity in your family. Go, my dear dean, take charge of the commission he turns
over

over to you, and do not doubt but by my diligence you shall find him such as he ought to be towards you, when we meet at Paris; for you may judge well, added she smiling, that I will make him lay aside his hatred for the world, and his resolution of flying it.

With whatever peevishness I listened to this long discourse, I found myself less afflicted at the injustice of my brother, which friendship made me immediately look on as the raving of a sick heart and mind, than I was piqued at the presumption of a woman, whom I never had seen four times in my life. How could she arrogate to herself the right of regulating my conduct and the interests of my family? Patrick had been her friend, and I could comprehend well enough, that during more than four months he had passed at Madrid, having been few days without seeing her familiarly, he might have placed in her a confidence, and made her some overtures upon which she might build a part of her hopes. But was she already so sure of his love, as to think herself authorized to assume an empire over every thing that related to him; and on the other hand could she fancy, that I had any other dependence on my brother, than that of an affection of blood and zeal for religion? Perhaps a little spice of jealousy had taken possession of him in this resentment; but could I think it just, when I considered, that Patrick had granted to a stranger those marks of confidence and friendship, which he had refused to me? The suspicion he had of my sentiments appeared pardonable in the first agitations of his grief; but I could not pass over his abandoning himself to his injustice, even to the making a noise of it by a behaviour so severe as his discourse. In fine, far from yielding to the proposal made me on his part, I protested to Donna Figuerrez, that nothing should oblige me to consent to forsake him a moment, and that I would not do him so much wrong as to finish a commission, of which the king could expect an account only from the person he had charged with it.

Without

Without doubt Donna Figuerrez had made a merit with him by the offenfive exactnefs with which fhe had reported to me his expreffions; and I durft not warrant it, that fhe had not added fomething to mine, with a view of poifoning my anfwer. The reft of the day paffed over without any incident, and I fpent it only in reflecting upon the unhappy reward of my zeal, which had yet drawn from my brother nothing but vexations and mortifications. Towards midnight, at the time when the bitternefs of my thoughts had banifhed fleep from my eyes, I heard the noife of horfes and carriages, which I took for the equipage of fome traveller. The kind of reft I enjoyed from the liberty I had at leaft of giving myfelf up to my forrowful reflections, was not difturbed by the noife, efpecially as I had not the leaft mifgiving of the new afflictions that threatened me. But on my uprifing, which was a little late, occafioned by the reftlefs night I had paffed, Jacin, my old valet, informed me, that Patrick was gone away with all his fervants, and that he had left a letter for me, which was not delivered to Jacin himfelf till he had got out of bed. I opened it with all the trouble that fuch an information could caufe me. It contained in a few lines, that not being able to bear the world, nor me, nor himfelf, he was going to retire into fome folitude, where he would have no further acquaintance but with mute and infenfible beings, who would not be capable of perfecuting and betraying him. He had left, added he, in his chamber a cafket, in which I fhould find the inftruments that he ought to have delivered to the king, with fome inftruction he had added to them for me, and that they would be fufficient for me to anfwer, as fully as he himfelf could, the expectations of that prince. He prayed me to make his excufes to him, building fo much on his goodnefs, as not to doubt but he would find them juft.

I had not the leaft doubt but Donna Figuerrez was gone with him, and this thought increafing my grief,

I let

I let fall before Jacin a thousand complaints, which made him discover one part of my troubles. In regard to Donna Figuerrez, he immediately informed me, that she was yet buried in sleep, and he was much deceived, if she had been better informed than I of the departure of my brother. I found my courage revive upon this assurance, and forming immediately a design, which would please me as much in relation to Donna Figuerrez, by giving me the opportunity of an innocent revenge on her, as on the part of my brother, by giving me some hopes of being useful to him in spite of himself, I gave orders to Jacin immediately to put the horses to my chaise. I was resolved to be gone on the spot, that is to say, before the Spanish lady should awake, and to follow Patrick with so much haste, that having no other road to go than that of the post, I should overtake him before the end of the day.

My orders were executed. I left the inn before Donna Figuerrez had called her servants, and pushing my revenge as far as I thought I could without injuring charity, I charged one of her train, as I got into my chaise, to tell her, that she owed me some thanks for the care I had taken of not disturbing her rest. When I had supposed, that the same motive, that had made her quit Spain had induced her immediately to follow us upon the track, I was sure, that there were not horses enough to be got at the post-house to furnish her for her journey before the return of ours, and I consequently reckoned that we should get the start of her so far, that she would find it difficult to overtake us.

This way of reasoning supposed nevertheless, that Patrick would pursue the road to Paris, out of which he could not always find regulated posts for a communication to other towns. With this thought I pursued forward as far as Orleans; continually inquiring at what distance he was before me, and if he had shewed no design of going out of the road. It was at Orleans I lost the track of him. They informed

formed me at the post-house that he had come there three or four hours before me, and that having committed his chaise, and some other parts of his equipage, to the care of the master of the house, he had gone away on foot with three servants he had in his train. I quitted the design of continuing my journey, and thinking of nothing further than to discover him, I flattered myself that his care would not require any long search in the provincial town. In the mean time, having to no purpose employed a part of the day, I learned towards evening, that he had hired a boat, into which he and one of his servants went, having dismissed the other two; and that not discovering himself either as to the place he was bound to, nor even the time that would be necessary for his passage, they could not give me any other information till the return of the boatmen.

What a new subject of embarrasment!——Prudence would not permit me to proceed further at a hazard. I was obliged to wait two days for a discovery which I could not get but by the way proposed to me. I passed these days in a thousand alarms, which the uncertainty of their duration yet rendered more cruel. At length the boatmen arrived, to put an end to them luckily. They had conducted Patrick to a benedictine abbey some leages from Orleans, situated on the banks of the Loire, and had returned very well contented with his mildness and liberality. Not being able to obtain any other informations, they only inflamed the desire I had of overtaking him. Could his despair, said I, have made him think of breaking absolutely with the world, and be capable of burying himself in solitude with a design never to come out of it, I should think ill of the resolution formed thus in the midst of his grief, and should apprehend bad consequences from it. These great sacrifices ought to be the fruits of a quiet meditation. Reason and grace would be but little able to support a violent choice, when they were

not

not the fruits of inspiration. I hastened to be gone with the same boatmen that had carried him.

BOOK XI.

UPON my arrival at the abbey, I was informed at the gate, that Patrick had presented himself to the superior under a name different from his own. He had not concealed his country nor his birth; but confessing that extraordinary troubles having driven him in quest of solitude, he requested it as a favour, that they would not attempt to dive further into them, and on his side he had promised, that he would give no trouble to the house by the kind of life he proposed to lead. Having agreed for the price of his pension, he pitched upon the most solitary and remote apartment in the house. The neighbourhood of a very thick wood had flattered his melancholy. He caused some books to be brought to him there, which he described by their titles; and agreeing with the superior, that he would not be disturbed by any person in the world in this retreat, if he did not sometimes request such an amusement himself, he shut himself up in it in a graceful manner, together with his valet de chambre, an hour after his arrival.

As an event so extraordinary had made a good deal of noise in the house, they could not hear that I was inquiring after it with much curiosity, without expressing as much earnestness to see and hear me. My design had been to send for the superior

superior, and learn from his own mouth what I feared I had only an imperfect information of before; but the porter, whom I was yet talking to, shewed him to me standing among others, whom curiosity had brought towards me. I took him aside with a good deal of precaution, in order that the rest should not see me; being apprehensive least the impression of so remarkable a figure as mine might continue in their minds, and from thence Patrick might sooner or latter come to understand that I had discovered the place of his retreat, and had come to the monastery two days after him. From the first notion I had taken of his project upon the porter's relation, far from finding it contrary to reason, I was convinced he might draw great advantage from it for the establishment of his repose; and I had taken up a resolution not only to avoid disturbing him by my visit in the first experiment of his solitude, but to leave him even ignorant that I had travelled so close on his heels. Yet I was well pleased to make an acquaintance with the superior, as well to assure myself of the means of receiving news from him regularly, as to engage him by my civilities to contribute all in his power to the recovery of my brother. Without discovering myself more than he did as to our name, and without as much as acquainting him how near I was related to him by blood, I omitted nothing that might make him dear and respectable to the community; and I had the satisfaction of learning from the superior, that at first sight he had taken all the sentiments of respect and friendship for him.

My heart was so comforted by this happy discovery, that daring to promise myself already the most agreeable fruits from it, I thought of nothing but going immediately to Paris to hasten the effects of them. Knowing the natural goodness and piety of the king, I had no fear that he would be offended at the choice my brother had made; and I had not the least doubt, but that with the instructions Patrick had left me I should easily supply his absence. But I found more
pleasure

pleasure yet in foreseeing that solitude, restoring him by little and little to that tranquillity of mind and heart, which he had for a long time lost, his reason would sooner or later assume strength enough to make him sensible of what he owed to Sarah Fincer, and to dispose him at length to re-establish her in all the rights that her rival had usurped. I forbore fearing any thing on the account of Donna Figuerrez. I had no doubt but she had continued her journey, and since I had left her, I could not defend myself from a fear that continually troubled me on the road. If I had in Spain but little dreaded the love she might have inspired my brother with; (because being there, as it were, on the theatre of her disorderly courses, I might every moment take off the veil from the eyes of Patrick, and let him know, either by my own account, or by the relations of a number of others, that her conduct rendered her unworthy of the hand of a man of honour;) I had not the same resource in France: On the contrary I apprehended, that the distinction, with which her personal merit, and the quality of relation to the ambassador was about making her shine in at Paris, was not so capable of dazzling the eyes of Patrick, as her removal from Madrid would without doubt be to shut them against those reproaches and accusations, which it would be difficult for me there to make good by proofs. The choice he had made dissipated all my mistrusts. He had but little affection for her, since his confusion and grief had made him capable of leaving her without regret; and though she should join to all the charms I knew she had, all the prudence she had not, to attack the heart of Patrick with such forcible arms, I should propose to myself to act so vigorously in favour of the unfortunate Sarah, and by ways to which he was naturally so sensible, that I thought myself already almost assured of victory.

I enter-

I entertained myself with those thoughts on my return to Orleans, where I had left my chaise, when putting into the banks of the Loire to get out of the boat, I saw Donna Figuerrez come out of a neighbouring house, attended by her servants, who immediately came up to me with as much joy to see me again, as I felt vexation at this meeting. I immediately understood what brought them there. Having pursued my brother's steps and mine, they had discovered, as I did, at the post-house of Orleans, that Patrick had left there his chaise; and an eagerness to find him out had laid hold of Donna Figuerrez. After a great many hasty searches, she came, as I had done, to get some imperfect accounts of him on the banks of the Loire. The boatmen, who had carried him to the abbey, not having had time at their return to relate the circumstances of their voyage, because my haste to make them go back the way they came, had not allowed them one moment to rest, Donna Figuerrez could from thence gather nothing clear and certain of the end of our journey. She waited, as I had done before her, 'til they should return, to ask them some questions; and although she had reason to be diffident of my presence, yet it never came into her mind, that I had the least interest in concealing from her the road my brother went.

Nevertheless, as much joy as I saw in her countenance, as much was I mortified at this meeting; and in my first perplexity not thinking on any thing ready enough to deliver me, I turned about to the two boatmen, to whom I promised double the sum I had agreed for my passage, if they would keep the secret two days. Even this precaution not appearing to me sufficient, I desired them to follow me, under pretence of paying them at the place where I had left my chaise; and I gave orders to my valet to carry them there, whilst I should stop a moment with Donna Figuerrez, whom it was impossible to avoid. Indeed she was already so near me, that having made me some hasty reproaches on my departure,

and

and continuing with the same nimbleness of tongue
to ask me where I had left my brother, I could find
no other medium, between the necessity of betraying my secret, or of deceiving her by a lye, than
to declare to her bluntly enough, that she asked me an
idle question. She was offended at my answer; but
as if my first harshness had disposed me further to
observe no measures with her, I reproached her
so briskly for the indecency of the motive that
made her go in quest of Patrick, that in the
confusion she felt at some of my words, she stood
speechless, and fell into tears, which she wiped
away with her handkerchief. I was left alone by
the departure of Jacin and the boatmen. One of
her servants, affronted at the insult I had offered
his mistress, advanced fiercely, and treating me with
an assurance that surprised me from a servant,
seemed only to wait for a word of her mouth, or a
wink of her eye, to follow his abusive language
with blows. His violence affrighted me. But Donna
Figuerrez commanded him to be silent, with an air of
authority, that obliged him to be so all at once;
and she even threatened to punish his impudence, that
made him fail in respect to an ecclesiastic.

I should have passed over this incident, if it had
not taught me an useful lesson, that I have found the
benefit of ever since. Although the vexation I felt
at being mal-treated, added to the hope of success
by the way I had taken of concealing the retreat of
my brother, made me immediately be gone, yet I
could not think on the impression my words had made
on Donna Figuerrez, and her goodness in taking part
with me against her servant, without acknowledging
myself more guilty than that saucy valet, whose in-
solence had offended me. Do then the customs of the
world, and the politeness of men, inspire more softness and sweetness of temper into our behaviour,
and more regard for decency, than the principles
which I have made my study all my life? Such was

my

my first reflection. But is it not I, continued I immediately, that have not penetrated far enough into the full extent of my principles? And passing through the discussion of this point in the same method I had often used, I found indeed, that in the principle of christian charity are included all the duties of politeness, which form the principal band of civil societies. Then pushing further this observation, I concluded from the motive of charity, which always tends to the good of our neighbours, with a proportion of that respect one owes to the weakest, that women, from an infinite number of reasons peculiar to their sex, have a particular right to this sort of regard, which is named politeness, and consequently, to neglect to pay them it, is in some sort a double failure of the precept of charity.

During the fervour of this reflection, I should have returned voluntarily to Donna Figuerrez, to make her an apology for the air and manner of speaking I had used to her, if I had not thought myself excused from this sort of reparation by the sentiment of my heart, wherewith I promised heaven to lay down to myself an invariable rule, and from the importance it was not to expose myself anew to be pressed to discover the retreat of Patrick. The merit of this lady appearing to me to be more dangerous, from the greatness of the perfections I observed in her, I began to fear more than ever for my brother; so that not thinking myself sure enough of the boatmen by their word, and the price I offered to pay for their fidelity, it came into my mind to send them far from Orleans for some days, to lay them under a necessity to keep their promises to me for so long a time. The only way was to engage them under some pretence to follow me to Paris. Interest being all powerful upon people who gain their livelihood only by their labour, I proposed to them, if they would go with me, such a sum of money as soon disposed them to it.

Thus

Thus events of affairs, and the neceſſity of providing for all circumſtances, formed in me from day to day a ſort of prudence, of which I never could find the rules in my ſtudy. It was from reaſonings of this nature that I prepared myſelf for the part which my brother had given me in charge to act at the court of St Germain. Politics had never made a part of my occupations; but conſidering, that even for the honour of Patrick, who had relied upon me for the execution of his commiſſion, I ought not to appear abſolutely without experience and judgment in the king's eyes, I ſtudied the inſtructions my brother left behind him with ſo much diligence, and from his care of incloſing in them a number of intereſting obſervations, I ſo perfectly put myſelf in a condition of making the beſt of them, that the king having done me the honour of diſcourſing me a long time in his cloſet, ſhewed a high ſatisfaction in my brother's and my ſervices. He ſeemed no leſs moved at the neceſſity, to which his misfortunes had reduced him, of retiring for ſome time into ſolitude. I gave no other colour to his choice, and the king's curioſity extending no further than to know he had loſt his wife, I luckily avoided a detail, which I feared his orders would have obliged me to have given.

Although I had not forgot, in leaving Madrid, to give notice of our departure to the count de S——— and to Sarah Fincer, my deſire of daily maintaining not only the liberty of regulating the duration of our journey, but that of managing the circumſtances of our arrival, and above all not to expoſe Patrick to a meeting perhaps with Sarah Fincer the moment we leaſt thought of it, had made me ſpeak of our journey, and of the day we might expect to be at Paris, as of two things equally uncertain. Without this precaution I could not doubt but Sarah would have come, it may be, a good way to meet us. But being obliged to moderate her impatience, I found her at the count's, taken up with her ordinary employments,

which

which were reading and working. My lord Tenermill had returned from Ireland some weeks before.
The noise of my arrival having spread all at once
through the house, every one the first moment gathered about me. They were not surprised to see me
without Patrick. He had gone away with so much
indifference to the count's country house, that six
months absence might not have dissipated it ; and
they could easily fancy that the news I had carried
him to Spain had made him feel, together with grief
for his loss, a very strong sense of shame for having
voluntarily drawn on himself his misfortunes by excess of prejudice, of which all the advice of his
friends could never cure him. It was not from the
first moment of my appearance that I discovered the
dispositions of all the dear persons who surrounded
me. But I could easily judge that Sarah burned with
a desire of drawing me aside to lay open her thoughts
to me.

I shewed this complaisance to her desires as soon as
I could obtain a moment's liberty. All my ardour
in relating to her what I had seen, or what other circumstances had thrown in my way, did not sufficiently
equal her eagerness. She wished to have heard
every thing at once, and pondering nevertheless on
each word I said, she would have the particulars over
again, where nothing was omitted or related slightly.
I could not avoid bringing Donna Figuerrez into my
story. Patrick's familiar acquaintance with that
lady made her tremble ; she asked me a hundred
questions about her character, even after I had drawn
a faithful picture of her ; and upon the whole, when I
had come to the events of our return, she asked me
at every word, if it were possible for Patrick not to
be moved at her resolution of following him ; and if
I were convinced that in the complaisances he had
shewn her there was no mixture of love. But having
at length laid open to her with the same exactness the
part he had chosen to act at Orleans, observing to her

only

only that this particular of my story was a confidence I had resolved to trust to no body but her, it seemed to me, that from the satisfaction she had hitherto shewed in hearing me, she passed all at once to give some tokens of inquietude and sorrow. During a long discourse, to which I added nothing of my own, she had perpetually hoped that some circumstance would happen, wherein she might hear me tell what I had done for her; but the separation of Patrick, and the recital of the journey I had made to the solitude he had retired to, making her plainly understand that I had not had any other opportunity of seeing him again, she accused me in her mind for having neglected her interests, and perhaps went so far as to suspect me of having favoured the pretensions of Donna Figuerrez. Nevertheless, she continued to look on me for some time with silence, even after I had finished my story, as if she yet flattered herself I was about adding something to it relating to her, or that having forgot something that regarded her, the attention I shewed to her concerns was about assisting me in recollecting it. At length, losing all hopes, Ah! my dear dean, said she, shedding some tears, you have not remembered either my entreaties or your promises; or if they have induced you to attempt any thing in the behalf of an unhappy friend, your silence gives me too well to understand that nothing has succeeded with you. This complaint moved me sensibly. I should have foreseen, answered I, that you would have thrown these reproaches on me, and I should not have failed in finding out just reasons to anticipate them. Nothing indeed had been so easy as to have observed in the course of my story, that having put off the discoveries I had made my brother to almost the end of my journey, there could be but little appearance that in a space so short I could have found means of making him other proposals. I had not seen him even once since I informed him of his misfortune. But being able in a manner to answer that he had

nothing

nothing in his heart but sorrow, and recalling the sentiments which I had known him always have for her, I could not have scrupled to flatter her by the most sweet conjectures. It was to this point I bent my strength, when I saw the need she had of such assistance; and had no difficulty in giving hope an entrance into a heart so much inflamed by its passions. I was about proposing to her to join ourselves together, to deliberate upon the discretion and caution that decency required of her; but she herself having more than one proposal to make, asked me what I thought of my lord Tenermill, who, without conceiving that she could preserve the least inclination for Patrick, had constantly pressed her since his return to shorten his amorous sufferings, which he believed she had manifestly determined to put an end to one day or other. He had affected openly to take a pride in his hopes, and declaring that he had forgot the conditions to which he had submitted before his departure, he had often employed the count and countess of S—— to sollicit Sarah to forget them as he had done. She (who had fancied herself obliged to a thousand managements in a house, which she had more interest than ever not to quit, and who not daring to promise herself any thing from Patrick, had yet less courage to open the desires of her heart) had lived under a perpetual constraint, having not even the consolation of disburdening herself, by imparting her grief to the trust of any friend.' I do not relate to you, said she, half of the persecutions I have suffered from my lord Tenermill, and I cannot think but they will increase, when he understands the affection I have always conserved for his brother.

I had seen by experience so many disorders caused by love, that I could not look on the apprehensions of Sarah as vain terrors. Nevertheless, the opinion I had of the disposition of Tenermill, squared but little with that excess of passion by which he was like to become troublesome or formidable to the person

he

he loved. I imparted this thought to Sarah. She agreed, that in his looks and applications she never remarked that air of passion which is the characteristick of hearts in love, and of which, she confessed to me with a smile, she had by long experience learned to judge. But his language, added she, is not therefore a whit the less pressing; and if it be not love that prevails on him to importune me by such eager solicitations, I should dread even more another passion, that should be strong enough to act so powerfully under the mask of a false pretended love. Without, answered I, believing his love to be false or pretended, one may attribute the effects, of which you complain, to some more powerful passion, from which it borrows a share of its ardour. My lord Tenermill interrupted us this moment, begging leave to make one in our conversation. The tone he assumed in my presence seemed to justify the complaints of Sarah. He upbraided her for the resistance she had made to his happiness, and calling me for a witness to the former vivacity of his love, he protested it with some military oaths, which his late expedition to Ireland had but too much increased. I confess, that being accustomed to the tender languors, and respectful eagerness, whether of Patrick and the count de S———, or whether of Sarah and the countess, I could not in this cavalier air discover the character of that love, of which I had formed to myself an idea from the example of others.

I soon unravelled this mystery. Going out with him from Sarah's apartment, he spoke of the design of his marriage with the same ardour, but with an air less studied. After some decent remarks on the notions he had of my friendship, he told me, that I was luckily arrived to take share in those things which he had in expectation, as the most advantageous for himself, and most glorious for his family; that it was a secret yet known to none but the king himself. While he was in Ireland, fortune had so far favoured him as to give him the opportunity of being useful to the king's service in an affair of great importance. His majesty, who did not think himself dispensed from shewing his gratitude for an obligation wherein his subjects were serviceable to him, had loaded him with caresses on his return, and giving him room to hope for every thing from his favours, had declared, under the obligation of secrecy, that if he could augment his fortune by an advantageous marriage; his design was to create him a duke. Judge, said he, if with the tender affections you have for a long time known me to have for Sarah, I am not strongly interested to press her to accept my hand. I dare not, added he, improve this motive, which would perhaps diminish something from the opinion she has of my love, and moreover the king's commands oblige me to silence. But to you, whose discretion equals your wisdom, I make no difficulty to discover myself, with the hopes that you will aid me in obtaining Sarah's consent, which must seal my fortune and happiness.

Words so clear and open would have removed all Sarah's doubts, if I had been at liberty to communicate to her what my brother imparted to me as a secret. But her reflection on the force of a passion, that was capable of lending ardour to love, became from hence more demonstrable to me. It seemed a matter indisputable, that Tenermill, looking on his marriage with her as the foundation of his fortune, would take every thing one might attempt against a hope so flattering to his ambition, as so many proofs of hatred. Haughty and imperious as he was, I doubted whether he would pardon even his brother the contest with him for a heart, to which he imagined his long services had given him a just claim. Thus nothing could become so delicate as my situation, under the necessity I was of coming to explanations with him in conducting the interest of Sarah, which all the world was not capable of

making

making me abandon. I drew myself nevertheless out of such a pressing perplexity by an equivocal answer, which I was convinced he would take in a sense the most favourable to his own love. Having first complimented him upon the king's favour, if Sarah, said I, has a relish for grandeur, she will without doubt be in haste to meet your eagerness, and without betraying the secret imposed on you, I promise you to give her room enough to guess at what your aims for her tend. He seemed satisfied with this promise. My design was indeed not to conceal from Sarah, that it was the ambition of Tenermill she ought to be upon her guard against, and having given her this advice the same day, I did not in the least perceive that these hopes of grandeur, which I explained to her in a loose and indeterminate manner, had made impression enough on her heart, to combat thereby for one moment her love.

On the contrary, if I had yielded to her proposals, she would have gone a few days after to live in Patrick's solitude. It came into her mind, that without letting him know she was in his neighbourhood, she could easily hire a house in the same village. From the thoughts alone of breathing there the same air with him, and of procuring there every day news of his situation, whereby to regulate her joy and grief from the accounts she should receive of his health and repose, she formed in her imagination the plan of a life most pleasant and happy. I had a good deal of difficulty to persuade her to lay aside this project; and I did so only by promising her immediately to take a journey to the abbey to see him, and talk to him, and to try his pulse whether he had yet remaining any inclination for her.

I should have postponed this journey but a short time, though I had made no such promise to Sarah. Besides the inquietude with which I was perpetually

petually filled for the health of so dear a brother; I had been under a necessity of excusing his delay under the pretext of sickness, which I should have badly supported, if I had let too long an interval slip without pretending at least to return to him. The count de S—— and my lord Tenermill had often desired to go and see him themselves in the neighbourhood of Orleans, where I had told them he had been obliged to stop. Nevertheless, not having explained myself to them upon the kind of sickness he had, or not having spoken to them of it in a manner capable of alarming them, they relied as to his situation upon the tranquillity I affected, and of which they could not have thought me capable, if he had been in the least danger. I pitched upon the day they least expected for my departure, to prevent the desire either of them might have had to bear me company. I nevertheless gave Sarah an account of it: What did she not say to me upon this occasion? With what ardour, with what affection did she not recommend to me the care of his happiness, and the concern of his life? I passed a whole night in receiving the sentiments of her heart, and in repeating the expressions she desired I would use to my brother.

I had nobody but Jacin with me. Before I shewed myself at the abbey, I thought proper to dispatch Jacin thither, to obtain some informations upon the changes that might have happened since my last journey to it. He reported indeed two pieces of news, which caused me more surprise than I could have ever expected from it: One was, that Patrick, whose name they did not yet know, had proposed to the superior to be admitted among the number of the religious; the other, that this worthy man had made a difficulty of doing so from this reason alone, that having conceived an high idea of my brother, from divers reasons, which had served as a foundation to his conjectures, he feared he should draw on himself

some

some reproach by complying with his instances, which did not seem to him to proceed from a tranquillity of heart and mind.

To what an excess of trouble did I not fancy the sorrowful Patrick was come, to be capable of submitting to such violent extremities? With an high respect to religion, I had always known him have so great an estrangement from those singular methods of piety, that I have been obliged a thousand times to oppose his aversion and prejudices against the generality of religious societies. In the disorder I imagined his reason to be, was it to grace I could ascribe the change of his notions, and did it not rather appear, that suffering himself to be vanquished by despair, he sought an end of it by a remedy even more terrible than his troubles; as a madman throws himself headlong into an abyss, or voluntarily buries a poinard in his heart? It was time then to force him from his solitude, and to make him hear against his inclinations every thing that my zeal had made me consider for calming his heart. But what advantages had I to expect for Sarah's hopes, and what little appearance did I see of being able to turn all the instructions she had given me in charge, at my departure, to a good use?

I repaired immediately to the abbey, and asking leave of the religious to talk to their solitary, I saw myself exposed to a refusal out of a fear of grieving him by a violation of his orders. Nevertheless, my intreaties, and the pretence of many important affairs, prevailed on the superior to undertake the trouble of making him consent to my visit. He conducted me to the door of the apartment, and going in before to tell him of my coming under the bare name of an ecclesiastic, who expressed a great desire to see him, he returned with permission to bring me in. Patrick had no sooner cast his eyes on me, than turning away his face, Ah! cried he, it is he himself, I mistrusted it at the first word of the superior.

superior. Ah! What interest do you find in pursuing me, added he, fixing on me at length his looks altered by his tedious trouble; how have you discovered a retreat, in which I thought myself forgotten by all men? But you do not come out of season, added he again, and you will find me in those dispositions which are agreeable to your principles.

For my part, I looked on him with an eye much more attentive than his, and scarce knowing him again under the sadness and dejection in which I saw him plunged, I admired that so short a space could make such an alteration in his face. Every thing about him seemed disposed to keep his grief in countenance; a suit of dark purple hangings, not capable of reflecting the rays of light; some chairs placed without order, upon which his cloaths and books were confusedly scattered; his windows half closed, to shut out the light of the sun, as if he feared it would dispell the natural gloominess; 'and in the neighbouring places a silence so profound, that one could not hear in them even the chirpings of birds, or the whisperings of the wind. These melancholy appearances inspired in me a share of that sorrow, that seemed to be diffused all around me. The answer I made Patrick expressed a feeling of this impression; it was short and mournful: Surprised myself that the senses had so great an empire over reason, I sat down sighing; and waited till he opened a conversation, that I had not the power to begin.

He kept silence for some moments, as if he had been moved by mine, or as if he were in search of terms proper to express himself in. At length breaking it with an air, in which tenderness seemed to take the upper-hand of grief, by whatever way, said he, you have discovered my retreat, I owe you my thanks and gratitude for the motive that has led you here. This can only be a sentiment of your ancient friendship, and I see moreover in your eyes.

eyes nothing but the pity which my situation has inspired you with. Do not think continued he, that it is love torments me with so much violence. The force of honour, and the power of a just resentment, have effaced even the last traces of that passion out of my heart. I think no more of that perfidious woman than to detest her memory; and when at first you saw in me an appearance of trouble, capable perhaps of carrying me to fatal extremities, I was torn in pieces much more cruelly by shame than grief. I even confess to you, that by retiring to this solitude, I thought of nothing but to avoid you, and every one else, whose looks could be to me a punishment: I could not bear the presence of so many virtuous and discreet friends, who had perhaps foreseen my infamy, when they opposed my fatal marriage, and who had in all appearance this reason only for condemning it. Alas! added he, interrupting his thoughts, you will agree nevertheless, that if I have been deceived by the most black perfidy, it was by an outside I was deceived, which might have plunged the wisest of men into the same error.

What then, added he, has brought me to this place, is no more than the fear of infamy and ridicule, a thought so dreadful and unsupportable to the heart of a man of honour, that it would have made me take all sorts of methods to deliver me from it, at least for so long a time as I have thought it necessarily fastened to my misfortune. Nevertheless, after having had my heart gnawed with it for some weeks, less confused notions have led me to other reflections; I am convinced, by shaking off the yoke of prejudice, that it is only a false and senseless opinion, that can make the honour of a man depend on the conduct of a wife and the success of a marriage. These arguments appear to me so manifest, according even to the weight and consideration of reason and religion, that exalting me above my firſt terrors, I ſhould without heſitation have quitted my retreat, if I had not had over and above another motive to ſtay me here. But it is now I am about informing you of my real weakneſſes, which you never yet have been able to penetrate. I diſcover them to you with ſo much the more confidence, as your arrival appears in my eyes a favour from heaven, in the neceſſity I ſtand of a guide.

I was ſo delighted to hear him ſpeak this language, that without foreſeeing to what point his diſcourſe was going to lead me, being equally moved by the aſſurance he gave me of his cure, and by the hope that ſprang up in me of being able to ſerve Sarah Fincer to purpoſe, I could not forbear interrupting him, to ſhew him marks as much of my ſurpriſe as joy. I even embraced him with a lightneſs of heart, which broke out in the moſt lively and affectionate congratulations. But, as if he was prepared to give me ſucceſſive proofs of all kinds of ſurpriſe, he haſtily enough drew himſelf from between my arms, and looking on me with the ſame air with which he had at firſt began his diſcourſe, For what do you congratulate me, ſaid he, and what ſubject of joy can you then find amidſt the griefs that devour me? This queſtion, and the gloomy and ſerious air that continued to ſway in his countenance, made me return to my chair, where I ſat down in a ſilence, that left him full liberty to reſume his diſcourſe.

If, ſaid he, any expreſſion has eſcaped me that bears a reſemblance of joy, it is much belied by the ſorrow of my thoughts. In recovering my heart to its natural ſtate, by the victory I have obtained over the paſſions I have deſcribed to you, I feel myſelf more unhappy a thouſand times, than when I was in ſo violent a ſituation. I am ignorant how it happens with the ordinary rank of men; but if any be found among them, to whom the common occupations of life, or even the wealth that depends on
fortune,

fortune, can procure a perfect tranquillity, I congratulate them for their happiness. My humour is to feel an unsurmountable heaviness in the midst of every thing that bears the name of pleasure and amusement. I have thought a long time, that this is a defect of which I ought to accuse nature; but the pangs I have found in love have taught me wherein she has placed for me my true happiness; and I have pitied the rest of mankind, when I have known myself to be so superior to them by those affections and relishes, to which no man in the world has ever yet been so sensible as I. Nevertheless, after an experiment full of charms, I have seen myself deprived all at once of my happiness, and my loss is so much the more terrible, that if the only object, to which I thought my happiness attached, could betray me with a shameful perfidy, I have no hopes ever to find one again, to whom my heart can surrender itself up with the same degree of confidence. Thus, whilst not only all my love remains, but I have even obtained a certainty, that it is only in the exercise of it I can be happy, I find myself condemned all my life to the want of so necessary a blessing, by a cruel mistrust, which will hinder me for ever to place the least reliance on the outside of a woman, after having been so barbarously deceived by mine. Perhaps, continued Patrick, this language may appear strange to you; but shew me a heart so tender as mine, it will easily understand me. My disgust for the world, since I thus despair to find in it the sole happiness on which I fix a real value, has arose to this point, so as to make me think of forsaking it by uniting myself for ever to this abbey. I shall not find in it those things that the world esteems most pleasurable; but I conceive that I may there hope for other blessings, to which the world is a stranger; and I shall be at least delivered from the necessity that my birth imposes on me of procuring riches, which I despise, or honours, of which I know

G 5   the

the vanity, or of subjecting myself to a thousand complaisances, which I look upon as the most childish and vain of all slaveries. They have here, added he, rejected my proposal, from some difficulties that you may remove; and I hope your zeal will induce you to favour a design which I think conformable to your maxims.

Upon finishing these words, he lightly skipped off his chair, as if he had found himself more at liberty from a discharge of his burden; and walking at a great rate about the chamber, he seemed to wait impatiently for my answer. Although Jacin's information had prepared me for what I had just heard, I yet ranked my ideas in order, that I might unfold myself with the more perspicuity and force. He turned to me with the air of a man, whose mind seemed to be taken up with some reflections. I will not at all conceal from you, said he, what has happened to me some days past. Donna Figuerrez, who, like you, has discovered the place of my retreat, has offered me her heart by a very affectionate letter; and would make me consider it as a happy lot to unite myself to her. But if the knowledge I have of her charms has awaked my natural tenderness, I am far from discovering in her all the qualities that my heart requires in being affected to her. Such as I know in her would never make me chuse her but for an agreeable friend, and of all women in the world it is she who could inspire me the most with mistrust and fear in love. I observed to her, added he, in my answer, that my present disposition did not indulge me in any thing for her but acknowledgment and esteem.

This discovery made me make some alteration in the answer I was musing upon; for in my design of feeling his pulse as to his inclination for Sarah, I had thoughts to have named Donna Figuerrez with her, to judge better of his sentiments by this trial. But I was from his words better satisfied to have one obstacle

obstacle the less to surmount, having always had some tendency to believe, that he was better disposed, than he was willing to be thought, for this Spanish lady. The description he had given me of his inward struggles, the idea he was willing to give me of his troubles, and even the resolution he had formed of quitting the world, gave me so little perplexity, that without staying to make him superfluous remonstrances, I was resolved to come all of a sudden to proposals more capable of flattering his heart. It sufficed me to think, that even with the character he had given of himself, and which I had long since discovered, religious solitude was what would be so little suitable to him, that I should think myself authorised by all sorts of rights, without any other explanation, to inspire him with such sentiments as should agree better with his age, his natural qualities, and the situation in which he already stood in the world. My zeal for religion had not so much blinded me as to make me take the agitations of an unquiet heart for the call of heaven; and notwithstanding the high opinion I had of a religious life, I never thought it was a choice to which all the world was called without distinction. In one word, the piety I required of my brothers was that which agreed with the duties of a civil life, under the different conditions in which the author of religion had placed us; and I thought the vocation marked out by their birth and personal qualities such as might render them useful to society.

According to these principles, upon which Patrick had not done me justice enough, I separated from my answer every thing different from the motive that brought me there; and seeking only to do a service to Sarah Fincer, the utility of which seemed to me to be equal as to him, I rested myself on that disposition of heart, which he had confessed to me, and that I had already known so well. I could not have believed, said I, that with the character you

ascribe

ascribe to yourself, an unhappy choice, which never had been made (if you will suffer me to call back the memory of it) with the cares and precautions required by wisdom, and which was only (to explain myself yet with more freedom) an inconsiderate passion of your early youth, ought to take away from you all hopes of succeeding more happily in satisfying your heart. There are women of merit and approved virtue; such who to the charms of beauty and wit have joined all those qualities, which you do not find in Donna Figuerrez; such as you might have found in Sarah Fincer, if your unhappy passion had not made you break those bonds, which ought to have united you for ever to a woman so amiable. During this time I observed his countenance, and not suffering his least motion to escape me, I hoped, in spite of him, to have penetrated into his inclinations. Never had artifice and subtilty of themselves taken possession of my mind; but when I had conceived, that without wounding probity or religion they might assure success to some honest or virtuous view; the ancient habit I had of regulating my outward appearance had made me apt and fit to compose the air of my countenance, and the tone of my voice, according to the end I had in prospect. Patrick, who never was capable even of this sort of dissimulation, sighed deeply at the name of Sarah, and, without mistrusting my intention, making even an excuse to interrupt me, I ought, said he, to regret the heart of the virtuous Sarah, and I blush to confess that I have done her injustice. But she is amply revenged for it by my abasement and mortification. He held his peace, to hear the sequel of my words. I did not let the desired opportunity slip. If it be true, said I, affecting to be moved by his reflection, you could have this opinion of Sarah, you should have excepted her from those subjects of mistrusts that you pretend to have against her sex; and I do not see from whence should proceed the despair, which makes you renounce

renounce all notions of happiness. Here his attention seemed to recollect itself, in order to examine what he had heard; and recovering immediately out of this meditation, no, no, said he, I should have despaired of nothing, if it had been permitted me to think——; and pausing at this word, beyond which it seemed he durst not extend his thoughts, but, added he, the enemy of her honour and repose, her tyrant, her executioner, the murderer of her father, and her uncle; in fine, the man, whom she has most reason to despise and hate, is not indeed made to be well received by her, especially when nothing but a forced repentance appears to bring him back..

This grief, though imperfectly expressed, seemed to me so natural, that I had need to strain myself to conceal my joy. I was pleased all at once in having discovered enough from hence to lay hold of the tender place in his heart, and lead him insensibly to my views by the use I should make of this knowledge. I always thought it would be a mortification for Sarah, and grievous to myself, that both of us should be reduced to solicit the return of Patrick as a favour; on the contrary, I now resumed hopes of making a merit of my services, and the compliances of Sarah, as a sort of pardon and indulgence, the certainty and extent of which should not be regulated but by his repentance. With this resolution, I made a new effort of throwing some coldness into my answer. You have caused Sarah, said I, (without looking on him) all the evils that spleen and hatred could invent, and I know not if there ever yet has been an example of so many cruelties to a woman, whom you have nothing to reproach with but an excess of love. Nevertheless, I know she has so much sweetness and goodness, that scarce have any other marks of impatience escaped her than sighs and tears. She consented however to our separation, interrupted he with warmth, and the loss of me soon ceased to afflict her. I admired this excess of injustice. How!
I could

I could not forbear anfwering him, do you impute the mortal violence fhe did herfelf as a crime, and do you look upon it as a flight to you? Do you upbraid her for having confented to pleafe you, to her own difgrace and misfortune? Tell me then what I ought to think of your humour, in which I more and more fee nothing but monftrous contradictions. This reproach made him however penfive and thoughtful. At length, changing his feat with a tranfport difcovered by the quicknefs of his motion, if I durft believe, faid he, the leaft fhare of what I defire, ah! far from hearkening to defpair, I fhould thank heaven for my happinefs.

I thought the victory over him fecure, and did not fail of addrefs to warm thefe firft fentiments; I gave him room to hope for every thing from my care, and added a thoufand reafons tending to make him underftand, that what he might look upon perhaps as a free and voluntary return, appeared to me as a duty of religion and honour. You fpeak, faid I, of taking on you here irrevocable engagements; but do you believe yourfelf fo difengaged from your firft bands, that you have the liberty of difpofing of yourfelf with fuch a forgetfulnefs of every thing that perhaps has ceafed to affect you? If you now look on your fecond marriage as the fruit of an irregular paffion, how can you perfuade yourfelf that it can ferve as a lawful reafon for breaking the firft? Without anfwering you, added I, as to the inclinations of Sarah, all my underftanding deceives me, if you be difpenfed by religion itfelf, to which you would make fo many facrifices from repairing, by amends at leaft and tenders, the outrage you have committed againft a virtuous woman, whofe rights all your injuftices have not had power to diminifh.

A motive fo fpecious, feconded by the inclination of his heart, difpofed him almoft the fame moment to offer me larger terms, than I could have dared to have afked him. I fhall try, faid he, whether heaven

ven has any favour in reserve for me. Do you become my guide, as I promised myself you would when I saw you arrive: but let it be in quest of that road to happiness, which you have inspired me with the boldness to pursue. He committed to me the conduct of regulating our departure, and of the measures he had to observe on his arrival at Paris. I judged it proper he should pass some days yet in the abbey, to avoid giving an air of inconstancy to his resolution; and I took care in this interval to justify by divers reasons the motives that obliged him to leave it. The religious, who had seen him plunged for so long a time in a profound grief, admired at the alteration that followed our first conversation. Curiosity, which is one of the principal vices of a cloister, induced then many to a desire of diving into his adventure, or of knowing at least by what charm I had assumed all of a sudden so great an ascendant over his mind. But I eluded their troublesome questions with so much care, that I even left them in ignorance that I was his brother. Whatever idea they might form of us, they had no reason to complain of our gratitude. It made us add to the quarter's pension, for which they had agreed with Patrick, such presents as surpassed their expectation.

Every step we made towards Paris gave as it were a fresh degree of hope to my brother, by the care I had taken of husbanding those hints, by which I thought proper to augment it. Nevertheless, I left him under uncertainty enough to exercise his desires; and the secret promising me more facility to conduct it by an open declaration of his sentiments, I advised him to retire to Saisons, whilst I went to Paris to assure myself of the dispositions of Sarah. He did not leave me without conjuring me to apply all my zeal to the success of an enterprize, the difficulties of which yet terrified him. His tender instances recalled to my mind those of Sarah, who used almost

the

the same expressions in recommending her interests to me; and for more than a moment it cost my heart much pain to delay to either one or the other of them a happiness, that seemed to depend on me. Nevertheless, with the desire I had of sparing the modesty of Sarah; I was held back by a fear of offending Tenermill, whose pretensions had made too great a glare for me to expect, that he would easily renounce them even in favour of his brother. I went into the count's house as much affected by this thought, as I had been by my commission to Patrick on my arrival at his abbey. Tenermill, not having returned to his own house, as being under a necessity of passing over to Ireland in the spring, I was apprehensive, that being lodged at the count's, he would appear to me before I could give an account of my journey to Sarah; or, that following me into her apartment, he might cast me into some perplexity still more to be dreaded, from the difficulty of satisfying those questions, which might proceed from such different motives.

The meeting of him, which I should thus have taken for the most unseasonable and unlucky accident I had to fear, ceased soon to appear so to me, when upon my going up stairs, I saw Donna Figuerrez coming down them, led by the count and countess of S———, who were eager in loading her with compliments. She shouted for joy at seeing me, and praying leave of the countess to go back into the apartment to hear an account of my journey, she gave me room to fear, I should get but badly off of this scrape, which I looked upon as one of the most painful moments of my life. I learned from her first words, that being arrived a few days before at Paris, she could not resist her impatience of becoming acquainted with Patrick's family. She had requested permission of my sister to visit her; and the title of my brother's friend, and niece to the Spanish ambassador, under which she had made herself

self known all at once, had obliged the count and countess to receive her both with caresses and distinction. No interest inducing them to conceal my journey from her, they had told her what they had learned from me before my departure; and her curiosity being much more brisk and of greater extent than theirs, made her hearken to my account with an eagerness she could not dissemble.

What dissimulation could be lucky enough to conceal from her the arrival of Patrick! For this was the point in which all my hopes centered. She might explain according to her fancy the marks I had discovered of my perplexity; but being little attentive to conceal them from her, I began an account that I should have ill conducted to the end, if my ideas had not been opened in proportion as I proceeded. After a relation exact enough in circumstances, that she had found the means of writing to Patrick, I spoke of the resolution my brother had taken of abandoning his retreat, as of an event which had given myself much surprise; and wrapping myself up in some equivocal expressions, I added, that he had quitted me on the road, letting me know that his design was not to return directly to Paris. As his health, said I, is perfectly restored, I am under no alarms, and I rely moreover upon his promise of letting me hear from him.

My sole design was to take Donna Figuerrez off the scent; and the manner in which I executed it succeded so well, that having led the count and countess into the same error, I resolved not only to hold them in it, but to let them impart it to Tenermill, and to all their house. I had an easy excuse, if any one should happen to surprise him at Saisons; and I should have thought it of good use to unfold the secret, when I could not possibly keep it such above two days. Donna Figuerrez,

dismayed

dismayed at what she had heard, asked me a hundred questions, which I got rid of with the same presence of mind; and Tenermill coming in during our conversation, I had room to praise the politeness of the count, who repeated to him my story, to spare me the trouble of going over it again.

Whilst I hugged myself with an invention, from which I reckoned to raise myself a merit with Sarah, Tenermill struck up an acquaintance with Donna Figuerrez, and added offers of services to his compliments, when he understood from herself the motives that had made her wish to be acquainted with the countess and all our family. She seemed well pleased at his offer to serve her as a guide in visiting the curiosities of Paris. They agreed upon a day. I saw without pain this commencement of their acquaintance; and if I had known Tenermill more capable of suffering himself to be surprised by the alurements of a woman, I should have flattered myself, that taking a relish for this fair stranger, whose humour seemed to me to be much more suitable to his than that of Sarah, it had relieved me from a share of the obstacles which I apprehended from him in my enterprize. But ambition would have served him as a curb, though he had been more sensible of the power of love. I obtained, from the esteem he took for Donna Figuerrez only, the liberty of a conversation with Sarah, without fear of being interrupted by his presence, for some hours that he employed in rambling about Paris to satisfy his engagements.

If I thought the time tedious till I saw Fincer's daughter, she could scarce moderate her ardour, which gave her in a manner wings to meet me upon receiving the first news of my arrival. I nevertheless watched with a good deal of precaution not to expose myself in my visit to any interruption from Tenermill; I therefore laid hold of the time wherein I knew he was employed. Sarah stretched out her arms to me as soon as she saw me appear. Come, said she, and do not be afraid to embrace your sister. But it is from you, added she, taking herself up, that I am going to hear, whether I ought to place my confidence in this transport. Do you bring me the confirmation of your happy presages, or am I condemned to pass the rest of my life in humiliation and tears?

The weakness of her health required me to manage her with some caution. Inured, as she was, to sorrow, I would not all at once heap on her an excess of joy, under which she might have a difficulty of supporting herself. I talked to her of the affections of my brother, as a tribute upon which she had always a right to reckon; and which he had never refused, even during the time he had forsaken her for another. Then taking notice, that far from exposing her to suffer any thing from an excess of joy, expressions so warily handled had left in her a secret grief, I assured her, that he was nevertheless melted down by compassion at hearing me speak of her. Thus endeavouring less to raise her by degrees to comfort, than to deliver her insensibly from what was capable of afflicting her, I without any violent impression, led her to the knowledge of the most happy news I had to tell her. The whole power of love did not then possess her heart in a less degree, although it made its entrance by such caution and management. Thus she was a long while as it were intoxicated with this fulness of pleasure, which sweetly diffused itself over all her senses. Her tongue was for some time without the power of moving; her eyes, although enlivened by the fire kindled up in her heart, had yet less of vivacity than of tenderness and languor. But having added under what uncertainty I left Patrick, when I had assured her, that it depended on her to hasten or retard the decision he expected, she roused herself out of this kind of dream; Ah! said she, why do you suffer him to continue

a moment

a moment under his doubts; why do you abandon him to thofe inquietudes, of which no-body in the world knows better than I do the torments? Ah! Who moreover knows, added fhe, whether thefe fentiments, which I owe perhaps only to the recital you have made him of mine, can hold out a long while in abfence? I will fee him, I will not give him time to forget me. Alas! His heart is but too much accuftomed to an emptinefs for me, and for the love that is my due. She would have been gone immediately for Saifons, and I was under the neceffity of ufing the ftrongeft reafons to detain her. Befides the motive of decency, which I would have her obferve for her own intereft, I reprefented to her, that not having for a long time ftirred out of the count's houfe, fhe could not take one ftep without exciting the curiofity of the whole family, and above all that of Tenermill, who perhaps would force his company on her whether fhe would or not.

Neverthelefs, as fomething muft be granted to her impatience, and that I had forefeen the fame difficulty in moderating that of Patrick, I yielded more readily to her propofal of bringing him at night to the count's. I had my apartment there, into which it would be an eafy matter to introduce him, and I did not fear a greater difficulty of getting him privately into hers. I undertook to do her this piece of fervice; only I annexed to it a condition, that inftead of giving herfelf up to the pleafure of feeing again her infidel, and of making with him too eafy a compofition, fhe fhould affect, if not a coldnefs and indifference, at leaft fuch a kind of refentment as fhould augment the grief and repentance of the criminal, and even hinder him from believing her pardon too eafy to be obtained, and the remembrance of his offences obliterated. She promifed me every thing that I thought neceffary to infift on; but the very

ardour

ardour of her engagements made me doubt whether they were sincere, or whether it was in her power to fulfil them.

I hoped nevertheless so much from this interview, that abandoning all other care, I immediately went to Saisons, to declare to Patrick a happiness, that he had no room to expect so soon. He received the news of it with transports. I spoke of Donna Figuerrez, and of the acquaintance she had made with the countess. This incident, which had disturbed myself, caused him no less inquietude. After the proposals she had openly made him by letter, he saw himself exposed, by the impatience she shewed to knit herself to our family, not only to see her under such circumstances that he could expect nothing from her but importunity, but to fear, that with so much wit and address she might raise some obstacle to his dearest hopes. Her acquaintance with Tenermill served only to redouble his fears. Not expecting to conceal from him long the renewal of his love for Sarah, he found himself in the front of two adversaries, who would have the same interest to traverse him, and who would from thence become only too terrible by an union of their resentment. This notion made us deliberate before-hand upon the conduct it was necessary for Patrick and Sarah to observe after their reconciliation. In the ardour of a thousand new sentiments, which already made this good-natured brother believe, that his happiness depended less on rank and station, than on the satisfaction of his desires, he spake of going over into Ireland, and burying himself in the county of Antrim. But I judged too well of the beginning of his fortune to suffer him to remove from St Germain. On the contrary, I proposed to him to go and throw himself at the king's feet, with her, whom I yet thought he had some right to call his spouse, and to demand from that prince his protection and permission immediately to renew his marriage. You shall continue at

St Germain, said I, under the eyes of a protector powerful enough to defend you, and if he has a design, as he has often declared to me, of engaging you to his person, you will have no occasion of seeking out another sanctuary.

He relished this advice. I had informed him in his retreat, that among the advantages mademoiselle de L—— had brought him on his marriage, there scarce remained enough to satisfy the debts she had left him to pay. The titles, upon which his pretensions were founded, were among those that had been conveyed out of sight; consequently he had only to depend on, for all his means, the dividend of the sum we had brought out of Ireland. See then, said I, if it be suitable to your circumstances to neglect the hopes you have from fortune.

His resolutions appearing to be fixed, we settled the hour for his coming to Paris, and the precautions he ought to observe for getting into my apartment. I trusted to the address of Jacin, whom I engaged to send for him. So lawful an enterprise having nothing in it that ought to alarm me, I was under no disturbance for the success, and I considered it only on the side that flattered my desires. I never thought of the innocent pleasure I might have had in leaving Sarah ignorant of the visit I had taken care to procure her. An unforeseen happiness might cause her too much confusion, and I wished that prudence might preside over all our resolutions. I gave Patrick notice of my design, and a caution to contribute all in his power to the concealing our secret.

The hour I had appointed my brother was that on which the company that supped at the count's used to separate. It often happened, that Tenermill went abroad when all the company were gone, and I observed also, that he sometimes shut himself up in his chamber. Either of these suppositions being equal to my purpose, I only wanted the time in which

which all the houſe was quiet. I had agreed with Jacin to give me notice of it by my window, that looked into the ſtreet; and he was ready to attend me towards twelve o'clock. I went down myſelf to open the door for my brother.

Among a thouſand reflections inſpired in me by ſuch a whimſical office, I made one upon Patrick's fortune, who was reduced to come by ſtealth, and as it were in the way of an intrigue, to a woman whoſe love and favours he had ſo long neglected. The experience of others made me alſo remark all the caprices of the paſſions. Sarah, who expected us, favoured our march by the care ſhe had taken of planting her chamber-maid in our paſſage. We at length gained her apartment, both agitated by different motions, he from a doubt of the diſpoſition he was about to find Sarah in, and I from a confuſion, which the novelty of the ſervice I was engaged in, gave me in ſpite of my teeth. Joy and hope neverthelefs got the better in my heart, when being very luckily got in, I ſaw myſelf almoſt ſure of the ſucceſs of my enterpriſe: But Patrick's perplexity continued longer. Although he affected a ſteady countenance, and that not daring to rely on his hopes, he ſeemed to pauſe upon regulating his firſt expreſſions, from the marks of pleaſure or diſſatisfaction ſhe ſhould diſcover at firſt ſeeing him, I obſerved that his confuſion did not leave him at liberty enough to make this diſtinction. Amazed at his ſilence, I was going to open my mouth to ſerve him as an interpreter, when ſeeming to recover himſelf rather from a natural effect of courage, than from the cure of his diffidence, he bent one knee to Sarah, who had riſen off her chair upon ſeeing us appear. He was about following this motion with ſome ſpeech; but the weak Sarah did not give him time to pronounce it; being as much abaſhed, as he appeared to humble himſelf, or rather tranſported by the inclination of her heart, which would

not

not exact so great a reparation for his satisfaction, she threw her arms about his neck, and with a broken voice, and her head fixed close to his bosom, Ah! my lord, cried she, with as many sighs as words, is it then permitted me to believe my eyes? This day which must be the most happy day of my life, if it makes me mistress of your heart, shall it answer my desires, and the promises Mr Dean has given me? How long a time have I expected it? What have my impatience and my tears cost me? But why this posture before me, added she, yet squeezing him close? Are not you the master of my heart, and my repose, as you are of my fortune and my life? Suffer me to take that situation, which becomes me better than it does you; for you never have yet for one single moment lost the domion I have given you over me. She would have cast herself on her knees, if Patrick had not bore her up and prevented her. He led her to a chair, where he pressed her to sit down, and placed himself near her. Vexed to see her yield so easily to her transport, and to give my brother so great an advantage over her, I had made her a sign from the beginning of her words, to remember my advice; and not seeing that this notice made any impression on her, I had even pushed her rudely, to make her mind me better. But insensible to either one or the other of my hints, she had shut her eyes upon every thing that might one moment divert her from her object.

I abandoned then this thought, and sat down near them, to share in their joy. Patrick, being recovered from all the fears that had tied his tongue, began to express himself with so many marks of repentance and love, that he would speedily have appeared in the eyes of Sarah to have merited that pardon, which he ought to have owed only to her indulgence. But the moment he had given himself up to his most sweet transports, and had the pleasure of seeing them hearkened unto with as much tenderness and satisfaction,

faction, a noise which we ourselves heard at the door of the apartment, obliged the chambermaid, whom we had left as a watch, to come in and interrupt us hastily. She gave us notice, that having heard the voice of my lord Tenermill, she had refused to open the door to him, telling him from the inside, that her mistress was in bed. But this answer served only to provoke him. In coming into the house, he had unluckily observed, that there were not only lights in her chamber, but that she had a man with her. He could not have been deceived in it; since Patrick being on the outside, he had seen him without being able to distinguish him. Jealousy had cast him into a furious transport, which carried him at first with as many threats as words to inquire of the porter, whether he had opened the gate to any one. Although I had used no other hands than my own in opening it, and even imagined I had not been heard by any body, yet the porter (who had thought he heard some noise, but was doubtful of it, as we had the luck to make much less passing through the court) not daring to conceal from Tenermill what he thought he had perceived in his drowsiness, this discovery increased his jealous fury. He came straight up to Sarah's apartment, and the black suspicions that disturbed him serving for a pretext plausible enough, after he had received his answer from the chambermaid, he insisted that the door should be opened for the security of Sarah herself, whom he pretended to be in danger of being robbed or insulted by some unknown person, that he had seen with his own eyes in her apartment.

Of the four that were in the room, there was no body but Patrick, to whom this cruel ill chosen time did not inspire with fear. Besides his courage, which would not suffer him to fear the insults or pride of any man, he could not persuade himself, that his brother would one moment keep up his pretensions to Sarah, when he knew, that far from approving of them, she thought of renewing her first engagements.

engagements. I submitted, said he, to your reasons without examining them, and consented to lay hold of this time of night in coming here out of deference to your advice; but as I am assured of my happiness from the generous goodness of my dear Sarah, I so little apprehend the presence of Tenermill, that on the contrary I am charmed to have him a witness of my joy. Sarah, who knew better than any body how far Tenermill had carried his presumption, the chambermaid, whom he had attempted a thousand times to draw over to his interest, and I myself, who had in my memory his former confidences, had all of us another notion of this incident; and his obstinacy to continue at the door threw us into a mortal alarm.

He continued to knock there; and although he did it with some caution, there was nevertheless but little appearance of his giving over the attempt. The apartment had no other door than that which he had besieged. In the manner I had conceived those things, the danger seemed to me so pressing, that without consulting either Patrick, who could not yet enter into my fears, or Sarah, who was only fit to increase them by her own, I prayed both of them to remain in the chamber we were in, and I determined to appear myself alone at the door. I had a light in my hand. Tenermill shewed an extreme surprise at seeing me. I observed his astonishment, and believed it would be the best way to take advantage of it by upbraiding him for his behaviour, whereby I was in hopes of throwing him into some perplexity. Is it, said I, to the fumes of wine that I ought to attribute the insults you have committed against a lady who deserves more respect, and for whom I thought you had other sentiments? He did not swallow the intended delusion. Let us leave insults alone, said he in a steady tone, and if you have no mind I should go in whether you will or not, let me know what person is within there so late. Is it possible, replied I, pursuing my first notion, that wine has so hurt

hurt your eye-fight as to hinder you from knowing me? What right have you to call me to an account for what I do here? You shall not deceive me, replied he, by your vain shifts; it is not you I am in search for: And laying hold of the door in such a manner as it was impossible for me to shut it, he seemed resolved to enter in spite of me. This violence having redoubled my alarms, I chose to confess to him that I was with Patrick, by giving him a plain and natural turn to the motive that brought him there. Ah! very well, said I, since your imperious humour imposes laws on me, to which the consideration of time and place obliges me to submit, know that I have here with me your brother, who upon his return to Paris thought himself obliged to make excuses for his past conduct to a lady, on whom he has multiplied misfortunes. My brother! interrupted he; Ah! I will be a witness what turn he gives to his excuses, and the manner in which they are received. In vain did I resist the effort he made to get in. He pushed into the anti-chamber in spite of me, and I ran the risque of being overturned by the shock he gave me, so that I had nothing else to do but follow him.

Sarah, who saw him appear at her chamber-door, came up to him with an air of fright, while Patrick, piqued at his boldness, remained in a musing posture on his chair. I opened my mouth instantly. Madam, said I to Sarah, it is without doubt a haste to salute Patrick that has given my lord the vivacity, you see in him. But without lending any attention to what I said, he addressed himself to Sarah. I do not ask you, madam, said he, what has engaged you to admit my brother at so late an hour: Your perplexity, and the familiar air in which I saw him sitting by you, gave me to understand, as much as the unseasonable time, what I ought to think of this rendezvous. You have thought me a proper person to make your May-game. But are you well assured that my patience can bear so much outrage? The menace included in these last words provoked Patrick in his turn. He arofe, perhaps, a little too haftily; and coming up to us, I never thought, faid he to Tenermill, that any body had a right to condemn the addreffes I pay my lady at whatever hour fhe pleafes to receive them, and I expected fewer obftacles from you than from any body elfe. Thefe words had nothing offenfive in them, although they were pronounced with a little fiercenefs. But the overheated imagination of Tenermill not laying a juft ftrefs on any thing, I faw anger fparkle in his eyes, from whence I was under mortal apprehenfions of the effects. He looked on Patrick for fome time in filence, and turning towards Sarah; your tafte, madam, faid he with an air of conftraint, will without doubt decide our pretenfions, and the circumftances make me much fear that this decifion is already made. But I fhall teach my brother the refpects he owes me, fince he feems to be ignorant of them. He turned his back to be gone. Patrick opened his mouth, and I do not know what anfwer his refentment would have been capable of dictating to him; but with a handkerchief I had in my hand, and with which I readily covered his face, I fucceeded fo luckily in ftopping his fpeech, that he could not pronounce the leaft word. Tenermill had time to go out, giving us at the fame time a new mark of his fury by the violence he ufed in fhutting the door.

A fcene thus crofs and unlucky gave me fo much uneafinefs, that without fuffering Patrick to continue the coverfation he would have refumed with Sarah, I exacted of him (with all the weight I could give my perfuafions) to retire immediately out of the apartment. Your hearts, faid I to both of them, have begun to difcover themfelves, and I look upon your reconciliation as a work brought to perfection: But I am not fo fure, that Tenermill, in the warmth of his firft refentment, does not threaten us this moment with fome revenge. Your defires and my cares fhall foon procure you
. the

the opportunity of meeting again. You shall follow me instantly, said I to Patrick, laying hold of his hand, and I give you but a moment for embracing your spouse. That tender name, which they were both charmed to hear, and the liberty of embracing that they would not have ventured at so soon, if I had not shortened their difficulties by this kind of permission, made them find less difficulty in obeying me. Patrick embraced his spouse a thousand times instead of once, and without having power, or rather without thinking there was any necessity of confirming a reconciliation by words, of which they had given such tender proofs, they consented to separate.

My chamber being not far distant from the apartment of Sarah, I led my brother to it, in order to deliberate together upon an incident, which obliged me no less than him to observe some measures. Without busying myself much about what Tenermill might attempt after the danger I had got out of, I thought of nothing but considering the justice and decency of our side, arising from a conduct which left us no reproach to fear. There was no doubt but that the next day all the house would ring of what had happened; and this thought made me consider whether I ought to advise Patrick to return to Saisons before day: His retreat might have the air of a flight, which would make people judge badly of the intentions that brought him there, or which would at least give Tenermill some right to complain of an enterprize, to which he would not fail giving names odious enough. Nevertheless, the perplexity, which the variance between two brothers was going to raise in the house, and the difficulty there would be in it to keep them from seeing one another, or of being assured they should see one another without anger and bitterness, made me take the resolution of sending Patrick away immediately. His chaise waited in the next street, and I pressed him to be gone. The only advice I recommended

mended to him was to go in the morning to court, and by his duty difpofe his majefty to give a favourable hearing to the explanations, with which I charged myfelf. I promifed to follow him in lefs than two days; and the only reafon I had indeed to defer my departure was, the defire of underftanding Tenermill's difpofitions.

He fpared me the difficulty I feared of finding the opportunity of a private converfation. Inftead of avoiding me, as I expected, he came in the morning to my chamber. His complaints were at firft moderate; but having had time to warm himfelf by the liberty I gave him of difburthening his heart to me without interruption, he reproached me openly for having abufed the confidence he repofed in me, in order to betray him, and of having preferred all my life the intereft of Patrick to his. I had forefeen the firft of thefe two reproaches. It was not by a denial of the charge that I undertook to defend myfelf; on the contrary, being in raptures that he had given me this opportunity of unfolding myfelf, I avoided to anfwer his accufations, and requefted him only to give a little attention to the difcourfe I had meditated. It contained at firft a plain relation of all the events that had paffed in our family while he was in Ireland, and of which the count had concealed from him the principal circumftances at my intreaty. My hopes were not only to melt him down in favour of his brother by the recital of his misfortunes, but to make him conceive, that the long paffion, which had made Patrick violate fo many rights, had been only a depravation of heart, which ftill left an exiftence of all his former duties, fince he could not fuppofe that it ever was from reafonable motives he had violated them. To make this conclufion more indubitable, I fummed up all the circumftances of Patrick's firft marriage; it was from me, by whofe miniftration it was effected, that he muft learn an account of them. There was nothing wanting in it to make the attachment facred, and of a
nature

nature inviolable. All these considerations that happened after, and which had their source only from the disorder of a violent passion, ought to pass for so many ridiculous devices in the eyes of reason, and perhaps for so many crimes in the eyes of religion. Thus, whatever time had passed in so palpable an error, it could make no change in the essential obligations on Patrick; and his first marriage, added I, appeared to me to be so little altered by the second, that if my sentiments of it had been believed, there had been no necessity to renew it.

This detail related to the main point of the dispute; but desiring no less to be justified upon account of the quarrel, I declared to him plainly, that he deceived himself, if he ever thought that Sarah Fincer had for one moment lost the hopes of being reconciled one day or other to her husband, or, that she had ever ceased to look upon herself as his wife. I had been a perpetual witness of her conduct, as much as a confident of her reflections and troubles. As to myself, who had in truth, against the light of my understanding, been inclined to give into the opinion, that she was free, and who, upon the united opinions of the king and our bishops had for the sake of peace countenanced her entering into another engagement, I in vain laboured to combat her obstinacy, and had been in the end reduced to allow that my sentiments were not different from hers. He had then flattered himself out of season, if he had thought her in a capacity voluntarily to receive his addresses; and in all those things that his inclinations had represented to him as most favourable to his love, he had seen nothing but the effect of an extreme complaisance for a brother-in-law whom she esteemed, or of a forced consideration for a man whom she had a thousand reasons to manage, and the more so, since she had obtained the favour of the count to make her retreat in his house, which was in a manner the center of our family. She had

had herself made me this confession; and when the death of her rival had revived all her hopes, she had conceived more than ever, that he might occasion her too much evil or good not to manage him in his weaknesses.

I saw Tenermill blush during this declaration, as if he had felt a sharp confusion for having been so long the bubble of some flattering appearances. But pretending not to take notice of his disorder, I continued to relate to him, with what ardour Sarah had given her interests in charge to me upon making my journey to Spain; which she had the thoughts of taking in my company, and it was with difficulty my objections stopped her. Since my return, I had scarce any other occupation than to make myself serviceable to her views; and at the very time he had taken me aside to discover to me the king's promises, and the method he would take to hasten the execution of them, I was charged with orders from Sarah to bring Patrick into her apartment. What other choice could I make, than to listen to him, as I had done, with all the complaisance he could desire, and to promise him an inviolable fidelity in keeping his secret? I had so perfectly observed my promise, that he had no need to fear either the raillery, that is the consequence of abortive projects, or even the triumph of his brother, who should never know from me what honour and friendship had enjoined me to conceal eternally. Thus, added I, did I reckon equally both to see him renounce his pretensions, of which he could hope for no further success, and to find in him the inclination, he ought to have, of living in a good understanding with his brother.

He hearkened to me with an attention that I could not be enough satisfied with, and which I began to take for an omen of my victory. I waited for his answer, which he made me with as much exactness as perspicuity. I will not take up my time, said he, rising off his chair, to disentangle your cavils and

and sophisms. I have no other laws to regard for this world, but those of the king, and for the other world, but those of the church: They are both united in my favour; this is the foundation of my pretensions. If Sarah is so little nice as to forget the outrages she has received from my brother, I hope the king will not so easily forget the word he has given me. But even under these two suppositions, added he, turning himself to the door, I shall always take care not to suffer my younger brother to obtain the ascendant over me, and to be upon my guard against the treachery of my elder. He left me, notwithstanding the instances I made to detain him.

I should have wanted nothing, if I had sought only to discover his dispositions. Never did an ulcerated heart betray itself by more manifest and undisguised passions, although he laboured all in his power to curb or conceal them. But the knowledge of the evil made me better perceive the necessity of a speedy remedy. After a number of reflections, I was convinced, that the most infallible method I had to take, was that I had mentioned at first to Patrick; that is to say, to engage Sarah to go to St Germain, and there marry him in the sight and under the protection of the king, by renewing the church ceremonies, which perhaps were not necessary to render their engagements more sacred, but which yet seemed to me capable of stopping all opposition. I went out of my chamber, to impart this thought to Sarah. But how great was my astonishment to learn at her door, that she had forbidden her servants to open it to me! I insisted to come in, that I might discover the cause of so unaccountable a refusal. Her servants knew nothing of it; but her chamber-maid, who came as if by chance at the noise of my voice, put a note privately into my hand, telling me that she had just received it, and had orders to give it me without letting any body know a word of the matter.

Retiring immediately, I read in the hand-writing of Sarah, that Tenermill, who had just left her, had

intreated

intreated her not to receive for some days either Pattick or me; and that having made her this requeſt with a great deal of politeneſs, he was reſolved to cut his brother's throat, and to ſeek an opportunity to offer me ſome public affront. He had quitted her, without adding a ſingle expoſtulation to this compliment. Sarah not doubting but ſhe was watched, had ſubmitted immediately to thoſe terrible orders. She prayed me by her letters to pretend, that I was ignorant of the cauſe of it, and to confeſs to nobody that I had the account from her.

It appeared very difficult to penetrate into this proceeding. Nevertheleſs, I have omitted one circumſtance of the letter, which made me find leſs injuſtice in it in appearance. Tenermill had promiſed, that on his ſide he would not expoſe Sarah to the importunities of his viſits, for ſo long a time at leaſt as ſhe ſhould make the ſacrifice he exacted continue.

Whatever view I could ſuppoſe he had, this kind of equality which he put between himſelf and us, perſuaded me, that it was not to violence he intended to have recourſe. I was retiring to my chamber much comforted with this thought, deſigning to make uſe alſo of the pen to let Sarah know what I had conſidered as moſt ſuitable to her intereſts: But my meeting Donna Figuerrez, whom Tenermill led by the hand, obliged me to ſtop in ſpite of me. She preſſed me with ſo many intreaties to afford her a moment's converſation, that not having it in my power to make her reliſh my pretences and excuſes, I was under the neceſſity of following her to the apartment of the counteſs of S————. Tenermill ſmiled at my embarraſment; and without doubt did not triumph leſs at the law he had impoſed on Sarah Fincer, of which he eaſily judged I had already undergone the rigour.

Donna Figuerrez was no ſooner got into my ſiſter's antichamber, than ordering all the ſervants of the houſe to delay for a moment giving the counteſs notice of her arrival, ſhe took me by the hand, and

and praying Tenermill to excuse her for talking apart with me, she drew me towards a window, where we could not be overheard. There looking on me with a steady eye, it is my impatience, said she, to talk to you, and the doubt whether you would consent to grant me that favour at my house, that brought me here this morning. After some compliments, that corresponded very well with this beginning, she reproached me with a wheedling air for having disguised from her the reasons that had made me oppose the inclinations she had discovered to me for my brother. I learned them yesterday, continued she, from my lord Tenermill, who has not concealed from me neither the passion he has for the fair Sarah Fincer, nor consequently the ardour with which he wishes to supplant his rival. Without opening to him my views, which he is yet ignorant of, and from the sole persuasion he is in, that you can do more than all mankind for our common satisfaction, I have contrived a plan, which will wonderfully conciliate all our interests. Join my lord Tenermill to Sarah Fincer, and Patrick to me. As a reward for this service, I dare promise you from the credit of the ambassador and my interest, that you shall have off hand one of the best bishopricks in Spain or France. She thought she had made so great an impression on me by this offer, that looking on me with a smile, she did not so much as add any reflection to make me sensible of the importance of the favour. I read in her eyes, that she already thought herself sure of my answer. But besides the temerity of her promise, which could seduce nobody but a man so much blinded by ambition as to shut his eyes upon all obstacles, I durst believe, that from the idea, which to the present time might be formed of my character, no body could be easily persuaded, that a motive of this nature was capable of affecting me: So I needed no effort to defend myself from the seduction. On the contrary, smiling in my turn at the confidence she had placed
in

in her artifice, I answered her with as much simplicity and sweetness, as was possible for me to bring into the air of my countenance and expressions, that she had offered me a superfluous motive to engage me in my duty, and that I should be disposed to spare no pains in establishing the honour and tranquillity of my family. Having given this answer I retired, without examing whether she had penetrated into the meaning of it. I had more curiosity in passing near Tenermill, who stepped forward to meet her. I lifted up my eyes on him, and sought to discover in his, whether he had as little share in the proposal of Donna Figuerrez, as she would have persuaded me. But the cold and serious air, with which he saluted me, made me judge that he was indeed ignorant of it.

This contrivance of Tenermill, into which I was even uncertain whether he had not the address of bringing the count and countess of S——, made me hasten only the more to give the explanation I desired of my views to Sarah Fincer. However, I was stopped by a difficulty to which I had given little attention in forming my project. I did not in the least doubt but Sarah would follow my advice, and that the bare reading of my letter would inspire her with a quick impatience to go to St Germain. But watched, as I supposed she was by the orders of Tenermill, what way could she take to steal off privately? And would it become a woman so reserved to go away from the count's house, without giving him notice of her departure? Nevertheless, as I could take upon me on the spot to make her excuses, this obstacle stopped me less than the other. I resolved at length to observe to her that I would keep a chaise ready whatever happened, and that if she consented to go, she should herself find out the opportunity of escaping with her chamber-maid and two lacqueys. I put my letter into safe hands, and went out immediately to get my chaise in readiness. The bearer of my note had orders to bring a positive answer,

answer, as to the hour and other circumstances which I ought not to be ignorant of.

In recollecting the offers of Donna Figuerrez, if I did not find myself actuated by ambition, I was disturbed by fear, for which I saw but too strong a foundation. This ardour of gaining my interest shewed so much vivacity in her desires, that being seconded, as I had no reason to doubt, by the counsels of Tenermill, she was capable of throwing us into some new embarrasment, which I had not at all foreseen. This was another motive to press the departure of Sarah. I gave her notice that the chaise was ready. The night, which was not far off, might favour her escape. She got out of the house indeed, but with such bad fortune in her passage, that the first object that struck her eyes, in two minutes which she passed under the gate waiting till they brought up the chaise, was my lord Tenermill's coach, whom a sort of misgiving had brought back to the count's. He perceived her, and alighting with transport when he saw the chaise advance, of which he knew the driver to be a man whom I employed, he had no occasion to have a confession of her design in order to discover at least a part of it. He nevertheless pressed her to inform him where she was going. The difficulty of hitting upon an answer ready enough, made her confess that she was going to St Germain. She added only, to give a colour to her journey, that not having yet had the honour of being presented to the king, whose protection might be necessary for her in France, she was going for the first time to make her court to him. Tenermill readily laid hold of this overture. It is strange, madam, said he, that you have no person to attend you: A thousand reasons should oblige you to think of this; and though I can well imagine you reckon upon some body at St Germain to present you to the king, yet I look upon it as a happiness to have come so seasonably, that I may take care at least of conducting you thither. She excused herself from accepting this offer by all the

reasons

reasons she could think of: But the ardent Tenermill added the two horses of my chaise to his coach, and taking her by the hand, without minding her resistance, went in with her, and gave orders to the coachman to drive forward.

He had two views; one to make sure of her in not letting her out of sight a moment; the other, which was not the effect of a sudden reflection, to take advantage of an opportunity he had a long time desired without being hitherto able to obtain, to engage the king to espouse immediately his interests with Sarah, and even to sollicit her to receive the hand of a man, on whom he intended to heap his favours. Thus chance forwarded his most eager desires. He had good hopes not to quit her, as he had given her to understand, upon his arrival at court, and his design being on the contrary to wait on the king next day with her, he would pass the night at St Germain, having first set her down at the place where he supposed she was expected. As to Sarah, whom I had promised an apartment at Mr de Sercine's, she had no means of concealing where she intended to alight; and this was a new subject of joy for Tenermill, who always, as Patrick also and I did, lodged in the same house.

But the idea one could conceive of the disquiet and vexation of Sarah could not make one sufficiently comprehend what were my own fears. I was mounted on horse-back to attend her, and desirous to avoid being seen in the count's street, I rode out of Paris to wait for her. The sight of my brother's coach, which I immediately knew, at first gave me only apprehensions of the cross and unseasonable time that his presence threatened us with at St Germain. However, as he most commonly made this journey in an evening to be at the king's couchee, and returned immediately to lie at Paris, I had hopes of concealing ourselves from him till his departure. But I instantly not only lost this expectation, but also fell into a mortal disquiet upon seeing Sarah sitting by his side. What could

could I think of such an unexpected fight? I had gone aside behind a hired coach, which luckily stopped on the road. Tenermill did not perceive me; but one of Sarah's lacquies knowing me, I gave him a sign to alight, and learned from him in an instant the violence that had been done his mistress. I recommended to him discretion, and immediately resolving what to do according to the circumstances, I put forward my horse with the speed of a jockey. My design was to get to St Germain before Tenermill and Sarah, to prepossess Mr de Sercine with notice of their arrival, to engage Patrick, whom I supposed to lodge there, to keep out of the way till the departure of his brother, and to wait there myself to observe what conduct he would hold with Sarah. He did not know me as I passed by, being wrapped up in my cloak. I found Patrick at Mr de Sercine's. I told them both by whom I was followed; and perceiving the impression this news made on Patrick, I immediately informed him of every thing that might serve to give him courage.

It was not without difficulty that I made him consent to give way to his brother. He murmured at a submission, which he did not at all think due to his years, and which moreover love was sufficient to make him dispense with. I laboured to make him consider it as a discretion necessary for himself, and without which I durst not answer for a thousand obstacles that might perhaps ruin his hopes. How? said he with bitterness, will the cruel Tenermill not yet be tired of pursuing me? He has in the first moment ravished me of a satisfaction, of which I had made only an essay. He scarce left me time to pronounce to Sarah the name of gratitude and love; and must I again find him here, to wrest from me the pleasure of seeing her, and perhaps to abuse the king's favour, whom he has disposed in my absence to embrace all his temerities? You fail, answered I, in your duty to the king, and in justice to your brother.

brother. He loves Sarah. He began to love her at a time he might do it without a crime. Judge of his sentiments by your own. I have heard you say a thousand times, that the motions of the heart are not easily kept in subjection. If he be transported beyond bounds, it is not by outrage or violence he must be reclaimed. Let us try the way I have proposed to you, and doubt not but he will yield more freely than you to the king's authority, if he sees it declared in our favour.

I was indeed persuaded that the ambition of Tenermill would soon cure him of his love, when he might find a merit with his master of a sacrifice he had to make to his pleasure. Patrick at length submitted to my reasons. He withdrew to another friend of our family, where I undertook to give him notice of what should pass in his absence. He had but just gone out when we saw Tenermill's coach appear. Mr de Sercine received Sarah with all the caresses necessary to inspire her with a confidence in his services. The evening passed over in a common cold conversation, occasioned by the care Tenermill had taken of diverting every thing that might give any suspicion of his design; and Sarah, being continually watched by his eyes, had difficulty to find an opportunity of making complaints to me of this tyranny.

The hopes I had conceived of seeing him go off that night, had prevented me from being as sensible as she was to the obstinacy he shewed in persecuting her. But when I understood in the morning not only that he was not returned to Paris, but that he had offered to Sarah his hand to lead her to the castle with madam de Sercine, I began to form suspicions, which made me observe in my turn his conduct and words. Having advertised Sarah, to mistrust his offers, and to pretend some indisposition to excuse her appearing at court, I laid myself out to follow him in all his steps, keeping at a little distance from him, especially in the king's chamber; where I indeed observed that this prince treated him

with

with extraordinary favour. I soon understood by his words, that he had informed his majesty of Sarah's arrival at St Germain, and that he had even prepossessed him of some design, of which he affected, to speak mysteriously in public. My fears did not give me liberty to seek to clear up the secret; but they were strong enough upon me to make me change the advice I had given Sarah. Instead of deferring her appearance longer, I thought she could not be too hasty, in executing the plan I had formed with Patrick. I gave her notice of it myself. Nothing pleasing better her impatience, the execution was put off no longer than that morning. I could have wished to have found out some moment when Tenermill should be absent from the king's apartment; but I even palled over this scruple, and fancied, if he had any thing to suffer from a scene, of which he should be a witness, it would help better to make him for ever turn his back to, all hopes, whereof we were desirous to stop up the course. We saw him go out to make his appearance at the levee. Sarah, more brilliant by her natural graces than her dress, though she had neglected nothing to set them off by the most courtly attire, was accompanied by monsieur and madame de Sercine; whilst Patrick, dressed out with the same air of magnificence and gallantry, took the same way to meet them at the door of the castle. I went alone into the king's apartment, almost as soon as Tenermill. Among many strangers, who had come to make their court to this prince, I observed the Spanish ambassador, with whom I was surprised to see Tenermill in familiar conversation. I was yet more so upon observing them both to smile when they saw me, and speak to the king with an air that convinced me I was the subject of their conversation. From thence I took occasion to be more shy and reserved in going forward. But the king having perceived me himself, beckoned to me to come near him. I was going to send for you, said he,

if

if you had not appeared so seasonably: and speaking to me, with his usual goodness, of the favourable intentions he had for my family; you ought not to oppose them, continued he, by the caprices of which they accuse you. They have proposed to me a plan, which assures your fortune, and that of your brother's. Mr ambassador will explain it to you; but I approve of it, such as it has been just told me, and I freely confirm the promises I have given of making you a bishop, if you do not remain obstinate in rejecting your own advantage and that of your family. A proposal so unlimited not obliging me to any thing but general declarations of respect and submission, I made no haste to ask the ambassador or my brother, what these explanations were, that I thought I knew before hand.

But the moment they seemed disposed to take me aside, probably to satisfy the impatience they imagined I was under, madame de Sercine and Sarah came forward, having demanded permission of the king; and Patrick, who followed them at some distance, pressed also to come up, to present himself as soon as they to the eyes of that prince. I observed the astonishment of Tenermill. He drew near the king again upon seeing Fincer's daughter appear; but with whatever design he had made this motion, his surprise seemed to be much increased, when he had perceived Patrick. It disturbed him to that degree as to make him anticipate the king, who seemed disposed to speak. Sire, said he, I flatter myself that your majesty will not forget what it is I have to fear from my brothers. It would be injustice, answered this good prince, to refuse hearing them. My confidence redoubling by this answer, I stepped forward immediately; and all the courtiers, who expected something entertaining in this scene, ranked themselves in order enough to leave us, as it were, exposed to open view in the middle of the circle formed about us.

Patrick

Patrick and Sarah took advantage also of a disposition so favourable; and laying hold of the opportunity, they bent one knee to the king Patrick's speech had more force and tenderness in it than length. Having made an acknowledgment of his errors, and lamented his misfortunes, he requested of the king as an only favour, to grant him a felicity, of which he had not before justly understood the value. And to remove all appearance of doubting his repentance, he confessed, that in the warmest ardour of an unhappy passion, by which he had suffered himself to be overcome, he had never smothered those sentiments of his heart, which in spite of him always represented to his memory the good offices and charms of the generous Sarah. He added, that in returning to her by the power of inclination, as much as by the force of duty, he had been so happy as to find in her the same inclinations, and that having no right to expect any thing from her but hatred, after so much ingratitude, it was incumbent on him to discharge all at once both the debts of love and gratitude.

This short harrangue, delivered with a good deal of gracefulness and genteel action, raised in the assembly such a favourable hum of approbation, that the omen from thence did not seem to be very fortunate for Tenermill. His indignation and confusion sparkled in his eyes. He requested permission of the king to speak; but that prince turning towards Sarah, and the disposition of the spectators, who seemed to expect some explanation from her, making him forsee that he should not be heard with the same favour, he chose still to endure this second mortification, which helped to take away from him all remains of hope: For Sarah made no delay to request the king's consent as a favour; and declaring to his majesty, that conscience and justice were equally interested in it, she implored the authority-royal to support her just rights, and from thence congratulated herself for having no opposition from Patrick,

who

who was the only person from whom she had dreaded any obstacle. The sense of this speech was so clear, that the king, addressing himself to Tenermill and the Spanish ambassador, demanded of them, if they had been aware of this obstacle to the plan they had proposed, and if they believed that there was any answer to be made to the requests of a husband and wife, who desired the permission of living well together. The ambassador, who was determined to nothing but an excess of compliance to the service of his niece, answered by a bow of his head, which seemed to discover as much submission as astonishment. I expected a greater resistance from Tenermill; but whether necessity of circumstances had taken away all his courage, or whether the opinion I always had of his love held good, he chose to act a part, that drew on him all our admiration, and that of the king himself. My pretensions, said he, (raising his voice, as if he had addressed himself to the whole assembly) have always supposed, that justice, religion, and all the rights which are this day sued for against me, were on the contrary united in my favour; and I had yet this further reason to submit to the inclination of my heart, that in the marriage I proposed, I thought to have found, with my own proper advantages, those of many persons most dear to me, and, if I durst venture to say it, those even of ———. He did not mention the name of Sarah, and looking only on the king, as if he had been sure of being heard; but I cannot resist, added he, when I have in opposition to me, the will of my master, and the happiness of my brother.

All the assembly applauded this speech. The king, pleased perhaps to see himself delivered from an embarrasment, which he had foreseen from the beginning of the scene, highly set off this generous resolution by great encomiums, and stooping as low as the ear of Tenermill, seemed to consult him a moment upon some point that was to me a secret. Afterwards, as if he had then resolved what to say, the

miscarriage

miscarriage of one project, said he to the Spanish ambassador, is sometimes repaired by another: What hinders you from giving your niece to lord Tenermill? He may inform you to what I have destined him: Moreover, I will not retract my promise to Mr Dean. The ambassador's answer was as polite as it ought to be; but not venturing to engage without the participation of his niece, he requested time of the king to know her thoughts.

Tenermill supported his promises with an air so disengaged and natural, that I thought them sincere. Upon our return to Mr de Sercine's, he gave his hand to Sarah, and turned the disturbances he had given her in her apartment into a banter. He made apologies to his brother upon the foot of his being ignorant that he had preserved so great an affection for her, and acknowledging that nobody could contest his prior rights. I might have suspected these protestations a little, who had taken the pains to give him these informations, of which he pretended to be ignorant; but distinguishing very well between what might be ascribed to his politeness, and to a desire of justifying himself, I never imputed it to him as a crime to exaggerate a little the integrity of his intentions. My friendship for him rekindled so lively by the sacrifice he had made to his brother, that beginning again to grow warm in his interests, I considered how far I ought to suffer him to lend an ear to the new proposal made by the king to the ambassador. The birth, the fortune, and even the merit of Donna Figuerrez could not make amends for the disorders which had been related to me of her conduct. I knew that Tenermill had too much honour to marry a woman disgraced in Spain by twenty scandalous intrigues; and if this reason had made me readily conceive why the ambassador had so easily consented to propose her to the king for a younger brother such as Patrick, I could not find but that the same motives ought to make upon us the same impression; or rather I was persuaded that he could not

from

from thence have conceived even any hopes, if he had imagined that I had brought back such good informations from Spain. On the other hand, the repugnance I had to difcover odious fecrets, which were not known in France by any body but me, the regards I had to chriftian charity, which created in me a law to conceal them, and even the fear of expofing myfelf, by difcovering them to the revenge of a woman, whofe addrefs and vivacity I knew, had caft me in the very beginning into a perplexity, from whence I forefaw it would not be eafy to get out.

It was not yet time to examine into the bottom of difficulties which feemed to be but little prefling, and I was not in hafte even to difcover by what new intrigue of Donna Figuerrez the Spanifh ambaffador came to St Germain a quarter of an hour before Sarah and Patrick were prefented to the king. Chance alone might have produced this meeting. I was more agreeably taken up at our arrival at M. de Sercine's by divers favours of heaven, which in one moment were heaped on my family A gentleman commiffioned from the king, beginning by compliments upon the marriage of Patrick, declared to him, that his majefty's pleafure was to have it celebrated in his prefence, and calling him by the name of earl of S———, he informed him, that he was juft before created a peer of Ireland by that title. I have obferved before, that Patrick had taken on him the title of the eldeft of our family upon his marriage with Sarah Fincer, and that according to the cuftoms of our iflands, this change could not be authorifed but by the prefumptive renunciation of Tenermill. The king, who had already formed fpecial views for all our family, was pleafed, that without having recourfe to a borrowed title, my two brothers fhould appear in Ireland under the fame diftinction. But perfifting no lefs in the defign of particularly engaging Patrick to his perfon, he ordered him to be informed, that with the dignity of his chamberlain, with which he had invefted him upon his departure

parture to Spain, he now granted to him that of his high-treasurer, to make him amends, by the emoluments of this office, for his trouble and slavery in the other, which was purely honorary. Among the small number of lords, of which the court of St Germain was composed, it ought not to appear surprising, that two employments of such consequence were united in the same person. They were even more important than could well be thought from the idea historians have given of this king's situation. The pensions he drew from the court of France and Spain did not require the creation of any extraordinary employment to receive them; because being paid regularly upon a bare order, they were not subject to perplexed accounts. But the king drew considerable sums from the catholics, and other subjects of England and Ireland. He had there in the several counties offices established with as much order and regularity as in the most peaceable years of his reign. It was over this kind of revenue that he constituted Patrick administrator, under the title of high-treasurer.

I was pressed down by this torrent of benefits: The bearer of these happy tidings had orders to declare to me from the king, that he had collated me to the bishopric of Cloyn. In truth, this was no more than a titular promotion, without any particular cure of souls, and without revenue: But the intention of this prince was not to remove me from continuing near his person; and proposing only to make me useful in his service in Ireland, his design was, that in the journeys I should undertake there, my dignity might give me more consideration among the catholics.

We should have returned immediately to the castle, to discharge ourselves of all our obligations of gratitude, if the same gentleman had not been commissioned to tell us, that the king gave us some days to regulate our domestic affairs, and that we should have notice whenever he judged it proper for us to

see

see him again. This order, which agreed so badly with our zeal, proceeded all at once from two different causes. We were informed of them by Tenermill before night. Not having the same reasons to absent himself from the king's presence, he returned to the castle. The Spanish ambassador remained there after us; and the king, who was under some concern to see the execution of one part of his designs retarded by the uncertainty of Tenermill's marriage, inquired particularly of that minister what expectations there were from the dispositions of his niece. He did not doubt but on losing all hopes of being married to Patrick, she would freely consent to receive the hand of his brother; and discovering to him his resolutions for the establishment of his fortune, he had encouraged the ambassador by this motive to use all means for hastening the marriage. The time he had given us to regulate our affairs was the same he was willing to allow Donna Figuerrez to come to a resolution. This excellent king carried his good nature so far as to acquaint Tenermill with this particular; and not being shy of letting him see how sensible he was of the pleasure of making us all happy, he declared further, that by depriving us for some days of the honour of seeing him, he had an eye to the satisfaction of seeing us all content, and of receiving the thanks of our whole family all at once. Tenermill, being already as expert a courtier as if he had learned that quality by long experience, took this opportunity of putting the king in mind of the countess of S——; and some words of praise, turned with as much address as truth, made those impressions on him, of which this dear sister felt also the effects.

The joy I received from so many agreeable events would have been pure and unmixed, if my reflections on the character of Donna Figuerrez had not stepped in to interrupt it. Nevertheless, I turned over the discussion of so serious a difficulty till my return to Paris. Tenermill being without love, I was sure of
having

having nothing to combat in his heart, if I should think myself under an obligation of making him drop the design of his marriage. I saw him nevertheless disposed to spare no pains in order to give it success. But I could not conceive, that ambition (which, he began to confess to me, was the only passion that possessed him intirely) had made him so ardent in the courtship of a woman, without the least degree of love. What I admired only as an effect of his lively imagination was, that the moment he turned his desires on that side, he mingled the charms of Donna Figuerrez in all his discourse, with as much satisfaction and relish, as if he had felt for her all the warmth of the most tender passion. He had seen her enough to be acquainted with her whole merit; and in the need she had thought she had of his aid, one may easily fancy she had practised every thing to gain his esteem. But having once penetrated the bottom of his heart, I thought I better knew his sentiments than himself.

He no sooner arrived at Paris, than he paid her a visit at her lodgings with the same ardour; and not going about the bush to declare his desires and hopes, he flattered himself, that with the king's protection, the approbation of the ambassador, and the declaration of his own love, he should easily obtain to be heard upon that point. But it was not ambition that tickled the heart of this beautiful Spaniard: She had just heard from her uncle the ruin of her love, and this news had cast her into a frightful despair. If she did herself a violence in receiving Tenermill with an undisturbed countenance, she could not hear that he built his happiness u̇p̣o̧n̨ the repulse Patrick had given to her passion, without ascribing to him a share of her misfortune; and this thought inspiring her with fury, she treated him with a pride which might have been capable of discouraging him. But according to the opinion he had of women, he looked upon their rigours as nothing; and not feeling for Donna Figuerrez that tender inclination which had given him hopes of finding in Sarah the satisfaction

Vol. III.   I   of

of his heart with the advantages of fortune, he did not from thence entertain lefs hopes of vanquifhing her. Thus the combat began between an ambitious man without affection, who would fain triumph over a heart, to make love ferve as a ftep to his preferment, and a woman paffionately tender and coquettifh, who preferring the fweet delights of love to all advantages of fortune, might eafily be foothed by his application and cares, yet could be moved only by fuch as ſhe thought fincere. With an experience and penetration, which gave her a better judgment of love than any other woman, ſhe brought into this kind of lifts a heart filled with another lover, and the moft unlucky prepoffeffion againſt him whom ſhe accufed of her ruin. A fevere fchool this for Tenermill, which neverthelefs furniſhed me with profitable leffons for the knowledge of paffions and characters.

He returned from this vifit with a difturbed air, which I took notice of. He did not even feek to difguife it from me; and giving me an account of the reception he had met with from his miftrefs, he afked my opinion of fo whimfical a fetting out. I had no other acquaintance with the difpofition of Donna Figuerrez but from the informations I had gathered up in Spain. Her character, fuch as I had then formed to myfelf an idea of, was that of a coquette; and not diftinguifhing all the forts of them, I placed her without doubt in the rank of madam de S——, whofe black artifices, and ſhameful irregularities, I fo well knew. It would have been a tafk too new for me to paint out in my imagination a woman, who had united in her character as many perfections as defects; —— one who lived according to her paffions and freaks, yet capable neverthelefs in her moments of ferious reflection of thinking with as much juftnefs and propriety as a man the moſt diftinguifhed by thefe two qualities; —— always poffeffed of a defire of pleafing; —— not thinking the glory of a woman to confift but in the multitude of her conquefts,

and

and even purchasing them by her voluntary foibles, when she could only find this way to put on or rivet the chains of a lover;—— but more tender and passionate than any body for the man whom she had the art of bringing to her love;— with all this — generous, good, subtile, but without malice in her wiles and artifices;——— always ready to oblige by her services, and to anticipate requests by her offers and diligence;——— as seducing also by the allurements of her humour and behaviour, as by the charms of her person; in fine, — one compounded of a thousand virtues and as many foibles. Such nevertheless was Donna Figuerrez, and I had to this time done extreme injustice to her, in comparing her to a woman so debauched and vicious as madame de S——.

However, as I was yet filled with this notion, and without coming to a resolution of the difficulty I had began to examine, the opportunity was too favourable not to found fully the principles of Tenermill; I ventured by chance upon some general reflections upon the danger of taking a wife, whose character and conduct one does not know. I could have cited for example mademoiselle de L————, if he had not been yet ignorant of the unfortunate adventure of his brother; but I found in the quality of a foreigner, and above all of a Spaniard, sufficient to give form enough to my way of reasoning. I know not, said I, whether the birth of Donna Figuerrez, her hopes of being heiress to the ambassador, and even the favours the king annexes to your marriage, are reasons strong enough to give you tranquillity under this sort of danger; and if you think upon it as I do, it will be at least a remedy for your consolation in the case, wherein the rigours you complain of may make you abandon your enterprize.

He had hearkned to me very attentively. You could have added, answered he, if the evils you have related are yet only matters of apprehension, or if they have already happened; for having been in Spain, where you have had as much acquaintance as Patrick with Donna Figuerrez, it is strange if you be not better informed than you are willing to appear. I found myself too far engaged. However, he himself furnished me with means to draw myself out of the perplexity. As much acquaintance with her as Patrick, replied I, in the way of defence! You may know from her and from him, that I never saw her but twice during my stay at Madrid. It is then to Patrick himself, replied he, that I must address myself, to clear up the doubts you would inspire me with. But while I wait for his testimony, I may confess to you, added he, that not desiring hereafter to look for more in a woman than those conveniences, which an advantageous marriage may afford for the advancement of my fortune, I shall perplex myself but little about the character of her who brings me birth and riches.

We were interrupted with the acclamations of the count and countess of S———, who returning home had been informed of the happy arrival of Sarah and Patrick, and who having yet had only uncertain accounts of their reconciliation and the king's goodness, were eager and hasty to find them out, to heap on them their caresses and congratulations. We went together to their apartment. They were there, and in a manner intoxicated with love and joy. Patrick, who had been so long a time a prey to grief and anguish, without excepting from them even the period of his fatal passion, which had been attended with too much vexation and trouble, not to have made some alteration in his manners and humour, seemed to have resumed all at once that sweetness and grace with which nature had adorned his character. He received the marks of our affection with such a frankness of heart as laid open his most inward sentiments; and he himself comparing his situation with that he remembered to have been in during the time of error, which his senseless preposession had made him call most happy, he agreed, that the pleasures annexed to duty are of quite another value than the irregular transports of the passions.

The

The conversation would have continued a long time upon a subject so conformable to the taste of the whole company, if word had not been brought the countess, that Donna Figuerrez wanted to see her. Tenermill instantly got up, and in great haste went to meet her. She received him with more indifference than anger. But when she saw the countess appear, she prayed him to leave them alone together. Their conversation continued a long time. We were told all the circumstances of it as soon as she went away.

Without dissembling her sentiments for Patrick, or concealing that she would not even have left Spain but for facilitating the means of becoming his wife, she confessed forthwith to the countess, that seeing him reconciled to Sarah by his own inclination, nothing remained to her but to make use of her reason to heal her heart. But not being at once able to renounce the pleasure of seeing a man who had been so dear to her, and finding not much less pleasure in living in strict union with our family, she requested of my sister two favours, both which she hoped to obtain; one, to make her that very day acquainted with Sarah, whose friendship she was desirous of cultivating; the other, to prevail on Patrick to treat her at least with the ordinary respect of politeness, without being so stifly determined, as he had been ever since his return to France, in refusing her a bare visit. The countess being willing to excuse my brother, as not having made any stay at Paris, I pardon him what is past, said Donna Figuerrez, smiling without affectation, but I desire him to repair his fault by a speedy visit, which I will even receive, if he absolutely insists on it, as his last adieu.

My sister, weighing these two requests, found less difficulty in the last than the first. She promised to lay before Patrick what he owed to a lady so well disposed towards him; and without doubt, added she, will have no need of entreaties to pay so reasonable a duty. But knowing what a little relish Sarah had for enlarging her acquaintance, or rather concealing under this pretext the fear of fretting her by the fight of a new rival, she civilly excused herself from complying with this requeſt. Her two propoſals nevertheleſs were of equal importance to her; and to lay open before-hand a ſhare of her views, she did not deſire to ſee Sarah, but to b convinced of what she had to fear from her charms, or to find by ſeeing her what it was that was capable of making an impreſſion on the heart of Patrick. Thus she was ſo offended at my ſiſter's refuſal, that having in vain often preſſed her requeſt with a number of freſh motives, she was not ſo far miſtreſs of her vexation as to keep in her tears; her reſentment muſt have been at its height. She took her leave of my ſiſter with a conſtrained ſhew of friendſhip and thanks, in order to pleaſe herſelf at leaſt with the expectation of a viſit from Patrick, upon which she depended ſo much the more, as not being able to obtain the other favour, she looked on the promiſe of this as infallible. The countefs ſurpriſed us very much with the relation of this converſation. Tenermill, for ever ſpurred on by the ſame zeal, obſerved the departure of Donna Figuerrez, and offered to wait on her home. His abſence leaving us more freedom of converſation, I was the firſt to commend my ſiſter for her refuſal, and to raiſe a doubt whether it were convenient for Patrick to hazard a viſit, of which I could not penetrate into the uſe. However, Sarah, who was never capable of a mean diffidence, and Patrick, who thought himſelf above danger, were of opinion that good manners made this viſit a duty. The count and countefs being of the ſame way of thinking, my advice paſſed only for an exceſs of ſcruple.

As this reſolution was not to be executed immediately, we waited for the return of Tenermill, who ſoon came and rejoined us. His countenance declared the tokens of his joy viſible to every body. He had been treated, as he told us, by Donna Figuerrez, with ſuch favour and indulgence, as she had not ſhewn him

in

in his first visit. But his happiness depended on his brother. You must, said he to him, take the trouble of seeing her, to oblige me. She has made me promise to engage you to it this very day. She has given me hopes, that when she had the explanations she expected and should receive with confidence from you, because she had known your character a long time, that our marriage should be the day after determined with all her heart and mind. He did not even call to mind the questions which he had promised me to ask Patrick; and thinking of nothing but to urge him to be gone, he thought it a tedious time to see him return, to give the last certainty to his hopes.

The night had already spread its shades over the earth; but we were in a season when the days were short. It was some time yet before Patrick had absolutely determined not to put off till next day a visit, which appeared to him burthensome under our circumstances. In fine, having sent to Donna Figuerrez, to know of herself if she approved of the hour he had pitched on, he went away alone in his own coach, and promised to be back at supper. We passed the time of his absence in reasoning upon the motives of Donna Figuerrez. Tenermill explained them to her advantage; and I confessed, after a great number of reflections, that I could discover nothing of the matter.

Towards nine o'clock, one of Patrick's servants came to us, to make apologies by his orders for the necessity he was under of supping with Donna Figuerrez. He ordered us to be told, that the Spanish ambassador, and some other persons of the same distinction, being come to her house the same moment that he did, she had not the opportunity of explaining to him the reasons that had made her desirous of seeing him. The time having insensibly slipped over, the ambassador had requested him to sup with her. Patrick attempted to retire; but the intreaties of the whole company, and particularly of Donna Figuerrez, who had promised to find an opportunity that night of a moment's conversation with him, had determined

him.

him, for Tenermill's interest, to suffer himself to be prevailed upon to stay.

This message, though little expected after his promise at parting, gave no disturbance to any of us. We supped with the most pure and perfect tranquillity and joy. Nevertheless, it came into my mind upon retiring, that every thing was to be feared from a woman so dextrous and violent as Donna Figuerrez. I was not capable of carrying any very powerful aid to my brother; but I might at least watch over the danger, and judge what measures were necessary to be taken to deliver him from it. From this thought alone, I chose between eleven and twelve o'clock to plant myself opposite to the lodgings of Donna Figuerrez, of which I had got an account from Tenermill and my sister. The solitude I immediately found in the street made me almost repent of my enterprize; for I could have but little hopes of getting admittance into a house, without having some pretence for it. I had my valet with me, whose conversation helped for some moments to divert me. Immediately some coaches drove up, which stopping before her door, convinced me yet further, that I was alarmed out of season. Patrick, said I, has submitted in spite of him to the constraint of decorum; the company that stayed him is going to leave him at liberty; his coach will be here soon, since the time appointed for the others is come; I will join him, and take advantage of his company home.

Whilst my thoughts were taken up with these hopes, I saw many persons come out of the house, who immediately drove off in their coaches. The Spanish ambassador appeared also; and as his hotel was only at a little distance in the same street, he went home on foot, attended by a great number of lacqueys with flambeaux in their hands. I concealed myself from their sight with great care. The door having been shut after him, I yet waited above an hour, and my impatience increased the more, as I did not see Patrick's coach come up, or the door
opened.

opened. It nevertheless soon after was opened, and I saw a gentleman come out of it on foot, who gave orders to the porter to wait for him a moment. By chance as I walked along the street, it appeared as if I had come out of the ambassador's hotel, which was not far behind me. The darkness of the night not suffering the gentleman to distinguish my face, he took me by my garb for the person he was going to call, and who must have come from the same place. Is it you, Mr Almoner, said he in Spanish? This title was familiar to me, since the king had granted me that office. A sudden impulse, that forestalled all reflection, made me answer, yes, in the same language. Let us make haste, answered the gentleman, turning about to walk before; our lovers are together, and this is an opportunity which perhaps will never offer again.

Indeed I opened my eyes at these words. I conceived if not an odious conspiracy against my brother, at least that he was menaced with some fatal accident, and that I had need to call up all my courage and zeal to aid him. The necessity of this did not appear to me to be yet urgent; but being resolved to risque every thing, I followed my guide without fear, and went with him into the house. By a special favour of providence the porter waited at the door without light. We went up stairs, which was lighted no better than the door. Wait here, said the gentleman, we shall have occasion for a cast of your office presently. It would have been too dreadful to me to fancy, that they had a design on my brother's life, and that they would not send for a man of my gown, but to receive his last breath: Heaven did not suffer such a thought to come into my mind. But I had a thousand other doubts to torment me mortally. At length the door next to that my guide went in was opened all of a sudden. Come in, Mr Almoner, cried somebody, you are waited for with impatience. Whatever trouble such long preparations had given me, I observed, as I went in, three men well dressed, who

held piſtols preſented to Patrick's breaſt, while Donna
Figuerrez, ſwooning in appearance, lay languiſhingly
ſtretched along on a couch. Come hither, Monſieur,
ſaid one of the gentlemen, come and repair the ho‐
nour of Spain, and that of Monſieur the ambaſſador,
by marrying this gentleman to Donna Figuerrez,
whom we have ſurpriſed together in a poſture not to
be juſtified but by a ſpeedy marriage. He is happy,
that in our firſt fury we had not imbrued our hands
in his blood. My face, which they had not at all
obſerved when firſt I advanced, my firſt exclamations,
conjuring them to ſtay their hands, and the words of
my brother himſelf (who under the ſurpriſe he was in
to ſee me, aſked immediately by what lucky chance I
was ſo near him, and if I did not wonder at this ſcene)
made them judge that there was ſome miſtake in their
adventure. They looked on each other with amaze‐
ment, without nevertheleſs forſaking the poſture they
were in. But one of them addreſſing himſelf to me,
you are a prieſt, Monſieur, ſaid he, with a bullying
air, it is of no conſeq..ence whether you be a Spa‐
niard or a Frenchman; give us a caſt of your office
by a moment's ceremony, which ſhall be rewarded
beyond your expectations by the generoſity of Mon‐
ſieur the Spaniſh ambaſſador. This is his niece,
whom that gentleman has diſhonoured; religion and
honour impoſe the ſame duty on you as upon us. I
came to myſelf again during their buſtle, and con‐
ceived their project in its full extent.' Fraternal
friendſhip, my hatred for all artifice, honour and
religion, by which they pretended to intereſt me,
actuated me with ſo much fortitude, that the ſight of
their arms, any more than the conſideration of their
numbers, did not hinder me from treating them with
all the ſcorn and contempt they deſerved for engaging
in ſuch a villainous attempt. I declared to them
without ſhift or ſubterfuge, that the gentleman
againſt whom they implored my aid was my brother,
and I threatened them with a puniſhment that all the
power of their ambaſſador ſhould not deliver them from.

Perhaps

Perhaps I abandoned myself too much to this first warmth: But whether it were that they were offended at my menaces; or whether, in reflecting upon circumstances, they imagined they were highly insulted, by this scorn of them; and that in spite of my teeth they could force from me the same service as they expected from their own almoner, one of them detached himself from Patrick, and coming up to me, in my turn presented his pistol at my breast; Monsieur, said he, you are a priest, that is enough for our purpose; come, perform here your function, if you would not rather chuse to be a dead man. I gave them no time to wait for my reply, but collecting together all my constancy, as much out of love to my brother, as zeal for my own duty, I shewed so much contempt for the death they threatened me with, and so much indignation against the authors of so base an attempt, that I saw astonishment painted on the faces of our enemies. They durst not persist in their design one moment longer, and laying a stress only on their generosity in sparing our lives, they protested, that if Patrick did not freely consent to what they called his duty, our punishment was only delayed. As to him, who was so much pressed down that he could not arise from his chair, he fretted at an abasement so unworthy of his courage; and when despair of success had obliged them to abandon their enterprise, he swore, as he went away, that he would make them repent their temerity.

They gave us liberty to be gone; but to disguise better their artifice, they affected to call the servants of Donna Figuerrez, and to press them to go to the aid of their mistress. Patrick expected to have found his coach at the gate; but not so much as one of his servants was in waiting. They had taken care to send them all away at a distance, by pretended orders from their master; and we were informed afterwards by the coachman, that having come at the hour Patrick had appointed him, they gave him notice to return two hours later. Jacin continued at the gate,

waiting

waiting my coming out, having no other road to get to the count's houfe.

Though the ambaffador's name had been often ufed by the three Spaniards, and that there was great likelihood they were of his train, without reckoning that his almoner was to act fo great a part in this odious fcene, it was to be prefumed the ambaffador had a knowledge of the undertaking; yet we could not perfuade ourfelves, that he had entered into a confpiracy difhonourable to his character. Being reduced then to accufe nobody of it, but the intriguing genius of Donna Figuerrez, we could not yet forbear admiring how fhe could build any hopes on an adventure, that carried in it not the leaft fhew of probability in the fuccefs. For who could be eafily perfuaded that Patrick could have the fmalleft tie of affection to her; at a time wherein he was taken up with nothing but his love for Sarah, and of which a thoufand perfons could give the ftrongeft proofs? and fo much pains taken to draw him into the fnare, and to difperfe his fervants far away from him, were not thefe things clear demonftrations in his favour?

All people reafoned thus who were informed of our adventure. Tenermill could fcarce get rid of his furprife; and the fhame of being inftrumental himfelf in cafting us into this perplexity by his inftances to his brother, chagrined him as much as the lofs of his hopes. It feemed to him indeed, that after a noife of this nature, he could not have the leaft appetite to renew his vifits to Donna Figuerrez. We all reafoned according to this fuppofition; and the fcheme of his marriage having been the only reafon that retarded Patrick's happinefs, we thought that without being defective in our fubmiffion to the king's pleafure, we might requeft his majefty to fhorten the time he himfelf had fixed for it. Sarah defired it impatiently, as the paft fears had infpired her with others to come. Patrick prayed me to requeft this new favour of the king, and even to obtain of his majefty that

that the ceremony might be performed without noise in any other place than St Germain.

I thought Tenermill so fully cured of his notions of marriage, that in going next day to court, it never came into my mind to ask him, whether I should relate Patrick's adventure to the king. As it was upon this foundation I went to solicit a revocation of his majesty's orders, it was natural for me to begin with this story, and I did not see further on Tenermill's side the least reason that could create in me any doubt of it. Nevertheless, coming to me the moment of my departure, he put to me a hundred questions, the meaning of which I did not at first conceive, and which at length all ended in asking me openly if I intended to mention the enterprise of the three Spaniard's to the king. This very care of ascribing our adventure to the three Spaniards, and not mixing a word of Donna Figuerrez in it, appeared to me to be a delicacy altogether new; but without giving me time to answer him, he added with the same absent air, that under whatever form he had considered the scene of the precedent day, he had found nothing in it that could make the least alteration in the situation of things; that the inclination of Donna Figuerrez to Patrick was known to every body; that in seeking to assure herself of his heart and hand, she did nothing but what every other woman with the same desires and the same power would not fail to attempt as well as she; in fine, that after the ill success of the artifice of the Spaniards, or of her, if I would have it so, she was not a whit different from what she was before the enterprise was undertaken. Is not she the very individual woman, added he (looking on me, as wondering I could make a doubt of it) with the same birth, with the same personal qualities, the same hopes of fortune? And as to the reasons I have had for marrying her, do they sul fill less?

He concluded from this way of reasoning, that if on the contrary they could bury our adventure in oblivion, and begin to do so by concealing it from the king,

king, no rub could stand in his way, after the marriage of Patrick, to hinder him from refuming his hopes of obtaining the Spanish lady. It is certain, added he (as if I yet could stand in need of this confirmation to convince me of it) that she will be under a necessity of renouncing my brother, when she shall see him irretrievably united to Sarah. Why then should she reject my offers, with all the advantages that attend them for her, of which her uncle has without question informed her?

I confess that with whatever surprise I could hear all this discourse, I could find nothing to put a stop to it, when my answer was necessarily required upon that point. I could not indeed convince him, that the enterprise of Donna Figuerrez was a blemish that made her more unworthy to be his than before, and that her love, which made her employ violence, was without doubt the same that had made her endeavour at first to obtain the heart of Patrick by more gentle and sweet methods. Nevertheless, an outrage of that nature seemed to me so rebellious, that at the very time I could not find expressions, or durst not use those that occurred to my mind, to express my horror, I admired that Tenermill did not feel the same impression from it. What I could find most moderate to say to him was, that he would not probably have any occasion to reproach himself for having submitted to an excess of jealousy. I reckoned I should pique him by this irony: But although he perfectly well comprehended it, yet it did not appear to affect him; and intrenching himself under the necessity that Donna Figuerrez would soon be in of stifling her affections for Patrick, he made no difficulty of confessing to me, that what he demanded of her was moreover very independent of the dispositions of her heart. She establishes my fortune, said he, she is capable of doing me credit by her birth, her wit and beauty; I acquit her of every thing else. Ambitious! interrupted I with a quick sentiment of compassion; that you should make me know the various springs and wheels in the

heart

heart of man! How did I deceive myſelf, when the example of your brother made me look on love as the only paſſion capable of blinding a man of underſtanding? How? Do not you perceive, continued I in the ſame tone, that an action ſo raſh as this of Donna Figuerrez, is not the firſt eſſay of impudence and coquettry? To what will you expoſe yourſelf, by uniting yourſelf to a woman of this character? And without explaining myſelf too freely upon the informations I had received at Madrid, I upbraided him for having ſo ſpeedily loſt the deſign he had of obtaining what inſight he could as to the conduct of a woman he had known but a few days. But far from anſwering my queſtions, think, my brother, ſaid he, that this abundance of reflections and pains will make me loſe thoſe advantages I ſhall never recover. The favour of the king may cool. It is probable that a lady of Donna Figuerrez's appearance has ever failed in the obligations due to her birth? Would the ambaſſador, her uncle, live in that good underſtanding with her? Suppoſe her to be a coquette: Are all the ladies of France leſs ſo? And her removal afterwards from Madrid, added he, might make an alteration in the nature of a great many things.

I made no reply to this laſt reaſon; and could not ſufficiently wonder at this contrariety of principles, which made him ſo eaſily ſubmit in an article ſo delicate; him, who appeared to be a man the leaſt tractable in the world in every thing that bore the name of a point of honour. Whimſical effect of violent paſſions, that finds nothing to be of importance but what has a relation to them! Love could make Patrick deſpiſe grandeur, and ambition could render Tenermill inſenſible to love. In the mean time, as I had no apprehenſion that he would advance too briſkly with Donna Figuerrez, I ſtill ſuſpended giving him thoſe explanations, that I thought moſt capable of making impreſſions on him, and reſolved to wait the return of Patrick before I took my own reſolutions upon the matter.

Neither

Neither Patrick nor I could be suspected of publishing our adventure, nor could we in the least accuse the count and countess of S———, whose discretion we well knew. Nevertheless, Tenermill had the vexation to hear rumours spread about, that gave him too much room to judge, that all the world had not observed the same silence; and as an addition to his grief, Patrick informed us at his return, that they had already reached as far as St Germain. The king, when he granted him the permission he sued for to hasten the renewal of his marriage, and to celebrate it without noise at our little house at Saisons, did not wait to hear his excuses and pretexts for justifying his petition. He had joked with him upon his fortune; and lamenting Tenermill for being less favoured by love, had added, that this was an incident that failed him in his establishment. With the bare income of his regiment, and twelve thousand livres pension, I should be very wary, said the king, in granting him a title, which would give him less honour, than it would cause him embarrasment in supporting it. He is young, and well made; Paris may present him with what he cannot obtain from Spain, if he does not rather choose to wait our return to England, where my friendship may perhaps yet help better to forward his establishment.

Thus this prince continued to promise himself success, that providence did not think proper to reserve for him. But the impatient Tenermill, who had not so much reliance on the future, looked on this declaration as a fatal wound to his hopes. All the chimeras, by which perhaps he had succeeded in cheating himself as to the conduct of Donna Figuerrez, became useless to him by the king's decision. What means had he to propose them to this prince, as he had ventured to do to me?—He never had one thought of making himself agreeable to the French ladies. His resolute and imperious humour could not suffer him to submit to the great attendances and complaisances, in which he saw the greatest part of them

them place their gallantry; and when his ambition to advance himself should make him descend to this sort of abasement, he thought that nature having not formed him for such a manner of making himself agreeable, he should run the risque of making himself ridiculous by his grimaces and affectations. As to England, he knew better than the king, how little his majesty could rely upon some slight advantages of the last campaign; and the notions of an expert officer, who had seen on the spot the dispositions of the country, were far different from the flattering language of the courtiers.

During some days I saw him so pensive and melancholy, that his grief would have inspired me with pity, if I had not thought it useful to make him open his eyes upon the folly of the passion that devoured him. He carefully avoided me, as if he had taken my looks for so many reproaches. Patrick's company did not appear to his brother less unsupportable. He received his words and caresses with an indifference, and sometimes with a haughtiness, at which the other would have had a right to take offence. As it was not upon occasions of this nature that Patrick was capable of hearkening to his resentment, I was not at all alarmed at their differences, but on the contrary I took a pleasure in seeing with what sweetness he would sacrifice his inclinations to fraternal friendship. When all the family went to Saisons to assist at the renewal of his marriage, Tenermill excused himself from accompanying us, under some very slight pretences. There was no person there to whom this affectation did not give as much trouble as amazement; but Patrick, who ought to have been more affected with it, contained himself so well as not to complain in the least of his behaviour; and not being discouraged at the first refusal, he endured more of them with the same moderation.

I knew, that from the hopes that our adventure had continued yet a secret, and perhaps from an opinion that Donna Figuerrez herself could not imagine we could yet have revealed it, Tenermill had gone to viſit her the day after, and had ſpent with her a part of the afternoon. His melancholy not having began till after the king's declaration, he ſtill continued to viſit her; and although he did not fail of paying his court regularly enough at St Germain, he ſeldom happened to paſs an entire day there without returning to Paris. We could not gueſs that this was on purpoſe to paſs a part of the day with her; for in the free and independent converſation we had eſtabliſhed at the count's, curioſity did not ſway any one there ſo as to make him remark upon the conduct of others. Nevertheleſs, by the indiſcretion of ſome one of his ſervants, I came to hear from my valet, that all the time he did not paſs at St Gemain or the count's, he ſpent with Donna Figuerrez, and that in the houſe of that lady no body talked of any thing elſe but of the favour he was in with her. This news gave me ſome reſtleſsneſs, of which I could not at firſt unravel the cauſe. What could be the foundation of an acquaintance ſo ſtrict? I knew Tenermill too well to ſuſpect him of becoming a ſlave to love. On the other hand, Patrick was from henceforth ſecured from all ſorts of attacks; and if Donna Figuerrez ſhould yet form any deſign againſt him, I ſhould be ſtrictly careful to make a ſhare of my diſtruſt fall upon his brother. I was fond of perſuading myſelf, that having found in this fair Spaniard more wit, than in the generality of the women of his acquaintance, he had by means of that quality reliſhed in her converſation the pleaſures of an innocent familiarity. He has renounced, ſaid I to myſelf, the appearances of love, which according to the deſign that made him ſubmit to it, had always ſomething uneaſy and troubleſome to a man of his humour; and not ſeeking any thing but to conſole himſelf for the ill ſucceſs of his ambition, he contents himſelf with the bare pleaſures of friendſhip. I could applaud this taſte, added I, if he has made choice of ſuch a remedy; for judging of it by the ſatisfaction Patrick himſelf had for a long time found in the friendſhip of Donna Figuerrez, he might have applied himſelf worſe.

Why

Why had I not this moment knowledge enough in the customs of the world to mistrust an evil which was beginning to arise? My zeal could have furnished me with a thousand ways to check it in its birth. If my own exhortations would not have been hearkened unto, I might have employed the aid of the Spanish ambassador, and even the king's authority. I could have engaged that religious prince to awaken the ambition of Tenermill by hopes less remote. Of two dangerous evils, why should I scruple to make one of them serve as a remedy to the other, which was the most formidable? If this aid had not been sufficient, I could have induced the king to have kept him in employment during the winter by some toilsome journey, or some negociation to a foreign court. In fine, I yet persuaded myself, that with the assistance of heaven, I could have succeeded in making him break an engagement, which had been a long time the cause of my zeal and the subject of my tears.

I did not begin too soon to deplore him, though I came much too late to the knowledge of him. My ignorance proceeded a long time from my security. I was without fear, because without suspicions. Far from being alarmed with just mistrusts, I no sooner fancied that Tenermill had taken for the Spanish lady the same taste that I had seen Patrick have for her in Spain, than drawing a good omen from the return of his tranquillity, and the healing of his ambition, which I had found dangerous by its excess, I sought an opportunity to congratulate him equally for these two blessings. He received my compliments with such an air of satisfaction, that it increased my confidence. As to ambition, said he, it is true I am much less tormented with it: The king has put me out of conceit with his favours by annexing them to impossible conditions; or at least what he turns over to times so distant begins to have less effect on my longing. And if, added he, I must confess to you this experiment, to which you have perhaps seen me too much affected, it helps every day to take

away

away even my taste for the court. I never shall appear there more but with regret. They loaded me with favours before I began to merit them; and I am put off with uncertainties at a time when my services, or, if you will, my good fortune, have perhaps made me worthy of some regard or attention: This is giving me almost an equal room to afford myself but small applause, either on account of the goodness, that was graciously before-hand with my merit, or of the justice that rewards it so ill. In regard to my acquaintance with Donna Figuerrez, you have reason, added he, to give it the name of friendship, and I am obliged to you for these compliments which it deserves. It is a long time since, instead of thinking of marriage or love, I should have established a commerce of this nature. If my fortune did not grow better by it, I should have found in it at least an advantage as to the pleasures of my life, and the tranquillity and calming of a great number of passions.

Who would not have believed, as I did, that this friendship, which had been capable of restoring tranquillity to his mind, and which upon the whole had served to cure him of ambition, was founded upon the most pure maxims of prudence? I thought of it so fully in this light, that I should have freely given thanks for it to Donna Figuerrez, to whom I ascribed this miracle. Although my knowledge of her had been formed from divers disadvantageous strokes and lineaments, I had nevertheless heard Patrick vaunt of her wit, and I knew he had all the qualities capable of making him a proper judge of it. If the lights and understanding of the mind do not always defend a heart against any disorder, they may be looked upon at least as resources, from whence one may always have some hopes of a return to virtue; because the most tumultuous passions having their intervals of relaxation and silence, they sometimes afford a time to sound and enlightened reason to see the precipice to which they lead, and consequently to arm themselves with new strength either to shun or to get out of it.

The

The very disorders and irrgularities of Donna Figuerrez, the trouble that had attended her passions, the disgusts and mortifications she had endured from her late enterprize, might not they have produced this effect on her, and by the brightness of her natural talents have made her a proper instrument to convey it to Tenermill?

The original of an event so remarkable in its nature and consequences deserved a relation of this extent, to prepare the readers for other particulars, which will make perhaps the most engaging part of this history. I find myself also under the necessity of deferring an account, which without doubt they have expected with impatience; that is, the celebration of the agreeable ceremony, which established the happiness of Sarah Fincer and Patrick upon a solid foundation. My pen is not fit to describe the transports of a new married couple, eager for each other, who had so much the higher relish of joy, as having been a long time, the one without desires, and the other without hopes, all the inclinations springing up in their hearts, were in a manner so many new impressions, which resembled almost in nothing their former trials. They seemed therefore to gaze on one another every moment, as if for the first time. Ah! that they had been seen always under the form they assumed that day the one for the other. Sarah saw in her husband a man as passionate for her, as she had for so long a time sued for from love; and in this lady, whom Patrick at another time had looked upon as the most invincible obstacle of his repose, he saw nothing but the object of his most tender complaisances, and the inexhaustible source of happiness no longer subject to a change. What prayers and vows did I not address to heaven in re-establishing their bands by a new benediction? With what ardour did I pray for a perseverance of so much affection, which I thought I read in their hearts, and which they promised so freely by their oaths? At another time they swore in the same terms of expression; but what

difference

difference was there now in the difpofition of Patrick and the fatisfaction of Sarah? What difference in my heart, which feemed to take fhare in their joy, and unite itfelf to their engagements, with as much inward fatisfaction, as I remembered to have felt grief and bitternefs in Dublin, when I was as it were obliged to drag an unhappy victim to the altar! How were the omens changed, and how did they alfo proclaim the change in their fate?

To fill up the meafure of our fatisfaction, the countefs, who was with child, without appearing to draw fo near her time, was the day following happily delivered of a fon. Nothing was wanting to the completion of our joy, but to fee Tenermill fharing in it with us there. In the black and melancholy grief, with which his heart was gnawed, he neglected to fend to Patrick and his wife even the compliments of decency, from which no reafon in the world could have excufed him; but this overfight was repaired afterwards by fincere apologies.

Some days after, Patrick having propofed to us to go to St Germain, to prefent there his fpoufe to the king, we confidered, if, notwithftanding the ill humour of Tenermill, we ought not to give him notice, that decency feemed to require him to go with us there. But after a fitting deliberation we agreed not to communicate our defign to him, and to take upon ourfelves to make his excufes to the king. We knew that in the firft warmth of the account Patrick had given him, he had let two days flip without appearing at St Germain. The king could not be deceived in the caufe of this abfence; and far from taking offence at it, he had talked the matter over with Mr de Sercine in a manner to convince us, that he himfelf regretted to have feen by the adventure of Donna Figuerrez a delay given to his views of advancing him. Thus we had very little fear of prejudicing him in the king's thoughts, by confeffing to his majefty, that the regret of having failed in the eftablifhment of his fortune had even deprived him of

the

the pleasure of being present at Patrick's marriage, and that our love for peace had made us apprehensive of irritating him, by proposing to him to join in company with us, which he would not have accepted.

Nevertheless, we were but little forward in our journey, when we had cause to repent of this resolution. The three Spaniards, who had assisted Donna Figuerrez, were hunting in the plain, with a man for their guard, who served them also as a guide; and seeing an equipage that shewed some air of distinction by the number of servants following us on horse-back, curiosity made them come near. Patrick knew them, and had not sufficient command over himself upon this occasion, wherein he need not have discovered that he was in the coach. He lifted up the glass: Messieurs, said he in their own language, you may inform Donna Figuerrez, that I was married two days ago, and may make my compliments to her for her having had such bad success in preventing it. This was a piece of raillery, from whence he protested to me he had no thoughts of drawing any further consequence: for, notwithstanding his menaces upon his leaving Donna Figuerrez, I had obliged him to come into my way of thinking, that honour did not oblige him to expect a reparation by arms for an insult of this nature; and that it would be even ridiculous to measure his sword with three men one after another, to whom we did a favour by not punishing them in a course of justice. However, there remained in his heart a foundation for resentment, which he could not get the better of upon meeting them, and which induced him thus to banter them, without reflecting on the consequences of it.

We had the count of S—— with us; so that we were two gentlemen against three. I will not accuse so brave a people as the Spaniards of desiring to take advantage of the inequality of numbers, or having designedly failed in respect for my sister-in-law, whose appearance alone was capable of inspiring them with it. Nevertheless, they were so offended at Patrick's words,

words, that one of them (alighting immediately) fiercely ordered the coachman to ſtop; and the two others followed his example. They honourably enough propoſed to my brother to come out of the coach. I oppoſed a motion he made to ſatisfy them. How, ſaid I, do you forget your promiſe, and can you be capable of any violence under the eyes of your ſpouſe? He laboured to perſuade me to ſilence by diverſe winks and ſigns; and I affecting not to hear him, he deſired me to explain what I meant by my ſuſpicions. This ſhift ſucceeded ill with him; my lady and the count apprehended all at once who were his aggreſſors. They had not forgot what we had before told them. The count, boiling with the ſame fire as Patrick, reproached me for the efforts I uſed to ſtop him, and ſaid to him that it was not a queſtion to be deliberated upon. But what gave me greater aſtoniſhment, Sarah, the tender Sarah, accuſing me herſelf of ſtopping him unſeaſonably, added, that it was not upon a point of honour that ſhe muſt oppoſe the courage of her huſband. I ſhould have ſuſpected her of ſome impulſe of revenge againſt the agents of Donna Figuerrez, if the knowledge I had of her principles had not convinced me, that it was owing to a greatneſs of heart, and a nobleneſs of ſentiments.

In the mean time, as it was not upon notions of this nature that the rules of my morality were eſtabliſhed, having in vain endeavoured to ſtop the count and Patrick, I turned my repreſentations and prayers to the three Spaniſh gentlemen. They received them as a banter; and when, being provoked at their anſwers, I did not ſpare to reproach them, that it was againſt all ſorts of rights to take advantage of their numbers, one of them exhorted me laughing to take a ſword and make the party equal. I confeſs this was the ſingle moment of my life wherein heat of blood made me find too much rigour in my duty; and if chance had thrown a ſword in my way, perhaps I ſhould have given way to the firſt motion that poſſeſſed my heart. I bitterly lamented, that Tenermill

mill was not at least with us to assist his brothers.
But the three Spaniards soon made me recover from
my diffidence. Having consulted together a moment,
they detached two of their body to attack the count
and Patrick; and the third drew near the coach, to
make an apology to my lady. She did not hearken
to him; but trembling, notwithstanding her resolution,
she advanced her head out of the coach with looks
so disquieted and troubled, that her life seemed to
hang on the fate of her husband. During this time
our servants consulted my eyes, to throw themselves
at the least sign upon their master's enemies; but
being under the necessity of enduring an evil that I
had not in my power to remedy, I took great care to
prevent the action from turning to the dishonour of
my brothers, by a succour so unworthy of their cou‑
rage.

The chance of arms was favourable to them.
Patrick, too well exercised in those sort of combats,
wounded his adversary dangerously. The count
disarmed his. I already had exhorted my lady to
pour up her thanks to heaven, when the third
Spaniard advancing towards Patrick, pressed him to
begin the battle again with him. Indignation seized
my sister‑in‑law; she thought her husband had satis‑
fied all the laws of honour; Ah! cried out she, ad‑
dressing herself to the servants in our train, will you
suffer them to assassinate your master twice? This fa‑
tal order produced a terrible effect. Our servants,
who were ten in number, from a desire my brother
had, that his wife should appear in some splendour at
St Germain, were Irishmen, whom we had brought
over with us, or had hired in France. They were
the more animated, for that at the very moment they
advanced to drive away the enemies of Patrick, they
saw him receive a slight wound, from whence the
blood sprang out. Then not giving any further heed
to the commands of the count or me, they threw
themselves upon the three Spaniards, who only pro‑
voked them the more, by making a defence; and by

the odds they had of being on horse-back, and armed with piſtols, they in a moment ſtretched them in the duſt.

The guard took to flight. Our only happineſs in ſuch a frightful diſaſter was, that not being known we might hope to get into a place of ſecurity, by marching off as ſpeedily as he. The place we were in being a croſs road, favoured yet more this hope. After ſome cutting reproaches, which we all four laid on our cruel Iriſhmen, I recommended to them above all things ſilence, as a precaution full as important to their ſecurity as ours; and, to conceal the better ſuch an horrible adventure, we drove through ſeveral turnings and windings to St Germain.

BOOK XII.

THUS the demonſtrations of joy and gratitude, which we were carrying to the king for his favours, were converted into grief for our misfortunes, and into urgent ſupplications to obtain pardon for our ſervants, having firſt made a private confeſſion to his majeſty of their barbarous zeal. He rejoiced to find, that we flattered ourſelves in not being known by the guard; but as he had an intereſt in giving no cauſe of complaint to the court of Spain, he immediately took a reſolution which we were far from expecting. You ſhall go for Ireland ſaid he to Patrick and me; this is the only way I have to hope, that you may not be ſoon diſcovered from the marks given of you by the guard, who muſt have had at leaſt the opportunity of obſerving you. I did not propoſe, added he, to make you ſo ſoon undertake this voyage, though I have already prepared

you

you for it by some overtures, which have made you comprehend a part of my views; but the present occasion determines my resolution. He proceeded to tell us in what particulars he thought us fit for his service. My brother having never carried arms against king William, and the perplexity from whence he was delivered at Dublin, making him fully hope that he would be but little suspected there, after the full proofs he had given of his innocence, the king's intentions were, that he should pass some months in Dublin, and should conduct himself without shewing any open affection to his party. He would neither make him a spy nor a conspirator: But in the new measures he had taken for the following campaign, too confidently flattering himself with success, he thought to establish at Dublin a head over his faithful subjects, who might unite them of a sudden in that city, when the advantages he promised himself by his arms should inspire them with courage to declare for him openly. He was sure of having a great number of partizans, whose zeal waited only to be animated by some lucky event; and in a town, whose example would become as it were a law for the whole kingdom, he wanted a man, whose merit and birth would be capable of making an impression on their minds. As to me: he hoped to draw the same advantages from my zeal in the provinces. The quality of bishop added to the weight of my name, gave him room to believe, that I should easily gain the confidence of the people, and that upon the least appearance of success to his arms, I should readily raise in his favour all those whom I should have already gained to his interest by my exhortations. He ordered me to hasten the ceremony of my consecration, and pressing Patrick yet further to prepare for his departure, he advised him not to put off till the morrow what might be executed the same day.

To the commission, with which he charged us, he added a power to take up the treasure of my lord Linch, and granted us liberty to apply to his service

vice such sums in specie, of which I had given him
an account from the memorandum intrusted to me.
His cares extended to my lady. Having congratulated her upon the conclusion of her marriage, he
exhorted her to use the credit she had in the county
of Antrim to reclaim that important part of the realm
to his obedience, and by the reputation her charms
would give her in Dublin, to second the zeal of her
husband in that city. He engaged his royal word,
that to recompence so great a service, he would make
her first lady of honour to the queen after his restoration, and that he would confirm my brother in his
two posts, of which he confessed the first was but an
empty title at St Germain. As to the second, it
being properly in our islands that the importance of it
consisted, he invested him with all the power proper to
faciliate the execution of it.

Patrick and his wife found nothing uneasy in these
dispositions, how remote soever they were from their
expectations. If the motives of obedience and zeal
had not been sufficient to prevail on them to embrace
those commands with joy, their private affairs requiring for some time their presence in Ireland, they
could not desire a more glorious opportunity to take
care of their own concerns, than by satisfying their
duty. They readily accepted the offer without excuses or delay. My sister-in-law, alarmed at the
reflection the king had made upon our adventure,
was the first to wish that he would take the road to
Dieppe the night following. They reposed on me
the care of setting their affairs in order in France,
and to transport their goods when I should leave it to
rejoin them.

The excuses of Tenermill, which I had not forgot to make to the king, were received by that prince
with goodness enough; but they produced nothing
else, that could make me discover what degree of
favour he retained in his mind. He shewed more
regard for the count de S———, and speaking to him
of his wife as a woman whose merit he had known a
long

long time, he gave him to understand, that he had prepared for her distinctions and graces when ever she should appear at court. A witness to so many favours would judge, that nothing was wanting to the fortune of our family; but I thought I had a glimpse, that in this profusion of benefits Tenermill was neglected.

He made this judgment of it himself, when (passing through Paris with the count) I informed him of the hasty departure of his brother, and the commission the king had charged him with. This preference of his brother to an employment of such importance, and the coldness with which the king answered me on his account, which I could not conceal from him, made him carry his suspicions much further than I did. See the price of my services, said he with a resentment, of which the half lay yet disguised in his heart; he punishes me with hopes, which he gave me room to conceive, and with promises which he has not thought seasonable to fulfil. I was ignorant that he had talked in the same manner in a thousand places of Paris, and that some part of it had been carried to the king. The answers, with which I laboured to console him, were drawn from the favourable intentions of that prince, who would reserve for him without doubt to another time what the circumstances of affairs would not yet permit him to grant. Can he complain, replied Tenermill boldly, that opportunities have failed him, when he has of his own accord torn two of them from me? Expressions so plain gave me too well to understand, that he had not looked upon the marriage of Patrick with an eye as undisturbed as I fancied, and that he was not more consoled in having missed the opportunity of marrying Donna Figuerrez, whom he looked upon at least as a resource. But what he added, made me judge, that the sort of forgetfulness with which he thought himself overlooked, whilst the king employed his brother with so much confidence, he finished the piercing him to the heart.

I did not expect, said he, any other explanation to declare to me my disgrace, and I will take care how I appear at St Germain to meet with a repetition of it.

All the reasons, by which I endeavoured to make him take up other notions of the king's goodness, not having had the power to reclaim him, I conjured him to give me time at least to dive into his proper situation, and I offered him to employ to that purpose all the ways he should himself judge seasonable to prescribe me. But his indignation seeming to redouble at this proposal; I! said he, Shall I by a shameful restlessness and servile excuses go and justify a treatment that I never deserved? This is a scandal I never will expose myself to. His pride thus combating his ambition, he seemed more to be pitied than he ever had been under the latter of these passions; but I hoped much better from thence for the time to come; because the natural effect of this opposition must be to moderate them both.

Nevertheless, not doubting but that with those sentiments he would soon fall under disgrace with the king, if he had not done so already, as he fancied, I had the curiosity to ask him, by what other views he hoped to supply the loss of his fortune? By the contempt of every thing that bears that name, said he with a gloomy air, and a scheme of life, by which I know how to render myself independent of the court. Not being able to get out of him any other explanation, I learned at the count's house, that during the few days we had passed at Saisons, he had gamed with so much good success, that at three sittings he had won four hundred thousand livres at Basset. They added, that with great prudence he had immediately placed it out at interest, from thence to raise himself a revenue as a proof against all chances. If I lamented him for having tried those ways of fortune so unworthy of him, I commended the use he had made of the favour of his good luck. But I avoided speaking to him of it; and far from be-

lieving

lieving him so sowered against the court as he had affected to appear, I did not at all doubt but that he would soon avail himself, through the advantages of gaming, to establish himself by an advantageous marriage, which would give a new birth to all his ambition. These also were the thoughts of the count de S——, to whom he did not discover his good fortune any more than he had done to me. In the mean time, as if the departure of his brother, and the near approach of mine, had been the time he waited for to execute his resolutions, he went to return thanks to the king the day following, and to surrender to him his pension and regiment.

I was not informed of this strange step but by the king himself, when, being consecrated in a private chapel without noise, I returned to St Germain to receive his majesty's last orders before my departure. Far from expecting such bad news, I thought of nothing but discovering, whether the sentiments of that prince were so cold towards Tenermill as I began to fear; and I had prepared in my discourse every thing that I thought necessary to revive them. But if it were true, that the king had been so offended at his complaints, as to diminish any thing of the affection with which he had honoured him, he had been much more sensibly moved, that an officer of his merit had forsaken his service, at a time when such sort of losses were not easy to repair. Without stooping so low as to let him perceive he was sensible of the offence, he conducted himself in such a manner as still to retain hopes of gaining him over by accepting only the half of what he came to surrender; and colouring with a good deal of address and goodness the laying down of his regiment, which surprised every body in a man of his age; although your infirmities, said the king, will not suffer you any longer to serve me, it would be unjust that your past services should remain unrewarded; I leave you your pension. Tenermill, notwithstanding all his resentment, which would have carried him perhaps to have refused this

favour,

favour, durft not violate fo far the refpect he owed his mafter; and, confounded at a favour fo little expected, he was obliged to fhew his gratitude by returning his majefty thanks.

The king having given me this account, carried the confidence, with which he honoured me, fo far as to afk me familiarly, if I found any juftice in the complaints of my brother. I was too much overwhelmed with the favours he had heaped on my whole family, not to acknowledge all the wrong Tenermill had done himfelf by an excefs of pride; neverthelefs, as much as it was poffible to juftify him from the mortal grief he felt in the lofs of fo great hopes, and by a panegyrick on the grandeur of his foul and his integrity, I laboured to make him appear lefs culpable. To give over meafure to fo much goodnefs, the king gave it me in charge to bring down this fiery fpirit by all the ways I could find, from the knowledge I had of his character. It is not, added he, within the compafs of a day that I expect you to bring about this change. Go you for Ireland; your fervices, and thofe of your other brother will help me with a pretext to awaken him to his duty by new favours.

Such powerful motives made a lively impreffion on my heart. I returned to Paris, and paffed there a few days more than I intended, with a defign to begin before my departure to caft into the mind of Tenermill the firft feeds of repentance, to which I did not defpair of engaging him. I found him employed in preparing furniture and every thing elfe that might help to make a houfe commodious and pleafant. Having quitted the king's fervice, and his fortune being confiderably augmented, it was natural for him to think of re-taking his houfe, and endeavouring to make it agreeable. I did not carry my views farther. I was informed that he propofed alfo to embellifh our little houfe at Saifons by a number of ornaments. The relifh for gardens and buildings makes the common amufement of a rich and retired man.

man. I found nothing very unexpected in his design; and on the contrary I commended him for turning his inclinations towards such innocent and plain objects. But I did not hear without amazement that Donna Figuerrez seemed to preside for the most part over those inclinations. It was added, that taking advantage of the absence of the count and countess of S——, she had oftentimes visited Tenermill even in his apartment; that she had supped there alone with him; that their entertainments always lasted very far in the night; that she kept up with him an air of familiarity, which presumed the most intimate acquaintance; in fine, that their interests appeared to be so united, that they seemed to put no difference between what was his or hers. Donna Figuerrez, though far from being so rich as she would one day be by the inheritance of her uncle, enjoyed nevertheless an estate considerable enough. She had noble inclinations, and a liberal humour. Tenermill being in that particular not inferior to any body, all the projects they formed in concert tasted of those two predominant qualities.

But the principal humour of establishment that they intended had escaped the eyes of those who gave me this notice. I did not penetrate it myself, or rather, my suspicions not turning on that side, I did not seek to discover it. But in sounding Tenermill, I found him so strengthened in the design of renouncing the court, that I had no hopes of making him easily enter into the king's intentions. He told me himself that he was clogged with the pension the king had forced him to keep, and that he considered it as the remains of a servitude, from which he grieved not to be intirely set free. If I had any hopes left, it proceeded only from the main bottom of his character, which I did not think more easy to reform in an ambitious man, than in a slave to every other passion: And I flattered myself, that if his ambition could be brought to spring up a new, the advantage of his vexations would be to reduce it within just bounds,

bounds, in making him retrench what he had vicious in his excesses.

My departure was forwarded some days by the noise of inquiries being made in the courts of law, who had taken cognizance of our unhappy rencounter. Although nothing had been made out by informations, and that the absence of Patrick, who they might have believed had gone for Ireland the day he quitted Paris for the celebration of his marriage, helped further to banish suspicions, yet my figure was so remarkable, that I ran the risque every moment to be known by the guard. I even excused myself from returning to Saisons; and taking leave of the count by letter, I recommended to him to keep some weeks from appearing in Paris, to give time to this storm to settle intirely. I made a prosperous journey. All hostilities having ceased during the winter, I found my passage open to Dublin. An ancient friend to our house, to whom I addressed myself on my arrival, shewed me a letter from Patrick, who by a prudent conduct thought proper to go first to the county of Antrim, before he appeared in the capital. He had writ to him from his mansion house, that, as if discouraged by the fatigue of his journeys, he had at length chose to fix himself in his own country, and to make Dublin his constant place of residence. He requested him to provide a house for him, such as would answer the design he had of appearing there in some splendour; and telling him the day he intended to come, he prayed him to inform himself of all persons who had any acquaintance with our family.

This generous friend was named Staberton. Being as faithful to the king as to friendship, it was not Patrick's business to conceal from him the secret of his commission: On the contrary, he made use of him as an instrument to spread abroad reports, which might make the government countenance him, by seeing him appear freely without diffidence or suspicion. I had much fewer precautions to observe; because not proposing to see indifferently all my acquaintance,

quaintance, the obscurity in which I was desirous of executing the king's orders, might keep me better concealed than my brother. Besides, my design was to stay but little in one place. I thought less of winning over partizans for the king, than in making sure those who were faithful to him, and confirming them in their loyalty. I must run over all the counties of Ireland, take from one town to another the names of every zealous Jacobite, to whom I could open myself with confidence, and keep an exact account of every one whose service was to be depended upon, as occasion offered. In looking thus more narrowly into my engagements, I found that religion had a less share in my labours than I had fancied; but my making myself useful in the restoration of the king, was serving religion indirectly.

I resolved nevertheless to depend upon the arrival of Patrick, for regulating my first enterprises in concert with him. It was during this interval that thinking before-hand of the means to put ourselves into possession of my lord Linch's treasure, chance threw in my way (in the house where I lodged) one of his old servants, who remembered to have seen me at his castle. Although he had not been intrusted by him so far as to know the spot in the wood where the treasure was concealed, he was not ignorant nevertheless that my lord was the trustee of a vast deal of wealth; and the opinion of people of his sort always enlarging facts of this nature, he fancied with the rest of the servants, that all the gold and silver in the kingdom was in the possession of their master. I was very cautious of discovering myself to him in the absence of my brother; but thinking this man useful to our views, by the knowledge he had of Linch's castle and the places about it, I gained him over by some liberalities that fixed him in my interest. Having afterwards had a full trial of him to build something upon his services, it came into my mind to employ with him the time that Patrick's delay gave me to visit Linch's wood, to refresh the confused

notions

notions I yet had of his cave. I took care nevertheless not to give him the least hint of our pretences or defigns; and in the vifit I propofed, I only intended to make ufe of my own eyes, without giving him even the opportunity of remarking upon what places I fixed my looks.

We began our journey together, under the fimple pretence of feeing once more a caftle where I had loft a friend, whofe memory was very dear to me. Having no reafon to conceal my route, I made an amufement of this journey, and did not ftop to obferve by whom I was followed; which neverthelefs I was, by fome fpies of the government. Neither the precautions I had taken, nor the reafons we had of fearing nothing from the jealoufies of the viceroy, prevented me on my arrival at Dublin from being fufpected. He had appointed two men to follow me from place to place, who never once loft the track of me, and had taken the refolution of travelling at my heels, when they faw me get on horfeback to leave Dublin. I had no miftruft of this convoy, and I arrived at Linch's caftle without obferving them.

The care I took of lodging in an inn apart from the highway, and of avoiding to meet any inhabitants of the town, having increafed the fufpicion of my guards, they did not lofe fight of me a moment; infomuch that rifing one morning very early, with a view of making a vifit alone to the wood, and of concealing myfelf even from the man whom I had brought with me, I was neverthelefs under their infpection without knowing it. The confidence I had of having no witneffes, made me lefs cautious than I had propofed. I not only knew the places I had vifited with my lord Linch, but removing the earth that covered the defcent to the cave, I went down as far as the ftone that ferved as a door to the entrance, and I endeavoured to lift it with all my ftrength; which not being enough for the purpofe, I began to fettle every thing in the fame condition I found it; when my two fpies, who took a high conceit

ceit of my attempt, and without doubt feared, that they should not easily find again what I took so much pains to cover, advanced to me with a cry that struck some terror into me. Without giving me time to return from thence, they shewed me the viceroy's order for watching me, and putting all their strength to lift up the stone, they went down into the cave, notwithstanding the darkness, which was capable of checking the eagerness of people less greedy.

In my first consternation I thought of nothing but lifting up my eyes and hands to the almighty, and putting under his protection against the prophanation of the wicked, a mass of consecrated wealth, that ought not to be employed but in his service. But when a moment's reflection had given me time to consider of some means to prevent the pillage, which I immediately expected, the sight of the stone which was set upon an edge near the mouth of the cave, and the turning over whereof was enough to shut up the entrance intirely, inspired me with a design of employing such an innocent artifice against force. The warmth that animated me increased my natural strength. I revenged heaven with more cruelty than I intended. My two enemies continued buried in the cave, and absolutely to take away any possibility of their getting out before I had considered of some way to save the treasure out of their clutches, I covered the stone not only with the earth I had before removed from thence, but with every thing I found near me proper to increase the weight. The descent into the cave being too narrow to admit of a passage for two at once, I was satisfied that the efforts of one alone would never be sufficient to disengage them.

My first thoughts nevertheless were not to leave them there long enough to die for want of food. I immediately returned to Dublin with a resolution of discovering myself to some of our most trusty friends. It did not seem impossible with their assistance to secure the two spies till the arrival of Patrick, and even to convey all the riches out of the cave into some place where

where avarice could have no access to it. Staberton, whom I first informed of my adventure, immediately gave notice of it to four of his best friends, for whose zeal and fidelity he engaged. I came to Dublin with so much expedition, that I made my journey in one day, and I took up no longer time on my return. A body of eight or ten gentlemen, tho' separated in many parties, being capable of giving some alarm in my lord Linch's territories, we took care to arrive there at night, and without stopping at the inn where I alighted before, we went directly to the wood, in which the treasure was concealed.

Among many precautions I took that of providing every thing to assist us in the dark. The uneasiness I was under for the life of my two spies made me hasten Staberton to lift up the stone that covered the cave. I had but a bad omen of their safety, when they did not appear at the entrance. We found them indeed motionless at the bottom of the cave; and all our endeavours were useless to bring them back to life. My heart was pierced with grief, and notwithstanding the integrity of my intentions, I thought myself guilty enough of their death to suspend for some time all the functions of my ministry. Nevertheless, my associates found nothing but a subject for joy in this unfortunate event; and confessing, that upon my recital, their design had been to rid themselves of these miserable wretches, they thanked heaven for having spared them a violence, which they had thought necessary for their safety.

The death of the only two witnesses, from whom we had reason to fear treachery, gave us more time and liberty than I durst have hoped for, to remove a great many large caskets, which had been difficult to carry away without carrs. Staberton was of opinion we should turn over that care to times less dangerous. But the meeting of so many honest gentlemen seemed to me to be an opportunity difficult to recover. I proposed to disperse ourselves about the neighbouring villages, from whence we might easily meet at the wood.

wood every night. Each of us succeſſively might take the charge of hiring one carr in the village where he was retired to, and to bring it in the morning at ſome diſtance from the wood. We might draw the caſkets out of the cave without other aid than our own hands, and carry them to each carr, and perſuade the carman they came from the neighbouring caſtle. Two gentlemen were ſufficient to conduct them alſo one after another to places of ſecurity. My friends came into my opinion, that they ſhould be depoſited in different houſes; and in theſe times, when zeal had ſtrictly united the king's faithful ſubjects together, it would not be difficult to find inviolable privacies for what was intended for his ſervice.

This ſcheme ſucceeded ſo luckily, that without meeting the leaſt obſtacle during eight days, I was at length maſter of all the riches of the cave. The ſums in ſpecie, which the king had commiſſioned us to employ in the execution of his orders, were tranſported to Dublin. Staberton, who had already provided a houſe for Patrick, depoſited them there himſelf in a cloſet, of which he kept the key. I obſerved to him, that after my misfortune of falling under the miſtruſt of the viceroy, there was no doubt but Patrick was watched in his turn. He came into my opinion; but nevertheleſs, the reſolution my brother in appearance had taken of ſettling in Ireland, beſides his having all his eſtate there, the little noiſe he had made at the court of St Germain, notwithſtanding all the favours the king had heaped on him, becauſe having been ſecretly enough ſent to Spain, during all the time he had not been employed on his private affairs, he had ſcarce appeared four times in the preſence of that prince; in fine, the ſweetneſs and agreeableneſs of his humour, which might make him be thought cut out rather for pleaſures than toilſome enterprizes; all theſe reaſons, that had been already weighed in France by the king and Patrick himſelf, made us hope that he would be leſs ſubject to ſuſpicion than I. In reality, arriving a few days after,

after, he waited on the viceroy, and all other persons of rank in Dublin, with so free an air, that they there looked on his return as the effect of a prudent resolution, which made him prefer the enjoyment of his estate in his own country to the barren honour of serving a dethroned king. The splendour with which he furnished and adorned his house made them further judge, that he had no politic designs in view; because the application they saw him make of his wealth this way, did not leave them room to suppose he had much remaining for other uses.

It is not my design to enter into a detail of the services he did the king during the rest of the winter, and to the end of the following campaign. Having spent some days in regulating with him such parts of our enterprize, as were in common between us, I thought of nothing but stealing as privately out of Dublin, as I had lived there since the removal of the treasure; and I had the precaution, in order to leave nothing to chance, to take with me my lord Linch's servant, whose indiscretion I feared during my absence. We made the tour of one part of Ireland, and had the satisfaction of finding there an infinite number of loyal subjects, who panted after the king's restoration. My employment in every town, and even in the meanest villages, when I applied to any one whose mind and behaviour inspired me with confidence, was not only to inform myself what assistance was to be expected from the place, in the cause we had to defend, but to take down in writing under fictitious names, in aid of my curiosity and the weakness of my memory, the age, qualities, degree of zeal, and the names of the principal inhabitants, whose fidelity I had gained assurance of. I did not hesitate to assemble them together, when I thought I could do it without danger. I laid before them the king's hopes, and the advantage they might be to his service. I made no distinction in my exhortations between the interests of the catholic religion, and that of the prince, who was the

defender

defender of it. My zeal did not draw upon me any mischievous incidents; and those who recommended me to their correspondents from town to town, were not deceived in the opinion they had of their fidelity. Nevertheless, a mistake, with which I can reproach no body, exposed me to a more dangerous accident, than I had to fear in the execution of my whole commission.

I left T—— in order to go to V—— charged with many letters of credence to procure me in that capital of the province of—— the same security and reception I had met with in the precedent places: such of my letters, as I thought necessary to make use of, being addressed to a catholic merchant of the town, whose riches and credit were celebrated through the whole province, I shewed to the first person I met, in order that he might direct me the way to Mr Filtely's which was the merchant's name; but there was in that town a counsellor of the same name, as opposite to the king's interest and to the catholic religion, as the other was attached to both; a man, moreover, extremely hurried away by his opinions, and capable of the greatest excess to make the best of his principles. Heaven, who was pleased to raise such opportunities for my labouring in its glory, as I did not conceive conformable enough to my zeal, permitted my guide to conduct me to Filtely the counsellor, instead of Filtely the merchant. Having no suspicion, I presented my letter to him, who, far from informing me of the mistake after he had read it, pretended to treat me with all the respect and friendship that I had been accustomed to receive from the catholics. But he had scarce shewed me the way into an apartment, which he pressed me to enter, to recover myself from the fatigue of my journey, than, not being longer able to moderate his hatred against an emissary of the church of Rome and St Germain, he declared to me, that I was fallen into the hands of my enemies, and that instead of a good reception, I had nothing to expect but punishment. But this shall not be,

be, added he, till you have made a confeſſion of your
deſigns, which without doubt are intended both
againſt my religion and country. He did not give
me time to get out of my amazement to anſwer him.
Having locked the door on me with great care, and
leaving me under the guard of his ſervants, he went
abroad himſelf, in order to prepare to have me carried
before a magiſtrate. Whatever obſcurity appeared to
me to be in this event, I could no longer doubt but I
was betrayed. The important memorandums I had
about me were the ſubject of my firſt fears. Notwithſtanding the pains I had taken to diſguiſe the names, a
hundred methods might be found out to diſcover them,
by the facility they had of going after me on the
track, and comparing from town to town the
circumſtances of times and places with my obſervations. The danger of my life alarming me much
leſs than this thought, I reſolved to take advantage
of all ſorts of riſques in that moment of my being
alone, and of the liberty he left me of ſecuring ſo
many precious intereſts. I had luckily about me the
moſt important of my papers. I had reſolved to
ſwallow them in bits, when caſting my eyes round on
every ſide of the chamber, I diſcovered a private
door, which did not ſeem thick enough to reſiſt my
efforts. I opened it as eaſily as I hoped; but finding
only a ladder faſtened at the foot, I was afraid of
rendering my flight more difficult by mounting to the
ſummit of the houſe, which was the only way it
led to; but as no other remedy offered, I followed this
feeble ray of hope.

The ladder led me indeed to the roof of the houſe,
where the difficulty of eſcaping ſeemed much to in-
creaſe. But nothing appearing to me ſo terrible as to
return back, I abandoned the care of my life to
providence, and expoſed myſelf to the danger of falling a thouſand times from ſo high a place, by deſiring
to get to the neighbouring houſe by the communication of roofs. A reſolution ſo hardy baniſhed from
me all fear, which might have ſtaggered me by looking

long

long on the danger. I not only gained the neighbouring roof, but, being become rash by my success, I ventured to go further, thinking only that I could not get far enough from the counsellor's house. It was heaven itself that inspired me, as it was heaven that without doubt watched over the preservation of my life in so strange an enterprise. I got also (by a way I never could be suspected to have chosen) upon the third roof, from whence the descent seemed so easy to a garret window, that I did not scruple to stop at this point. I got without difficulty into the garret, and finding no body in it, I immediately thanked heaven for having afforded me so visible a protection.

Having rejoiced nevertheless for escaping so many dangers, I did not know whether I ought not to tremble yet at those that were to come. The garret door was open, and I could not in the least hesitate in following the stairs that led me down. But where would they lead me, and into what hands was I going to fall? I went down by chance, and had scarce taken four steps, when I saw a woman dissolved in tears, and so filled with the subject of her grief, that without appearing to be struck at the sight of me, she went into a room at the foot of the stairs. Distracted and afflicted as she was, I thought her from that cause more proper to receive me without mistrust or fear. I appeared before her door, and seeing her all in tears, I turned my words in a manner capable of moving her in my favour, by the resemblance that my misfortunes bore to her's.

She began to look on me more attentively, and her tears seemed to stop by the impression my presence made on her, when a sudden noise giving her fresh alarms, she left me without speaking one word, and without seeming even embarrased at my staying in the chamber after her. I made no haste to follow her, but reflecting on so whimsical an adventure, I cast my eyes upon some letters which lay scattered upon a table, and was surprised beyond all expression to find them in the hand-writing of my lord Tenermill.

What

What enchantment! said I to myself, and who will aid me to comprehend an adventure so extraordinary? I did not think myself bound by the ordinary duties of good manners and discretion, in circumstances of this nature, and especially in regard to letters. I laid hold of some of them, which I read over hastily; and my astonishment much increased in finding them all to be letters of love; they were without direction, and without date. Whatever difficulty I might find in this mystery, I lost half my fears as to my own security, and I thought my danger at an end in a house where my brother was known. My boldness increased, even so far as to make me find no difficulty in looking after the lady who had just escaped me. Whether love had a part in her tears, or whether they proceeded from some more violent passion, I fancied she would find a pleasure in knowing me, and explaining to me the cause of her troubles.

Building upon this notion, I went down to the first door I found open, and did not scruple to go in. The sight of me could not strike so sharply the person who looked on me, as I was moved in knowing Anglesey; and the furious air, in which I saw him, adding a quick fear to my surprise, I remained for some moments without the power of advancing a step further. Recovering however, soon, he had not the same perplexity in taking immediately his resolution. Ah! Is it you, said he, fetching his breath, as if even his astonishment had given him some relief. Come near, come near, said he, you can help without doubt to clear up a secret, that touches you as near as it does me. I had not known the younger of his two sisters as easily as I had him. She stood nevertheless opposite to him, in so mortified a posture, that I easily remarked she was the cause of his troubles, and that she thought herself perhaps threatened with some effects of his fury. The woman, whom I met on the stairs, was her chamber-maid, who continued to testify by her tears, that she apprehended something terrible for her mistress and herself.

Encouraged

Encouraged at length by the invitation of Anglefey, I came up to him. Without lofing any thing of his warmth, he told me, that Tenermill being reconciled to him after his laſt journey to Ireland, ſeemed to have a particular fondneſs for his ſiſter. Though this inclination, added he, agreed ill with his pretenſions to Sarah Fincer, whoſe hand he had confeſſed to me he had the hopes of obtaining, yet I was not ſurpriſed, that an officer, fatigued with his military expeditions, ſhould ſeek ſometimes for amuſement in the company of an amiable young lady. His quarters not being far diſtant from my houſe, I freely ſuffered him to come privately, and paſs with us ſome intervals of repoſe, which he could ſpare from his duty. He went away at the end of the campaign, and I thought his amours finiſhed, when his reſidence in Ireland was ſo.

In the mean time, added Angleſey, having obſerved after his departure, that this virtuous lady ſhewed extraordinary uneaſineſs, I was ſurpriſed one morning to find ſhe diſappeared in the night, without any other company than her chamber-maid; and not having given any notice of her deſign, I imagined all at once, that her enterpriſe was not a matter of prudence. I in vain went in ſearch of her for many days; at length I diſcovered here her retreat, though this town be twenty leagues from my houſe; and immediately following her, I ſurpriſed her to-day in the place you ſee her. She has hired this houſe for ſix months. It is only by force of menaces that I have got out of her a confeſſion of her ſhame. She baſely abandoned herſelf to your brother, who has forſaken her with the fruits of his perfidious amours. It belongs to you, added he, whom I find in this place, without diſcovering what brought you here, to decide her fate: For ſhe ſhall periſh this day by my hands, if you inform me that my lord Tenermill has no thoughts of marrying her.

I have preſſed her to declare, ſtill proceeded he, if ſhe were ſeduced under the ſhadow at leaſt of

ſome

some promises. She speaks to me of his letters, which I will read in your presence. Where are they? interrupted he himself, looking furiously on the chamber-maid. This wench, who had gone up only to bring them, and who upon hearing the noise increase, had as soon come down, being fearful lest he should be transported to some excess against her mistress, went off immediately for them.

During this time, from every thing I had heard I was at such a stand, that not daring to venture even at the least answer, I waited with great impatience till the letters were produced. Such as I had read, were only common protestations of love, in which I observed no proposal of marriage. Moreover I had a thorough knowledge of Tenermill. If he were capable of having looked on the debauching of a young lady as a joke, he was not a man that would deceive her by false promises; and with the hopes he had moreover to marry Sarah Fincer, I could not be persuaded that he had made Anglesey's sister any other promises than those of love, of which she herself ought to have discovered the illusion. The reading of the letters, which was not deferred a moment, confirmed me in this notion. Nevertheless, not believing from thence that my brother was less obliged to repair the honour of a young lady of quality, whose ruin he had to reproach himself with, I made no difficulty of agreeing, that I looked on this obligation as an indispensible duty, and of promising that I would press him to comply with it. These words, and the exhortations I added to them to inspire Anglesey with more gentleness, restored him a little to a calmness of mind; and his sister got up from his feet, to cast herself at mine with transports of joy and gratitude.

The reliance he had on my promise restored him so far to tranquillity as to inquire what strange chance had brought me to V——, and into the house of his sister. I had not so much difficulty to inform him of the truth of my adventure, as he he had to believe it seriously. However, having considered with me what might be the consequences of it, he agreed, that they were dangerous enough to have inspired me with all the fear that had induced me to such extraordinary resolutions. Without making a profession of an open adherence to the king's party, he desired his restoration, provided that when he favoured his interest it was not acting against his inclination; and the service he expected from me engaged him moreover not to refuse me his assistance. He proposed himself to take his coach, and carry me out of the way without being taken notice of. I should have little regreted my horse and luggage, which I was obliged to leave behind me; but Anglesey gave me yet room to hope, that by re-demanding them himself of the counsellor, he might have them delivered to him with so much the more ease, as I had assured him I had left nothing in my valise that could betray the secret of my commission. Being a native of Ireland, my zeal for the catholicks of that country, and even my quality of bishop, which were the only discoveries the counsellor could make by my letter, did not expose me at all to the rigour of many new laws, which related only to foreign missionaries. My gratitude for the assistance Anglesy offered me with so good a grace inspired me with the intention of rendering to his sister that service which agreed best with her situation. As there was little appearance, that after having been so unluckily discovered, I could much longer execute my commission without falling at least into some new snare, which might be as prejudicial to the king's cause, as to the safety of my own life, I proposed to return to Dublin the shortest way, and to wait there privately the king's orders, to whom I would give an account of the truth of my adventure. Under the hope I am, said I to Anglesey, of engaging Tenermill to act as becomes him to your sister, I believe I may offer you for her a private retreat in Patrick's house, who is come a little while past

past to settle in Ireland. If you lend me your coach, I will take charge of her to Dublin, and I do not despair even of carrying her to France, as soon as I have prepossessed Tenermill of the obligation he lies under to repair his fault. He embraced me with great gratitude; and his sister, yet further moved than he by my offers, did not forbear to shew me hers, by the most affectionate acknowledgments.

Having with me Jacin and the old servant of my lord Linch, I had been lucky enough to send them to an inn before I went to the counsellor's; and this was a custom I followed in all my journeys, that I might not be troublesome to those who entertained me. It was easy to give them both notice to go out of the town, and wait for me on the road I was to take. I went immediately into Anglesey's coach with his sister and chamber-maid, being persuaded, that if the counsellor should search for me, he would make his inquiries among the catholick houses of the town, or at least in any other place than on the high road to Dublin. I made all the haste could be expected from the carriage I was in; and Patrick was under an extreme surprise to see me return so soon to his house, contrary to his expectations and mine.

I found him so well established in the minds of the people, and already so much considered by the viceroy and all the nobility, that as to the designs the king had communicated to me, it appeared demonstrable, that his majesty could not have made a better choice. But I had not perceived in my journey, that the number of his partizans was so considerable as he had fancied at St Germain, nor that they were filled with that ardour on which he relied so much for the next campaign. I made this observation to Patrick, who had already remarked the same thing in Dublin. If king James had a number of subjects well intentioned enough to wish ardently for his return, he had but few whose zeal was capable of making them expose their lives or fortunes in his quarrel.

quarrel. On the contrary, having nothing more dear and precious to defire than the converfation and fecurity of thofe two advantages, they feemed to be much better affured of them under the new government; and the intereft of religion being then the only confideration capable of warning them, even this motive could not infpire them with all the fpirit the king defired, as long at leaft as the prince of Orange fhewed himfelf difpofed not to difturb them in their worfhip. The fear of giving offence at the court of St Germain by fuch free accounts, did not hinder me from communicating all my obfervations to the king. He did not fhew that my fincerity had at all offended him; but without giving me an anfwer to the particulars of my reflections, he gave me orders immediately to return to France, under this pretence alone, that my enterprife having been fo unluckily difturbed, he could not doubt but that the government had been well informed of it, and that my refidence in Ireland might bring fome prejudice to my brother's commiſſion.

With whatever devotion I was refolved to facrifice myfelf to the interefts of my religion and king, I found nothing irkfome to me in this change. My zeal could not want an object in France. The more I reflected on the misfortune of mademoifelle Anglefey, the more my inclination increafed to ferve her with Tenermill. Notwithftanding all the hopes he had from his endeavours and underftanding, I faw him the only one of my family who yet wanted an eftablifhment; for I would not willingly give that name to an income he had obtained by gaming. Might not the fame chance, to which he owed a fortune fo unworthy of us, deprive him of it by the fame ways? In truth, fhe could not be a match very advantageous for him, being the younger fifter of a family lefs rich than noble, who could bring him only hopes at a great diftance. But befides the obligation of honour, with which I did not think

think' he could easily dispense, I much flattered myself that (by making the marriage agreeable to the king) I could engage his majesty to resume all the views he formerly had for the advancement of my brother. Without being in a condition to enrich his servants, he had a thousand ways to employ them in a manner advantageous for their fortunes; (witness the example of Patrick;) and I did not doubt but the desire of attaching to him all the house of Anglesey would induce him, as much as his inclination for ours, to signalize his bounty by new favours.

In the mean time other reflections made me change the thoughts I had taken up of prepossessing Tenermill with my design. Although I did not think him capable of disowning his engagements with mademoiselle Anglesey, I imagined nevertheless that having never proposed any thing by it but an amusement, he would immediately reject a marriage, that he must look upon as an obstacle to all his pretensions; and his refusal of it once during his absence would perhaps oblige mademoiselle Anglesey to remain in Ireland. Instead of which, her passing into France in my company, without giving him any notice of it, and surprising him in some sort before he had time to think of defending himself, she might hope, that her presence and tears might soften a heart which had made no preparations for resistance. We went off together, having first imparted our views to her brother. He proposed to go with us; but I was afraid of too sharp expostulations, and too violent instances from a man so fiery, who would have the honour of his family to support; and I conjured him to repose his interests upon the integrity of my intentions.

To return to St Germain with some agreeable fruits of my journey, it would have been necessary to have found means of transporting thither a part of Linch's treasure; but this would have been risquing too much, at a time that the approach of a bloody campaign made the government redouble their vigilance in all the ports. We had difficulty enough

to

to escape ourselves, without giving any other cause of suspicion, that might be prejudicial to my brother. Heaven took care to conduct us through a thousand dangers; and not being able to gain France but by making many long circuits, our delay made my friends, who had been advertised of my departure, fear, that some very unlucky accident had happened to me on the road. As an addition to my embarrasment, mademoiselle Anglesey, who was far advanced in her pregnancy, was surprised with her first pains in Flanders, (for it was by that way I was forced to return) and the indispensible care I had for her retarded our arrival six weeks more.

I give the name of embarrasment to this last unseasonable accident, because I could not look upon it but as a subject of vexation. Notwithstanding the ardour with which I had embraced the interest of mademoiselle Anglesey, and even the persuasion that induced me to make it an indispensible duty, I was sometimes scared by the indecency of being seen with her in her situation, and I apprehended that she would be looked upon in the same ridiculous light as I. What appearance was there of presenting her in this condition, whether at court, where I could willingly have fortified her pretensions by the king's authority, or whether to Tenermill himself, who not having yet heard any thing of the consequences of his amour, might be rather disgusted than softened by such a sight? Not that mademoiselle Anglesey wanted any of those allurements that are natural to her sex. I have already made an encomium on her charms; and the opportunity I had of diving into her character, gave me room to discover in it merit enough to make amends for a transient slip, which did not lessen her natural principles of modesty and virtue. But I was delighted to see her after lying-in resume that air of decorum suitable to a young lady, and which I thought had been extremely impaired by her big belly.

The end of my journey inspiring me thus with more hope and joy, than I had felt since my departure, I communicated my thoughts to her, by tracing over before-hand the plan I had formed for hastening her marriage. Tenermill, said I, shall have no notice of our arrival but by our visit. I will prepossess the king with your adventure, and will interest his religion and goodness to afford you his protection. Of the many friends I know my brother has, I will intreat such, whose weight is capable of making an impression on his mind, to be with him the moment of our visit, to back your prayers by their solicitations and advice. I will procure an officer of the king to go with us, whom I will intreat his majesty to charge with his recommendation, or even commands, if it be possible to obtain them; and I doubt not but by this mixture of supplications, advices and authority, we shall in an instant force our way through all obstacles, that Tenermill can possibly think to oppose to us.

I said nothing to her but what I was persuaded of myself. In an affair of this nature, wherein humanity and religion make the foundation of our rights, I could not imagine that the principles of many of my brother's friends, who were known to be men of honour, were different from mine; and I already had cast my eyes upon those whom I thought most proper to do us the service I expected from them. Being arrived at Paris, I thought it seasonable to prepossess some of them with this business before I went to St Germain. But having began with him, upon whom I relied the most, how great was my astonishment to hear him resist all my proposals? He was an old general officer, who had passed through all the military preferments, and who had in the world the reputation of being irreproachable in his honour. Having heard me with great attention; Was this debauching, asked he, supported by any promises? I answered, that mademoiselle Anglesey did not lay a stress upon any. Ah! replied

plied he laughing, who has not had in the course of his life twenty adventures of this sort? Honour does not oblige one to observe what one does not promise. Women would be too happy, if, by forgetting their duty, they could acquire a right over our liberty and fortune. Ah! Where is the man of gallantry, that would not be exposed to ruin himself by a mischievous marriage? No, no, added he, I shall never advise your brother to make good a simple piece of gallantry, by the sacrifice of his fortune, and perhaps his happiness.

So formal a refusal taking from me all hopes on that side, I was vexed for having addressed myself to a military man, whom I ought to suppose much less knowing in certain duties, or more indulgent than others to this sort of disorder, which the world honours with the name of gallantry. I knew Tenermill had another friend, whose sentiments I hoped would better correspond with my expectations. This was a financer, extremely rich, but one whose riches did not take from him the name of an honest, nor even of a good-natured and generous man. I laid the fact before him, and intreated him, as I did the other, to join with me to prevail over the mind of Tenermill. He looked on me with a nice and sensual air; I am not at all surprised, said he, that an ecclesiastic of your age and piety should refer every thing to the severe maxims of the gospel; but it would be hard to expect so much strictness from laymen, such as we are. You do not consider well to what you would reduce us, if you would oblige us to marry a woman, because we have taken for her a slight and transient inclination. Ah! what advantage would it be to us, that nature has made so great a number of them? She was willing to afford us the means of making trials to chuse the better: moreover, added he in a serious tone, I think we ought always to make a just destinction between objects of pleasure and those of duty. If my lord

lord Tenermill had found in the choice you proposed to him every thing suitable to his fortune and happiness, and that by a forgetfulness of his interests, he was stiff and obstinate in rejecting it, I should undertake perhaps to make him open his eyes upon what he owed to himself: But as this cannot be supposed to be the case without a contradiction, I will not endeavour to incline him to a marriage, from which on the contrary his refusal or coldness should make me judge that he has few advantages to gather.

Such plain language persuaded me that my applications were yet but indifferent. I called to mind the judgment the gospel gives of the rich men of the world, and I was much less surprised to find this opposition to these maxims in him whom I had consulted, than to have forgot myself, how uncommon it is for the spirit of religion to agree with riches. But as those two errors I had successively fallen into were no reasons for making me give over my project, I recollected the name of a third friend of Tenermill, whose rigorous probity I had heard himself boast of. Such ought to be the lot of all of his profession; for he was a man of the robe, of a distinguished character. I had greater hopes of success in applying to him, which his gravity in hearing me yet further increased. When I had ended, he paused for some moments, as if he had considered the case in all its circumstances. At length he asked me, if there had been a formal contract under my brother's hand. Having answered him, that there was not, but that it was no less true, he interrupted me in haste—Have you any thing to found a proof on by writing? No, said I again, and the damsel confesses herself, that she has nothing but some tender letters to build upon in her favour. Ah! replied he, without seeming attentive to the impression his answer would make on me, cast away your fears, that she can ever force my lord to marry her; and take you care how you advise your brother to a match, which can never be

of

of any advantage to him. In the rigour of the law, he will be acquitted for some damages, which will bear a less proportion to the birth of your Irish lady, than to her weakness in forgetting her duty.

My astonishment was so great after this third decision, that having neither power nor will to reply, I chose to retire without speaking one word. What strange consent and agreement, said I to myself, in all ranks and conditions of men, to wound openly the most sacred law of nature and religion? How? Must there be promises to a woman, must they be in writing, to oblige a man to marry her after having drawn her into a precipice, from whence she cannot possibly disengage herself but by marriage? Do not then the very attempts to debauch her amount to so many promises, and is not the meaning of them clear and manifest to both sexes? The weakness of a woman in surrendering, and the pleasure a man finds in vanquishing, are not they in a manner the seal that ought to confirm them? Is it before the eyes of men, that proofs must be here produced, and must the principles of fidelity and good faith depend on their opinions? But I came to myself by thinking, that a grave magistrate might fail in his attention to the plain duties of morality, from an excess of attachment to the objects of his profession. It is the fault of the greatest part of men to refer every thing to the knowledge of those particulars that they are most employed about. Without being yet discouraged by these three experiments so opposite to my expectations, I resolved to make a new one upon the mind of an honest citizen, whom I knew to be well affected to my brother, and who had even acquired some ascendant over him by many important services. I shall have nothing to fear here, said I, neither from the false customs of the world, nor from the corruption of riches, nor from the prejudices of study and learning. The citizen, to whom I went immediately, seemed at first well pleased at the confidence I put in him: But having listened to my proposals—I shall not, said

said he roughly enough, make so bad a use of the little power I have over my lord's mind. This is the way infallibly to draw on me his hatred, when he shall come to be sensible of the injury I shall have done him by my advice. And, added he, to lay open to you all my thoughts at once, I do not pity, so much as you do, a young lady who has forgot herself so far as to throw behind her back the care of her honour. To what should we be exposed in our families, if they were assured of repairing immediately their faults by a good marriage: We must abandon the guilty to their infamy, to frighten, by their example, those who should be tempted to imitate them.

Without examining his manner of reasoning, the fallacy of which was besides manifest, since the question only turned on the duty of Tenermill, and that the fault of mademoiselle Anglesey did not in the least diminish the obligation he was under to repair his, I observed that I had little assistance to expect from other friends of Tenermill, since I could obtain none from those I had pitched upon out of choice. Not being able nevertheless to persuade myself that my opinion was false, nor that I was the only man in the world that had thought justly upon a point so material, I admired the care my brother had taken, in chusing, for his best friends, those whose principles appeared to me so conformable to his own; and I pitied them all in a lump for neglecting the precepts of religion, even so as not to make any use of them in their manner of reasoning and advice. There remained another conclusion for me to draw from the ill success of my hopes, which was, that for the same reason I ought to be apprehensive of finding much more resistance from Tenermill; and, seeing nothing more powerful to move him than the methods that had failed me, I was in danger, as the reward of my zeal, to have on my hands the charge of a young lady and her infant, for whom there remained no other resource than my compassion. Nevertheless, I yet flattered myself with some aid from the king's authority;

rity; and though Tenermill had taken the resolution of forsaking the court, in order to pass a life more free and independent, yet I could not imagine, he had shaken off the yoke of respect and obedience so far as to shut his ears against his master's orders.

Thus, with the same view that had made me avoid seeing my family on my coming to Paris, I went to St Germain without giving any body the least notice of my arrival. Having given the king an account of all the circumstances of my journey, I had nothing so urgent on me as to put into his majesty's hands the cause of mademoiselle Anglesey; and concealing from him neither my fears nor the reasons of them, I interested him in favour of an unfortunate young lady, by such motives as might make an impression on a religious prince. He was more moved by it, than the friends of Tenermill had been. But not having seen him at court since he formerly left it, he shewed some mistrust of his attachment and submission. I know not, said that prince, what kind of life he has cut out for himself in a sort of retreat, wherein I apprehend he confines himself to the society of some women, and a small number of friends. He had won something by gaming; he has lost much more during your absence, and not having any substance more than the pension I continued to him, I cannot conceive by what methods he maintains at his house that plenty, and those pleasures, of which I have had a description made me. I am sorry, added the king, that a man whom I esteem, and who might qualify himself for the greatest things, should corrupt himself with luxury and idleness.

All these objections not being capable of discouraging me, I redoubled my instances to procure from the king at least a recommendation, shewing the desire he had to see mademoiselle Anglesey speedily settled in her rights. He consented to this request; but it was after I had given him a taste of the dispositions of Tenermill, in order to regulate the tenor

tenor of his orders upon the difficulties I should find in succeeding.

I thought myself so fortified with these hopes, that returning in haste to Paris, I did not scruple to intreat the count and countess of S―― to receive mademoiselle Anglesey in their house, as a young person, who one day or other might have a relation to our family by her marriage with my brother. I nevertheless recommended to them secrecy upon a project which yet required some contrivance on the king's part as well as Tenermill's. But having received my compliment, and the thanks of mademoiselle Anglesey with their usual politeness, the count expressed some earnestness to have a private conversation with me. I judged by his uneasiness, that he had some important overture to make me, and without waiting in reality till I laid the matter before him— Is it, said he, with the concurrence and consent of my lord Tenermill, that you have had it in your thoughts to marry him? A question so much to the purpose, to which I could make no answer, without entering into a long detail, made me chuse to ask the count what difficulties he found in this marriage? You are ignorant, replied he, what changes have happened during your absence; and engaging me in a detail capable of surprising me, he said, that my brother had made an open profession of renouncing all hopes of establishment and fortune, by his discontents, which he took no pains to conceal, and that being engaged in a strict familiarity with Donna Figuerrez, they had formed together a society, which perhaps was without example. They had both gloried in being without love, as well as without ambition, and to have no relish but for a certain number of amusements, which they spared no cost to procure. They had furnished without ostentation, yet with the greatest elegance, a house in town, and that of Saifons, which served them as a country seat. Their expences had been supported in common, and though they had affected to cut off all air of love

from

from their intercourse, they had been seldom asunder, their pleasures being all the same, which consisted in good cheer, music, reading, gaming, and associating together five or six persons of both sexes, whose humour and wit were alike, they had affected to despise the world, with which they pretended to be unacquainted. The Spanish ambassador, astonished at the choice he saw his niece embrace, had taken much pains to prevail on her to forsake such strange notions; but had not been able to overcome her resolution.

This life had continued some months with all the pleasure they had proposed from it; but Tenermill, naturally liberal and generous, not having justly enough calculated to what his expences might amount, found himself so shortened, that he had been forced to think of other resources. Gaming, which had been at first so favourable to him, had not continued with the same good fortune. Having played high, he had suffered such considerable losses, that to pay off many debts of honour, he had quite exhausted his annual income. This misfortune would have laid him under an absolute necessity of breaking off his project, if Donna Figuerrez, to whom he had been constrained to make a confession of the perplexity of his affairs, had not applied herself with the like generosity to repair his losses. Hitherto he had not suffered her to contribute much to the expences of their settlement; but not finding any great difference between the necessity of breaking off, and that of consenting to her entering into the common disbursements, he was overcome by her entreaties. An agreement of this nature became as it were a new tie, which had united them more strictly than ever; and if Tenermill had absented himself from court out of resentment, on the score of ambition, he had also extended his forgetfulness to every thing different from this society, even to avoid seeing his own family.

You

You see, added the count, after finishing this recital, if I have room to doubt whether he be informed of your views, and whether I have not yet more reason to believe, that it will be difficult to bring him to embrace them. The relish for an effeminate life has succeded his former activity. I admire to what pass his humour is changed. This Spaniard besieges him: and whatever sort of engagement he may have with her, I am persuaded you will not succeed in breaking it.

The evil appeared to me as dangerous as to the count; and although the reserve with which he discovered himself had yet hindered me from penetrating into the full extent of it, yet the perils alone attending such a life of sensuality cast me into a sharp alarm. However, I did not from thence see, as he did, such strong reasons to fear that she would be an obstacle to Tenermill's marriage. I had boldly laid hold of the notion, that his engagement with Donna Figuerrez was not that of love; and not conceiving any other cause that could attach him too strongly to her, I had so much the greater hope that the loss of his fortune, and the necessity he was under of taking advantage of that of a woman, without which he could not live in that plenty for which he had taken a relish, appeared to me an infallible motive to separate him from her, when I should make him look upon, together with the hand of mademoiselle Anglesey, the king's new favours, which I did not despair to see him obtain. I left the count with this notion, without having judged it seasonable to communicate to him yet the truth of our adventure. It was not my diffidence of him that engaged me to this dissimulation; but I thought myself obliged to it out of a cautious management for mademoiselle Anglesy.

I learned at my lord Tenermill's house, that he had been at Saisons for some weeks past, enjoying there the early pleasures of the spring, with his usual

usual company. The sight of the hurry they were in at his house in Paris, in making preparation of a thousand things to serve his table and pleasures, gave me all at once an idea of his settlement. I made no delay in going to him. Besides, that decency required this visit of me after a long absence, I had an interest, as well as he, in the seat of Saisons, and I thought myself authorised at all times to examine into the condition it was in. I might pretend to be ignorant of the alterations made there since my departure, and that it was inhabited by such a numerous company. Resting upon this point, I discovered as much surprise upon my arrival there, as if I had not been forestalled by the count's recital. And this pretext was but little different from the truth, since, with the hints I had received, I found yet at every step some subject of astonishment and admiration. The house, the gardens, every thing had taken a new form. Tenermill had few servants whom I knew; insomuch that having met many of them, of whom I inquired where I might find their master, I was to them a sight as new, as the ornaments of the place were to me.

Among some tokens of joy, and a few caresses, Tenermill discovered embarrasment enough to convince me, that he was under some constraint at my presence. I was shewed into his closet, where by chance he was gone upon some business. I did not lose the opportunity I came in search of. Instead of giving him answers to his first questions, by which he thought perhaps to rid himself from mine, I prayed him to hear me upon a subject important enough to merit his whole attention; and without going about the bush, speaking to him of the condition he had left Anglesey's sister in, I asked him what he thought of the misfortune of a youg lady so amiable and well born. A discourse so little expected, and the steady and serious air with which I accompanied it (for I dare not call it a remorse

for

for a fault which he then called to mind) threw him into a confusion, which declared itself for some moments by his blushes. However, this disorder continued but a short time, since, immediately turning the matter into a banter, he spoke to me of this adventure, as of an amusement, from whence, said he, he had no thoughts that the effect would have been the production of a new being. I stopped him: Do you know, said I, that with this effect, which nevertheless you ought to expect, another ought to be produced, which I am vexed not to see brought to pass as soon as I could wish? and remarking, that this question made him more attentive, I spoke to him with resolution of the pretensions of mademoiselle Anglesey, and even of the hopes she had of turning them to account. He stopped me in his turn, and seeming sensible of every thing that I had only expressed by halves, he assumed a more serious tone, to defend himself. His reasons were those I had already commiserated in the mouths of his four friends. He was engaged by no promises; he thought of nothing but amusing himself in Ireland; Could any one pretend that the weakness of a girl could give her power over the fortune and liberty of a man? Strange arguments, which always presumes the fault to be only on the side of the weakest sex, and that there is no reparation necessary in these sort of adventures from him whom the world is pleased to call the glory and ornament of a woman! It was not nevertheless upon Tenermill that I was in hopes of making impressions by other trials. It did not even come into my mind to make the experiment. I had executed the king's orders in assuring myself of Tenermill's dispositions, and if I added any thing, it was only to make him unfold them more clearly by force of objections and instances.

He fortified himself in such a manner against his first confusion, that pressing me at length not to trouble him longer with proposals that fatigued him, he
passed

passed suddenly to ask me news of Patrick and Ireland. I satisfied him plainly, and taking a cold leave of him, returned to Paris, notwithstanding his persuasions to keep me with him at Saisons for some days. It would have been but little agreeable to me to engage in a society, such as his was represented to me to be. Though I had not intirely entered into the sense of the count's expressions, I did not fancy there could be much innocence and prudence in a retreat, wherein they had nothing but pleasure for their object. My design, upon my return to Paris, was to take mademoiselle Anglesey and present her to the king, whom I yet hoped to engage more powerfully in her interest, after his majesty had seen her. Her form and her tears in reality touched him so much as to make him take a resolution to send one of his gentlemen immediately to Saisons. The king interpreted the refusal of Tenermill more favourably than I did. Seeing nothing was wanting in mademoiselle Anglesey to please him, and imagining in reason that she must have been agreeable to him, since she had drawn on her his attentions, he was convinced that the only reason which could inspire him with a repugnance to marry her, was her poverty; and without having him told what his views were in proposing to him to receive her hand, he charged his gentlemen to assure him, as from himself, that he would find his advantages in submission. But opening his mind further to me, he told me, that without having any thoughts of making him a duke, until he was rich enough to sustain that dignity, he would in favour of his marriage grant him an employment, that should enrich him by ways very speedy. You may inform him, said he, that I have declared my mind to you upon the matter, and engage to him my word, that I shall reckon his obedience in the rank of his services.

With the piety that animated all his actions, the king had a motive for his proceedings that I was a stranger to. Anglesey, not daring to promise himself the full effects of every thing I had given him

room

room to hope from my good offices, had writ to
the king from Ireland, supplicating his royal protection for his sister; and in an affair wherein the
honour of his family was concerned, he made no
difficulty to promise his majesty, that to shew him
his acknowledgment and gratitude, he would by
himself and his friends before the end of the campaign, bring over all the province of Munster to his
authority. The submission of this part of Ireland
was of great importance, as much for the facility
of landing his forces, as for the quarters of his
troops, who might there pass the winter in security.
Moreover, it was of no small consequence to engage
openly in his interests a family so numerous and so
considerable as that of Anglesey. Without penetrating so far, I had myself made this last reflection to
the king, and if he did not confess that it was capable of warming him, I no less remarked, that it had
increased his heat and zeal. I had soon other proofs
of this from the eagerness he shewed upon the return
of the gentleman, whom he had dispatched to my
brother. Being informed, that Tenermill had received his orders with all the respect due to the name
of his master, and that notwithstanding the address
whereby he had avoided to engage himself by a positive answer, he yet expressed himself in terms of perfect submission, he pressed me to make him another
visit, and to declare to him openly what he was resolved
to do for him. I was afraid, said the king to me with
a freedom worthy of so great a soul, that he would
have taken advantage of my situation to insist upon
his old discontents; but knowing his humour, I
think him disposed to obedience, since he has received my orders with so good a grace. In reality,
divers examples had daily taught this good prince,
that the title of a king is but a slender check to
violent passions, when it is not supported by power;
and the late treason of my lord ——— made him
fear every moment, that he should not find more

loyalty

loyalty in the greatest part of those who appeared to be attached to him.

This confidence of my king, and the desire he let me see he had of reclaiming to him the mind of my brother, animated me with so brisk an ardour, that not thinking I could too soon execute his orders, I pressed him in my turn to licence my departure, that I might go directly to Saisons. I imparted all my hopes to mademoiselle Angelesy by an air of satisfaction with which I prayed her to wait for me at Paris. It was night when I arrived at our seat; but I made no distinction of times, and thought every season proper for my negociation. Being informed at my arrival that Tenermill had got up from table, I sent in notice, that I had affairs of importance to communicate to him, and desired to talk to him alone. I was ignorant whether he had already discovered my proposals and the king's orders to Donna Figuerrez; but his slowness in coming to me made me so impatient, that putting my head out of the door of the closet where I waited for him, I saw her with him in the next chamber; and the air of secrecy, as much as the heat with which they appeared engaged in the discussion of some matter of importance, gave me room to think, that my visit was the subject of their discourse.

Tenermill did not appear to me with a countenance less disengaged; I removed also from mine every thing that might look like constraint, and anticipating all useless questions, I told him, that my visit to him was by the king's orders. You have been informed lately, said I, from the mouth of one of his gentlemen of the interest he takes in the marriage of mademoiselle Anglesey: But that explanation had relation only to things in general; I am now here from his majesty, added I, to declare to you more particularly his intentions. With a wife, whom he presses you to receive as from his hand, he promises you an employment that may soon make you rich,

and

and which will one day put you into the condition he is defirous of feeing you, in order to create you a duke.

This entrance into my difcourfe, in which I alfo had included every thing that I had moſt prevailing to offer him, made a greater impreffion on him than I expected from it. He fixed his eyes on me, and not being able for a confiderable time to moderate the affections of his foul—How, faid he, foftening his voice, does the king vouchfafe to return to me, and (far from being offended at my haughtinefs) is he not apprehenfive of abafing himfelf too much, in calling me back to him by new favours? Ah! So much goodnefs will never be repaid but by my blood, which I will empty all in his fervice. His tranfport made me judge, that I had moſt luckily taken him by his two foibles; of which the laſt itfelf had a greater poffeffion of him than he imagined. Thefe were generofity and ambition. But when I was ready to hug myfelf for them, he added, that he was in defpair as to the marriage of mademoifelle Anglefy, for that this method of complying with the king's goodnefs was abfolutely fhut out from him; that without finding in his heart the leaſt repugnance for a lady fo amiable; upon the whole, that though fhe be offered to him by the king with all thofe advantages, yet he had other engagements which he was not at liberty to break, and that the moſt glorious fortune in the world fhould never make him fail in his engagements of honour. Struck with this language, I afked him, with a good deal of aftonifhment, whether he were married? No, anfwered he ingenuoufly; but he put little difference between his engagement and marriage. He feparated from me, and took fome turns about the clofet in a profound meditation, whilſt I confidered with myfelf what anſwer to make him. Then coming up to me, he requefted me to hear him without interruption. I am pierced faid he, with the king's goodnefs, and I doubt not but they raife in you the fame admiration. I have a thoufand ways

left

left to render me worthy of them, and they are not the most easy I would chuse. Nevertheless, forced as I am to reject her whom he daigns to offer me himself, I am sensible that my refusal will expose me not only to his just indignation, but to the censure of all men of honour, if it be not justified by some excuse. At the same time, I do not flatter myself, that I can make you relish my apology, and under the necessity I am nevertheless to employ you in my justification, this difficulty has appeared to me embarrassing enough to throw me into the reverie out of which I am just recovered.

Notwithstanding the promise I had made to hear him without interruption, I thought myself obliged to remove a doubt, which appeared offensive to my friendship. I complained that he thought it justly founded, and conjured him to conceive a better opinion of my affections. No, no, replied he smiling, it is not of your friendship that I have any diffidence; but do not be tired of the silence I require. Then continuing his discourse, he related to me, that since he had lost the desire of espousing Donna Figuerrez by the king's refusal, of consenting to that marriage, or at least annexing to it the favours he had been made to hope for, he had never ceased visiting that lady. He had found from day to day new pleasures in her conversation; and his good fortune had so favoured him, that she being obliged to renounce her inclination for Patrick, had taken for him a share of the affections she had for his brother. He had not been at all sorry for being beloved by her, as long as the proposals of marriage continued in a manner buried; but upon renewing them by the Spanish ambassador at her instance, he did not hesitate to declare to her, that he did not think himself cut out to bear the name of a husband, and that the reasons inducing him to think of marrying her, having ceased by the king's pleasure, he was come to a resolution never more to submit to chains, of which nature was afraid. He had neverthless softened

this

this refusal by some polite compliments, and owning, that he had seen few women whose wit and humour had such a number of charms as her's had, he confessed, that he laboured to inspire her with an intercourse and correspondence established in freedom and independence, by which he sought after a remedy for those sufferings he had just experienced from the court. Gaming had at this interval brought him in sums considerable enough to settle his affairs upon a solid foundation; and the king having forced him to keep his pension, he found himself in a condition of forming a plan, which he had the good luck to make agreeable to Donna Figuerrez. In fine, surprised himself, said he, at the facility he had found to bring her into it, and judging even from thence, that this could not be her first essay of gallantry, he accustomed himself to live with her, and to enjoy a very pleasant situation both in town and country. You will ask me, continued he, what could render such an engagement so inviolable as I have represented it to you! Hear me, for one part of what I have to say to you will appear difficult to comprehend. First, you can never conceive how great is the power of an habitual society between two persons, who have for a long time had only the same house, the same table, the same occupations, the same pleasures, and who, in one word, passing the day and night without quitting each other even a moment, have learned mutually to know their faults, to pass them over, to look on themselves in relation to each other as dispensed from all sorts of decorums and constraints, to speak to each other when they will, and to be silent when they will, not to conceal nevertheless from each other their thoughts, and to place their satisfactions and their troubles in common; it is not interest that links them together since they may live an easy life without the assistance of one another; it is not exactly a relish for the same pleasures, since they do not seek after it in those that are the most

brisk

brisk and poignant, and that the half of their time is spent in discovering the foibles of every thing that carries that name; it is not an inclination for good cheer, for though nothing be wanting to set off their table, they have not the greater appetite for it, and very often rise from thence without touching the best dishes; there is yet even less of love in it, since they see each other without eagerness, are absent from each other without grief, they scarce happen to say to each other a word of kindness or tenderness, that they often avoid those plain respects of complaisance which they would have for the greatest stranger; and if they use only one and the same bed, they commonly lie down and rise up without thinking of those rights which they consented to yield to each other. Nevertheless, you may attempt, if you think it seasonable, to make them renounce living together, you will see they will laugh at all your efforts. In the whole conduct of life they are as necessary to each other, as if they were bound by interest, by pleasure, by good cheer, and by love. I would not speak to you so positively, added he, if I could not add to my example that of a thousand people of worth and honour, who are in the same case at Paris.

He was about proceeding; but I had began to have a misgiving of something, that had not hitherto entered into my mind, and which he seemed to be desirous of concealing from me. I did him wrong by this last suspicion; he never thought but of sparing my delicacy by covering under a sort of veil something that he imagined I could not be ignorant of; and in the principles wherein he was hardened, this proceeded from a respect he had for me, much rather than for himself. However, the simplicity of my heart making me attribute this discovery to my own penetration, I found my blood stirred enough to make me forget the promise I had even renewed not to interrupt him; my first expressions had as little caution and management in them as they well could have in an impulse of surprise mingled with anger and grief. But when he had understood by the terms debauchery and fornication, which had dropped from me, upon what point my warmth and reproaches fell—I had strong expectations, said he smiling, that this conversation would have passed without a storm; but you ought to be cured, at least as I am, of those transports of morality. However it be, added he immediately, in a more serious tone, I will leave you this moment, and renounce speaking to or hearing you, if you do not give me liberty of proceeding to a conclusion without interrupting me. Imperious brother! Haughty and inducible heart! (I could not forbear answering him with the most bitter passion) continue then a discourse which offends and outrages me, and which discovers only too much the riot and debauchery you are in.

He replied, shaking his head with a sneer—I agree that the engagement and ties, of which I tell you, will not appear of equal force to all the world; and it is not to persuade you the more to forward them, that I have laboured to make you comprehend them. My intentions only were, that as you have offered to serve me, you should not be ignorant of any of my dispositions. Two engagements, much more strong, have bound me to Donna Figuèrrez; one of which proceeds from my promises: For if my friendship for her was free in its original, can I think it changed from its nature, since the satisfaction we have mutually found in it has made us take a thousand oaths never to dissolve it? What difference do you put between a life of this sort and that of marriage? For what reason will you not find it as indissoluble as that, if the essence of the other consists of itself in the consent only of the will? Why does it not appear as respectable to you? Is it not the state of nature, which is the first and most holy of all laws.—Forbear, forbear, interrupted I, seeing him grow warm upon a subject that he had an interest in supporting, and lamenting still more his corruptions than

his

his sophisms. He was piqued at the air of compassion to which I affected to confine myself in these two words. I do not demand it but as a favour of you, said he; and, when you please, I will defend this doctrine against all your prepossessions. But you will not disagree at least, but that my promises draw after them some duty, and impose on me some obligation.

Then, as if he had thought this reason not only unanswerable, but sufficient to justify him against the king's instances and mine, he told me, that what remained for him to inform me of, was one of those difficulties of delicacy, of which he did not love to boast, and which of all others he should have most trouble to insist on, because it would oblige him to mortifying confessions of self love. Nevertheless, added he, as his character had placed him above common weaknesses, and that he did not know how to blush at what he thought he might accept without shame, he confessed to me, that Donna Figuerrez acquired over him such rights, to which he could oppose nothing without rendering himself guilty of the greatest ingratitude. In thinking to augment his fortune by gaming, he had ruined it without resource. All his settlement, the expences of which had been till then divided between her and him, would have been at an end by this misfortune, if she had not had the generosity to turn over to him the management and disposition of all her estate. He had been under a necessity of consenting to it at her instances, and since that time their society was not supported but at the expence of this generous lady. With what front could he propose to her to break off a commerce, in which he knew she had placed all her happiness? He was not capable of such a baseness, though it should gain him the empire of the world? and if I would give an account of his motives to the king, he was persuaded they would be approved of by his majesty, and all men of honour.

I made no haste in my answer, that I might leave him

him at liberty to give all the force he desired to his apology. I could so easily have destroyed it, (and I was so fully satisfied, that after he had declared to me his reasons as invincible obstacles, they were reduced to very frivolous arguments) that I began to think myself certain of my victory. I laid no stress on his first article, with which I was even astonished, that he could have busied himself one moment. I contented myself with remarking to him mildly, that he ought to reproach himself with a kind of life, which had been capable of enervating him even so far as to make him reckon such childish reasons for something. I avoided with the same care employing any expressions too harsh to attack a commerce, which I saw manifestly condemned by all my principles. But by whatever exceptions and lenitives he thought to excuse it, I obliged him to agree, that it was contrary to all the common laws of religion, to which he made a profession of being attached; and leading him much further than he had foreseen by his making this confession, I forced him to conclude with me in spite of his teeth, that all the promises, by which he had undertaken to support it, were so many illusions, which could not be seriously alledged. In relation to the gratitude, by which he thought himself indebted to Donna Figuerrez, I did not pretend to oppose it, and I pushed my indulgence so far as to acknowledge that he ought not to seek to excuse himself from it. . But had he not a more honourable method, and a way more worthy of him, than that of increasing this debt from day to day, and laying himself under the necessity of enjoying perpetually the same favours? Conserve, said I, all the esteem you owe to the affections and sentiments of your Spanish lady. Ennoble your own, by endeavouring to render them independent of her's. Will not the fortunate time in future, which is destined to you, open a thousand means to preserve you from ingratitude? and cannot you this day do it by

promising

promising her an eternal friendship? This manner
of answering him produced one part of the effect I
hoped for from it. Though he endeavoured to en-
trench himself under natural right, which he looked
upon, he said, as the rule of a man of honour, and
that he thought himself well defended by this pretext
against the strongest of my objections, he nevertheless
entreated me to suspend for a few days the answer I
intended to give the king, and to assure his majesty
how feelingly he had received the first news of his
goodness. I could not doubt, but that the time he
seemed to take for deliberation would increase the
impression, from whence he could not defend himself,
upon understanding the favours the king had intended
for him. By supposing his love for Donna Figuerrez,
I might perhaps have been apprehensive, that it would
too strongly have combated his ambition: But considerations so weak as those he had offered, could not
inspire me with the same fears.

It was a more unseasonable time than ever for me
to stay at Saisons. I should not have been willing to
expose myself to the sight of Donna Figuerrez, nor
to delay mademoiselle Anglesey the pleasure of hearing, that I began to flatter myself with solid hopes.
In giving her an account of this happy news, I could
not conceal from whence the obstacles proceeded.
She was ignorant of my brother's engagements, and
not ascribing the coldness he shewed for her to any
thing but her unhappiness of being without wealth,
she had hitherto accused him less than she did fortune.
I had admired the moderation of her complaints, and
had a difficulty to conceive, that having loved enough
to be capable of so much weakness, she yet waited for
her fate with a tranquillity that did not discover a
violent passion. But I had scarce informed her that
she had a rival, than assuming another countenance,
and with eyes sparkling with fire, which I never
before observed in her, she let a thousand odious
names escape her, of which I easily comprehended
that she made the application to my brother; and
addressing

addreſſing herſelf to me, I give you thanks for your pains, ſaid ſhe, and ſhall never forget what I owe you; but the moſt inſtant death, and even the certainty of my diſhonour, which I ſhall find more inſupportable than death, ſhall never induce me to marry a man, who has been capable of abandoning me for another woman. Though I could not condemn this noble pride, I repreſented to her, in order to appeaſe her reſentment, that love had but a ſmall ſhare in the infidelity of Tenermill; and that even his repentance was not at a great diſtance, ſince I thought myſelf on the point of breaking all the engagements that ſeemed to ſtand in the way of his duty. Theſe two conſiderations, which ſhe made me explain to her with all their circumſtances, had the power of calming her paſſion; but I ſtill continued fully convinced, that without an abſolute ſacrifice, Tenermill would have a difficulty to ſatisfy her.

I did not make two hours ſtay at Paris; neverthelefs, upon my arrival at St Germain, I found a lacquey of Donna Figuerrez, waiting for me at Mr de Sercine's, who having left Saiſons a quarter of an hour after me, confeſſed, that he had made an extraordinary haſte, to overtake me before I could wait on the king. He had received this order from his miſtreſs, from whom he put a letter into my hands, which he preſſed me to read immediately. It contained but four lines. Before I gave myſelf up to my zeal with ſo much confidence, ſhe exhorted me to remember the death of the three Spaniards, and of the power ſhe had to deſtroy me, and all thoſe who had a ſhare in that tragical event.

Such an unexpected menace froze my blood: I had thought that unhappy adventure was for ever buried; and ſo it was as to the public, and the law itſelf, which was tired of making inquiries and ſearches after it to no purpoſe. But Donna Figuerrez had not forgot the menaces of Patrick. At the firſt news of ſuch a fatal accident, ſhe had the curioſity of interrogating the guard who attended the three Spaniards;
and

and although the caution and difcretion fhe thought
fhe owed to the brothers of my lord Tenermill, had
prevented her from making a noife of her fufpicions,
fhe could not miftake us, by the defcription the guard
gave of us. What a frightful obftacle was this to
my enterprife! Could I be ignorant how far jealoufy
is capable of carrying its furies?

Preffed by the courier, who waited only for my
anfwer to return the way he came, I chofe to make
my letter as fhort and loofe as that I had received.
I writ to Donna Figuerrez, that without fancying I
had entered into the full meaning of her's, I could
affure her of two things equally certain; one, that
I had nothing to reproach myfelf with, in having had
any fhare in the deaths of the three Spaniards; and
the other, that I was not capable of failing in my
refpect and difcretion for her. This did not hinder
me from making my court to the king; but in the
fright I was yet under, I took great care of pro-
voking her to make her advances too brifkly, and
notwithftanding all the murmurs of my zeal, I thought
I owed this facrifice to prudence. Having given him
an account of my brother's fentiments, I humbly
entreated him to fufpend his bounty to him for a
few days, and for divers indifpenfible reafons to
pardon him the delay of throwing himfelf at his
majefty's feet. This excellent prince faw nothing
in this excufe capable of offending him. He imparted to me fome letters from Patrick, which at that
time drew his principal intentions towards Ireland.
The firft operations of the campaign had not anfwered his hopes, and from the expectations of many
enterprifes, which had been prepared in the winter, he
feared that fuch an unfortunate prefage would cool
thofe whom he had commiffioned for the execution
of them. Neverthelefs, he took occafion from his
very embarrafment to talk to me of Tenermill. I
have need, faid he, of a refolute and intelligent man.
Your brother is the character of him I want. If
you think him difpofed to ferve me, added he, lay
before

before him this new motive, how far he may reckon upon my favours. He did not finish what he had to discover to me; but I had no need of any further explanation, nor of any more pressing orders to enter into views so glorious for my brother. I determined to go back immediately, with this difference only, that instead of going to Saisons, my desire of avoiding a meeting with Donna Figuerrez made me chuse to dispatch to him my valet, to propose his meeting me in Paris.

I went to wait for him at his own house; and the haste he made in coming there made me judge, that his impatience was equal to mine. He embraced me with the most free air, and anticipating the interesting news I brought him by a declaration which was no less so, he assured me, that he was resolved to marry mademoiselle Anglesey, to begin by this mark of submission to merit the king's goodness. The joy I felt from it was so great as to make me forget what I had burned to tell him; and filling myself only with hopes and fears, which this protestation raised in me all at once, I asked him with some embarrasment, if he had no more obstacles to fear from Donna Figuerrez. Have no fear, added he, and you need not doubt but I am assured of her consent. I embraced him, in my turn, with transports that I could not moderate; and not in the least imagining that he had any other meaning to give his words than what answered my desires, nor any other notion to take off his resolution, than that of an heroic sacrifice, which he made to religion and his fortune, I used the most lively expressions to demonstrate to him as much esteem as zeal and friendship.

The explication I afterwards gave him of the king's intentions not serving for any other purpose than to redouble his ardour, he proposed to me himself to carry the account of his consent to mademoiselle Anglesey, and engage her to meet him next day at court, to obtain together the king's approbation. Such formal offers did not suffer me to doubt any longer his sincerity.

sincerity. I was not willing to give time for this heat to grow cool, and promising him to be the next morning at the king's levee with mademoiselle Anglesey, I exhorted him to support with glory such noble resolutions. A little more reflection upon circumstances would have made me think it strange, that he had not yet spoke to me of seeing her that very day; and I might have asked him also, when Donna Figuerrez proposed to leave Saisons: But the motions of my joy left me only attention for the matters that had caused me such an agreeable surprise, which however was not equal to what I imparted to mademoiselle Anglesey.

A discovery so plain and so little expected dissipating all her mistrusts, she thanked heaven for her happiness with the most moving expressions, and the delay of a single day seemed to her a torment. It did not enter into her mind, any more than it did into mine, that she had measures to take yet on the part of her rival. We employed ourselves only on the other project, which seemed to us to be the masterwork of our prudence, and of which the success perfectly answered our pains. With an impatience to see Tenermill fixed by the ceremonies of the church, we took the resolution of going that evening to St Germain, and of disposing every thing for the celebration of his marriage, as soon as he should be engaged to it by the step to be taken next morning. We prepossessed the king of our desires, who had the goodness to enter into all our views, and to promise us every assistance that depended upon his authority. Tenermill, faithful to his promise, arrived at Mr de Sercine's at the hour appointed. He shewed a great deal of satisfaction at seeing us there. Without affecting over fond caresses, he treated mademoiselle Anglesey with a consideration that contented her enough, and confirming to her every thing he had said to me the evening before, he immediately offered her his hand to lead her with us to the castle.

Let us no longer suspend the explanation of a mystery, in which the reader perhaps begins to find too much obscurity. Tenermill was seriously resolved to marry mademoiselle Anglesey; but what marriage, and what cruel conditions did he annex to this sacrifice? He had taken all his resolutions in concert with Donna Figuerrez. This lady, to whom he had communicated the arrival and pretensions of mademoiselle Anglesey, had not thought at first that she had much to struggle with to deliver herself from such a troublesome counter mine; and far from beginning with reproaches and complaints, she had affected to shew but little alarm. Nevertheless, when the king's messenger, and the hopes his majesty had ordered to be given my brother, had apppeared to awaken his ambition, she had judged the danger more pressing, and, in the interval of this deputation and my visit, had employed all her address to assure herself of the state she held in his heart, and if under the supposition of his resuming the design of marriage, she might not flatter herself with being preferred to her rival. She had found in the natural integrity of Tenermill wherewith to satisfy readily her doubts. He had declared to her, that he was not capable of changing his dispositions, and that if he should happen to think of marriage, it should be on conditions too difficult to flatter himself with, that in the disfavour he stood, he should ever obtain them. However, the day after these conditions had been proposed to him by my mouth, and he was as much affected by them as I have related, Donna Figuerrez perceived the matter. To the lively inquietudes shewed by her he had answered in the same tone, that he would never sacrifice her to love; but that owing something to his fortune and advancement, he would not engage to resist the king's offers long, if his majesty would keep his word with him; and knowing from herself in what terms she had written to me, he had pressed her in the name of a friendship as firm and as philosophical as what united them,

not

not to oppose herself to the great hopes, for which he thought himself indebted to my pains, by considerations unworthy of them. Such an open declaration, and the knowledge Donna Figuerrez had of his character, had with her the force of a decisive refusal. But not being able to relinquish an engagement, which was become in a manner necessary to her, she had equally improved the rights of her affection, and the power she had of injuring me, to draw from him two promises, to which he had consented with so much the more ease, as they were agreeable enough to his own inclinations: The one, that he would not finish his marriage, without being ascertained of the king's views to his fortune, and without having received indubitable pledges of it from the mouth of that prince; the other, that in giving up this step to ambition, he should not only grant nothing to love, but should accustom mademoiselle Anglesey to content herself to bear his name, and to suffer him, without murmuring, to continue to live in the ordinary exercises of their society. It was after this unaccountable engagement that Tenermill had appeared so determined on his marriage, and that he had made no difficulty of assuring me that Donna Figuerrez would give no opposition to it.

Thus, by conducting mademoiselle Anglesey with so free an air to the castle, his first design was to learn from the king upon what fortune he might depend, and to regulate his offers and engagements upon the surety he should discover in that particular. The king's goodness did not leave him in a state of uncertainty long. He had scarce kissed his hand, and made some excuses for his long absence, and the uselesness he had lived in for the king's service, when his majesty raising him up with the most affectionate air, proposed the views he had formed for him. You shall repair, said he, the sloth with which you reproach yourself; and I am not sorry that, joined to your natural qualities, you have a motive of this nature to animate you in my service. I have

M 4   appointed

appointed for you two employments, which will call for no lefs than the full extent of your wit and courage. One is, intendant general of all the enterprifes tending to re-eftablifh my affairs, and particularly of all the military aids that I expect from catholic princes. The other, which is nearer at hand, and which is only the firft exercife of the other, relates fingly to Ireland. The title is of little importance, and the neceffity of avoiding a noife will hinder me perhaps from creating fuch an officer. But it could not contain any thing too grand to anfwer my views. I give you full power over a thoufand things, the explanation of which I referve to myfelf. This is, added the king, to fhew you a confidence that I fhould not have for you, if I had known any body merit it better.

Such diftinguifhed favours, offered with fo much noblenefs and bounty, would have made Tenermill throw himfelf into the midft of flames. His gratitude and zeal fhone out in a thoufand expreffions full of ardour. The king having interrupted him to fpeak of his marriage, he fubmitted to his whole pleafure without exception. He feemed neverthelefs a little furprifed, when upon his confent alone he heard the order given me to repair to the chapel, to conclude the ceremony there. But he was immediately relieved by the king's promife of carrying his fubmiffions to account, and looking on them as a new engagement to heap more favours on him.

Never had my hand exercifed the ecclefiaftical functions with more fatisfaction to my heart. Mademoifelle Anglefey was a fharer in my joy. Tenermill carried himfelf through the whole ceremony with fuch an air of gaiety that impofed on me. Thus, added I inwardly, addreffing myfelf to heaven, all the felicity that is lawful to defire upon earth is fhowered down together on my profperous family! finifh, great God, what is yet wanting to its happinefs, by heaping on it a full meafure of thy bleffings. We returned to the king's apartment, who

did

did the bride and bridegroom the honour of kissing
them; and signed the instrument of their marriage.
As he had not yet fixed the appointment of my
brother's two employments, or rather as he had reserved to himself to inform him upon what particulars he would assign them, he made him a present of
twenty thousand crowns, as an earnest penny, said
he joking, of a revenue that ought to be much
more considerable. He gave him five days to prepare himself for his journey to Ireland, with orders
only to attend often at St Germain during that time,
where he would confer with him upon the projects he
was resolved to intrust to him.

Who would not have believed, that I was now at
an end of so many agitations, and such great troubles, which my affection to my family had cost me,
and that seeing it happily established in its three
branches, I had nothing remaining but to consult the
king's pleasure, in order peaceably to discharge the
duties of my employment at court, or the functions
of my ministry in Ireland? I had this idea of my
lot when I arrived at the count de S⸺'s, where
we alighted at Paris. Although it had not yet come
into my thoughts to make the least doubt, whether
mademoiselle Anglesey, to whom I shall henceforth
give the name of spouse to my lord Tenermill,
ought not to be the same day lodged in his house,
it was nevertheless natural, that, having continued at
the count's since our arrival from Ireland, she should
carry him the news of her marriage, and the thanks
she owed to his friendship. The satisfaction he had
at seeing so many happy events, shewed more than ever
how much the happiness of our family was dear to
him. But whilst he was abandoning himself to joy,
and the countess did not deliver herself up to it with
less reserve, Tenermill prayed his new spouse to step
alone with him into the apartment she had hitherto
used. Every body was inclined to joke pleasantly
upon his haste to have her alone, which it was natural
to attribute to the ardours of love. Their absence

M 5 *continued.*

continued but a short time. My brother quitted her after some moments discourse, and returning to us, said with a gloomy air, addressing himself to the count, that divers reasons, which he had just discovered to his wife, did not permit him to continue with her, and especially on the eve of a journey, which probably would be of some duration; and that having already provided for her maintenance with a liberality which she could not complain of, he prayed us to preserve for her those inclinations we had always shewed her. The surprise these words gave, silencing us, or at least putting us in a condition to throw off the answering it upon one another, Tenermill took his leave handsomely, stepped into his coach, and drove off immediately.

Our first surprise induced us to go immediately into his wife's apartment, whom we found dissolved in tears, and ready to swoon away for grief and fear. She did not wait being pressed to inform us of the cause of her amazement. He has treated me, said she, redoubling her tears, with a contempt that has pierced my heart. If he has not loaded me with outrages, he has clearly given me to understand that he has forbore them out of moderation only. In fine, he has declared, that thinking he had done enough in giving me the name of his wife, he had no thoughts either of seeing me or living with me. Ah! continued she, I know to whom I ought to ascribe his hatred. I am betrayed, I am undone; death would be much less cruel to me than the sorrowful condition into which I have voluntarily cast myself. You could not but know it, added she, turning her eyes on me, Why did not you give me notice of it? Why have you made me the most unfortunate of all women?

I interrupted her, to console her with better hopes. Though the hasty retreat of my brother had left me much embarrassed, yet I fancied he might be excused by the nearness of his departure for Ireland, which did not allow him much time to settle a young wife in his house, whom he should be obliged to leave
alone

alone during his absence. The care he had taken of providing for her maintenance, and the explanation moreover I asked of herself, supported me yet in an opinion so favourable. My lady informed me, that he had allotted her, for the first year, the thirds of the sum the king had just granted him, in the interim, said he, till his affairs were enough regulated to assign her a settled revenue upon his appointments. I took occasion to console her even from this generosity, by making her look with a better eye on her lot; and promised her to spare no pains to dive into the intentions of her husband.

The count de S—— judged less advantageously of this matter than I did. He knew by a thousand experiences how difficult some certain kinds of engagements are to be broken through, and he moreover repeated to me a part of what I heard Tenermill say: This was, to discover sufficiently that he had no thoughts of separating himself from Donna Figuerrez, and to give one room to judge, that it would be a less obstacle to his attachment to her, than a reason to tie the knot closer. You see, said the count, that having entered into marriage without love, he will take no more of it than he sees suitable to his own repose, and that all he has done for his wife aims only, as she fears, at making her miserable by the vexation she will perpetually have of seeing her rival preferred to her. These predictions, which from the mouth of a man so sensible as the count had the power to frighten me, did not nevertheless hinder me from executing the promise I had made my lady. I saw Tenermill before he returned to Saisons; but I had the vexation to hear from his own mouth, with much haughtiness, every thing he had told his wife, without being able by my intreaties or reproaches to bend him.

Although he was not frank enough to declare what conduct he intended to hold with Donna Figuerrez, and that he had even affected not to make me any answer to some words I ventured to say against this union, yet the evil seemed (to me) so urgent, that the

only.

only remedy I thought of applying was, to see Donna Figuerrez herself, and to scare her by my menaces, if I could not gain her over by my exhortations. Tenermill not having disowned that he would return immediately to Saisons, this was not the time proper to pitch upon for my enterprise. Yet not doubting but he would begin again more regularly than ever to make his court to the king, it was easy to lay hold of the time of his absence. I moreover took measures that could not deceive me; and far from imparting my design to his wife, I drew from a thousand considerations intirely different, those hopes with which I continued to sooth her. I did not in the least mistrust that she would on her side form the same project, and that, having reasoned as I did, she would take the same day for executing it. Motives, such as she had, not suffering her to neglect any thing, she was accompanied by an Irish gentleman, called Viterbb, with whom she had made some acquaintance at Paris, as being near allied to her family. Without any other assistance than than of Viterbb, and a chamber-maid, she proposed to confront all dangers, and at least to treat Donna Figuerrez with all the haughtiness that a wife could draw from the most lawful rights of honour and religion. I know not what would have been the consequences of an enterprize so ill concerted, especially on a day that Tenermill had left with Donna Figuerrez three of his best friends. But it happened, that having arrived in my chaise the same moment with Viterbb's coach, I immediately knew my sister-in-law, and learned her design, which she could no longer conceal. I found her scheme less blameable in itself than dangerous to her own desires; and representing to her a thousand reasons for my fearing, that so bold a step would estrange the mind and heart of her husband more than ever from her, I proposed another method to reclaim him to her, which the present circumstances inspired me with, and which the power of love made her relish notwithstanding her resolution. Instead of reproaches, and

and perhaps outrages, with which she was resolved to load her rival, I advised her to assume power enough over herself to attack her by the sweeter methods of flattery and friendship. The heart of my brother, said I, and that of Donna Figuerrez herself, are not the hearts of tygers. Modesty and gentleness make an impression on the most insensible. Try at least this way, which must be less painful to a reasonable and virtuous woman than that of violence. I will lead the way, added I, to the course you are to take, by a conversation of some moments, which I am going to have with Donna Figuerrez, whilst you may consider on what you are to say to her. Without prepossessing her with your visit, I will prepare her mind in your favour by a panegyric on your character. In fine, it is from her I expect your happiness; and notwithstanding my views in coming here, I know no better way than what I have proposed.

Nothing has convinced me so much, that the heart of a woman is capable of all sorts of impressions, and that their faults and virtues depend almost always on the manner in which one has the art of representing objects to them, as the facility with which my sister-in-law submitted to my advice. One may draw from it, if one pleases, another consequence in favour of her natural humour. The forgetfulness of herself, which before her marriage had made her fall into a mortifying slip, did not hinder her from joining to a great deal of wit and to her education those principles of virtue and modesty, to which I cannot help thinking but she must have returned again. A violent passion sometimes gives place to reason, which after having been sacrificed to that affection, becomes more strong than it. But in the heat of resentment, which brought her to Saisons, I did not flatter myself with a false glory in ascribing the moderation, which she returned to in a moment, to the power or probability of my advice. Having once got the possession of this idea, she extended it by her reflections, and what she added

added to it became still a more powerful help to the furtherance of her desires.

I prayed her to continue in her coach at some distance from our house; and agreeing upon a certain sign to my valet, that he should give her notice the moment it would be proper for them to appear, I made no delay in paying my visit to Donna Figuerrez. I requested to see her alone, and she kept me a long time waiting; which slowness I ascribed to her embarrasment. Nevertheless, full of the notions with which I had just inspired my sister-in-law, my design was to relieve her with my civilities; and I executed it so happily, that the air of tranquillity, with which I accosted her, having helped to dissipate her suspicions, she recovered all at once from a slight emotion, that seized her at the sight of me, and received my first compliments with the most open air. I did not go about the bush to let her know the occasion of my visit. Continuing to observe the same moderation and civility in my words, I proceeded to mention her familiarity with my brother, as a friendship which alarmed all my family, and, upon the whole, caused mortal inquietudes to my sister-in-law. She interrupted me; and, foreseeing to what point this discourse was going to lead me, she used all the address in her power to avoid such offensive declarations. I thought of nothing less than to offend her; but I imagined she had given me some advantage over her, in letting me see this delicacy; or rather, I must confess, that having given her a hint of the idea I had formed of her from so many accounts, which gave me no very favourable judgment of her virtue, I was very far from expecting she could so sensibly feel the confusion arising from her irregularities; and charmed to see in her at least these appearances of reservedness, I did not despair of making them turn to the advantage of my project. So I did not insist one moment on my reproaches. On the contrary, giving a quite different turn to my discourse, I attributed to detraction those reports, which were as injurious

to.

to her as vexatious to my lady Tenermill. Then taking occasion from the name of my sister-in-law to speak of her person in terms of praise and panegyrick, I represented her as one of the women of the world who the least merited the indifference of her husband.

The opinion Donna Figueriez had of my character helped her without doubt to find a greater probability in the representation I had given of her. How could she fancy, that a man, whose steadiness she had experienced many times, and whom Tenermill had without doubt never painted in the softest colours, should lay such a constraint upon himself as to imprison within his own mind the impulses of his zeal, if he had been well informed of the nature of the habitual commerce of her society? She drew so great a confidence from this relation, that looking perhaps on my error as a favourable incident to all her desires, she gave herself the pleasure of confirming me in it, by a description of the amusements which employed her in that solitude. The picture shewed nothing but innocence, and when she blended in it Tenermill and his friends, she laboured to represent to me all their pleasures in a light most capable of flattering judgment and reason, as if they were the only particulars of which the society had any relish. She could not avoid speaking of my lady; but far from contradicting the praises I had given of her merit, she added to them many strokes, which she related, as she said, with pleasure, and she made no difficulty of assuring me, that she burned with the desire of knowing her.

I had given orders to my valet to post himself in some place from whence he could see me. Upon giving him the signal agreed on, he ran in haste to give notice to my sister-in-law. I could have wished she had been already present, at the instant wherein her rival was so luckily engaged in my views. I applied all my pains to keep up the conversation on the same subject, and I continued to draw from her new expressions of esteem and affection for the wife of her lover, when a servant came to give her notice of

the

the arrival of my lady Tenermill, who asked to see her. Her blushes and embarrasment made me immediately resume the discourse, by shewing the joy I felt at such an agreeable meeting. My lady, said I, would be extremely pleased at your expressions, if she had heard them. Perhaps she does not expect to find here a friend already so openly professed, at a time that without doubt she comes to request your esteem and friendship; but I am resolved, added I, that as soon as she comes into this parlour she shall know from me all at once from whom she may expect them. Donna Figuerrez, being put more to a nonplus, than I could have thought possible for a woman of her birth, who to a good deal of wit had joined a subtlety and refinement drawn from a conversation with the world and coquetry, remained some moments without finding any words to answer me.

In the mean time my lady came forward, led by Viterbb; and as far off as they could see me, I observed both of them seeking in my eyes what they had to judge from my first cares. I assumed a smiling countenance, and advancing to my sister-in-law, I said thus to her, loud enough to be heard by Donna Figuerrez; Whatever motive, madam, brings you, you are here better known, and better beloved, than you can imagine. I am charmed with every thing I have just heard; and if you can be sensible of esteem and friendship, you owe gratitude and acknowlegments for the sentiments they profess to you here. My sister-in-law, who had sufficient time to study her part, immediately embraced her rival, and requested her friendship in so easy a manner, that nothing could excuse Donna Figuerrez from promising it in the same way. Their conversation also engaged them in the most affectionate expressions. It was in the midst of this ardour, that my lady Tenermill seeming to turn her reflections upon her happiness, asked Viterbb with admiration, whether he would not confess that public fame is subject to much imposture, and if he had expected, after what

people

people had told him, that she should so easily make a friend of Donna Figuerrez? Viterbb had naturally a voice as rough, as his person was tall and bullylike. Pretending to soften his voice, and to accompany it with a gracious smile, he confessed that he could not easily return from his astonishment. What I see, said he, shall be a lesson to me all my life to teach me to mistrust reports and scandal; and when I proposed to you, continued he, addressing himself to my sister-in-law, to come and inform yourself by your own eyes of the character of madame, I did not tell you either all the injury her enemies had done her, or the great impression their malice had made on me. I was afraid of causing you too much vexation by telling them, and giving you too much fear for my project. For if you will pardon this freedom, added he, giving his air and his voice all their natural harshness, I had been so offended to hear that madame lived in a scandalous commerce with your husband, of which you were the victim,— that I came here with a design of grievously insulting her, and cutting my lord Tenermill's throat, if I had seen him disposed to take her part—Pardon, madame, added he, turning himself with an affected politeness to Donna Figuerrez, pardon such coarse expressions in the mouth of an Irishman, whose humour has always been a little boisterous. I think it is sufficient to see and to hear you, to take up a quite different opinion of you.

A compliment of this nature, which would have frightned myself, if I had thought I had not penetrated into the intention of Viterbb, finished the disconcerting Donna Figuerrez. Whether she imagined that they were ignorant of her familiarity with my brother, and that confusion produced in her the effect of repentance, or whether having in her less blackness and enormity, than levity and inclination to pleasure, she could see nothing happy for her in the consequences of an intrigue so openly opposed. In recovering from her perplexity, she contented herself with making

bitter

bitter complaints of the injuſtice the public did her ſentiments. You ſee, replied Viterbb coldly, that all this is founded upon the familiarity in which perhaps you live with my lord; and if you can think me capable of giving good advice, you will cut off this pretext for calumny. The embarraſment of Dohna Figuerrez would have begun again, if my ſiſter-in-law, contented enough to ſee her trembling and mortified, had not affected to redouble her careſſes, to take away from her all ſuſpicions ſhe might apprehend of any intelligence between us. I was uncertain where this ſcene would end, and I was meditating on ſome means to aſſure it of ſucceſs, when word was brought us that my lord Tenermill was come from St Germain. Donna Figuerrez ſeemed to fetch her breath again, whilſt fear was viſibly painted on the countenance of my ſiſter-in-law. As to myſelf, the ſurpriſe of an incident ſo little expected, put me in ſuſpense what part I had to act. But Tenermill had already got into the apartment, and the informations he had received from his porter, making him haſten his ſteps, his walk ſeemed to declare as much fury as impatience.

How great was his aſtoniſhment to ſee his wife ſitting cloſe to Donna Figuerrez, and me oppoſite to them. I endeavoured to ſupport the appearance of gaiety, which I had affected during our whole converſation. We got up when we ſaw him appear; but his ſurpriſe had detained him ſome moments, at the entrance of the chamber we were in. I apprehended that this inſtant was deciſive. I encouraged my ſiſter-in-law with my looks, and quickening myſelf up to aſſurance, I advanced ſome paces to meet him.—There have happened, ſaid I, great alterations in your abſence. Heaven has diſpoſed your domeſtic affairs with ſo much care, that it has eſtabliſhed your fortune at court. Donna Figuerrez apprehends, that ſhe is obliged to return to Spain: She could not tell us the news without grief, continued I, caſting on him a ſtolen and ſmiling look, to let him know, that I thought myſelf in a good underſtanding with her, but

her

her departure is necessary. She will leave you, besides your own liberty, that of lodging my lady with you. You will have the satisfaction, added I, of seeing two persons very dear to you, linked in a strict friendship, the moment they begin to know one another. I was going to proceed; and I confess, that in the confusion I was, I spoke almost at random, following only the impression made on me from the method we had taken with Donna Figuerrez. I flattered myself, that staggered, as she gave me room to think her, and out of fear and shame, she would follow the path chalked out for her, to disengage herself decently from a place, where from henceforth she could not hope for more security than honour. From this thought, I did not even fear to fortify the motive, which I took for granted he had to part, by throwing out some ambiguous words that might give Tenermill room to understand, she had wished for the occasion of it; and that it was less her own inclination, than a forced complaisance, that detained her at Saisons, after the marriage of my lady. My discourse, though little considered, produced a greater effect than I durst have hoped from it. Tenermill, taking all my expressions in the sense they were spoken, and not being able to conceive, that I had lent to Donna Figuerrez such sentiments as were not indeed her own, or that she could have disavowed, was piqued so much at those that I had attributed to her, that he pretended to receive them with a good deal of indifference. His pride assisted us so much the better, that proceeding so far as not to cast on her a single look, from a fear of giving her room to discover his vexation, he, on the contrary, thought of nothing but how to disguise the chagrin that devoured him. Having sat down, he testified by some cold expressions, and the most disengaged air he could affect, that having never pretended to detain her against her will, he should do her no violence in stopping her. She was offended in her turn at a moderation which so strongly resembled a contempt; but not being less haughty,

or

or less capable of concealing her weakness, she made an effort to answer him in the same tone; that she could perceive nothing more than he to hinder her parting without regret, and that she was charmed to have such worthy people witnesses of her dispositions, who were capable of justifying them by their testimony. She arose off her chair, and redoubled her compliments to my sister-in law. I know not whether he had suspected her of thinking to be gone immediately, or whether he would be so much alarmed at it as to make any motion to stop her; but the same moment a servant brought in word, that the count and countess of S—— were come from Paris; (without having foreseen indeed that they should find him at Saisons, but reckoning nevertheless that he would return there in the evening, and proposing to join their persuasions, to mine and to my lady's instances, to call him back to the obligations of his marriage.) It was from her this thought proceeded, after she had relished the plan that heaven had inspired me with. She had dispatched one of her servants to Paris, to press them to come immediately to Saisons. She had even entreated them to bring her son with them, whom she had put out to nurse, in one of the suburbs of Paris, to an Irish woman, whom I myself had recommended. Tenermill had never yet seen his son, although we had not concealed from him that she was delivered of it in a town in Flanders. In chusing to follow the most sweet ways of tenderness to move her husband, she had thought, with reason, that the sight of an infant of that age would make some impression on the heart of a father. The rest of this scheme was the invention of Viterbb.

Tenermill having returned more speedily than we expected from St Germain, because he had missed the king, who was gone that morning to Fountainbleau, was so amazed at every thing he had seen in his house, that a mind less firm and steady would have shewn more perplexity in the same situation. When to the trouble, from which he could not defend himself, they came to add that which he felt from the arrival

val of the count and countess, he lost all the attention he had given to the answer of Donna Figuerrez. Whilst he went out in haste to meet the count, he did not at all observe that she had stole out of the apartment, and he even less mistrusted her resolution, of being gone immediately to Paris. I thought I penetrated the views that made her fly. I even took advantage of the motion, that the arrival of the count and countess had caused, privately to order my valet to watch her steps; and when a moment after he had signified to me by a token, that she had forsaken the house, I found my mind more at liberty; and I did not doubt but my lady's party was much the stronger for it.

Indeed, as if heaven had taken care to guide the count's tongue, his first compliments were congratulations on the happiness of the good understanding he saw between my brother and his wife; and, not in the least doubting but I had fortunately atchieved what he had hoped to have given success to by his aid, he assumed the most serious voice of reason and friendship to assure Tenermill, that the side, to which he had supposed him determined, was the only one agreeable to his fortune and honour. A discourse, which so seasonably seconded our efforts, produced without doubt a new motion in the heart of my brother. I read in his eyes the excess of his agitation; and my lady made the same observation. She thought, that all the happiness of her life depended on that lucky moment; and quitting her chair to cast herself at the knees of her husband, she embraced them with an ardour in which one could easily perceive that even interest had a less share than love, with which she appeared to be entirely possessed. She requested of him repose, honour, life, which all depended on those sentiments, which she conjured him to have for her. Was it submission which he desired in a wife? She would not live but to obey and please him. Was it gratitude and love? She had consecrated her heart to those

two

two tender paſſions, and duty could not make a la
for her more binding than her own deſires. Wh;
then muſt ſhe do to obtain that which ſhe demande
by ſo many titles? Muſt ſhe forget all her rights, b
confeſſing that ſhe held nothing but from his goodneſs
She was ready to look on every thing as a favour.

We interrupted this ardent effuſion of affectionat
ſentiments, as much to relieve the tenderneſs c
our own hearts as the embarraſment of Tenermil
Mine was pierced with what I heard. Ah! m
lord, cried I, ſhedding ſome tears, you would b
too great an enemy to virtue, if duty ſhould ap
pear to you rigorous under this form. How? ſai
the counteſs with the ſame compaſſion, can you b
ſo inſenſible, as to reſiſt ſo much ſweetneſs and ſ
many charms? The count joined us with a voic
more compoſed; my lord, ſaid he to my brothei
I ſhould have a difficulty to comprehend what it i
you look for in a wife, if you be not moved by ſ
much merit and love, when the king's goodneſ
annexes to it all the advantages of fortune. In fine
Viterbb, who hitherto had the power of containin;
himſelf, added with an impatient air; my lord
my lord, meaſures are not always kept with a gii
whom a man has deceived, but honour lays dow;
different rules in marriage; and moreover do yoı
conſider, that what may be let alone with reſpect t
a wife, is due to her family?

Tenermill was going to anſwer, and I was in th·
mean time perſuaded, that yielding already to thı
force of circumſtances, he was only ſeeking for ex
preſſions to explain to us the change of his notions
But the counteſs prevented him, by preſenting to hiɔ
his ſon, whom ſhe took out of the arms of his nurſe
I was ſurpriſed myſelf at a ſight I by no mean
expected, and I ſhould have laughed at the fancy o
my ſiſter, if the effect of this new ſcene had not per
ſuaded me that ſhe knew the ſecrets of nature bette
than I did. Tenermill looked on the infant ſomı
moments, whom they ſhewed him for his ſon. Hı
theı

then cast his eyes on his wife. His looks were enlivened in a moment; his very countenance kindled up. If not a single word escaped him, it seemed to be confusion, or some other subject of awe, that tied his tongue. At length, inclining his head on the face of his son, he fastened to it for a moment his lips, and with the same motion raised himself up with a passionate air, and a thousand times embraced his wife. She made no answer to such dear caresses but by tears of tenderness, with which we mingled ours.

The END.

www.ingramcontent.com/pod-product-compliance
Lightning Source LLC
Chambersburg PA
CBHW032105220426
43664CB00008B/1140